"This book tries to remind us of the solid, positive, *right* things we have in America. You can read it anyway you want to. Forward, backward, or even from inside out. It's put together like a mosaic. There are literally thousands of facts and figures about our country put together in these pages. But if you step back and view the whole, the hundred separate pieces come together to make a rather surprising picture of the greatest, most complex country in the world."
—from the Introduction to
What's Right With America

"I'm amazed at the thousands of facts and figures in this book. Facts we can use to build the future, as we finish our country's first 200 years and begin the second. Every one of us will learn something new from this book about his own country."
—Sol Polk, President, Polk Brothers

WHAT'S RIGHT WITH AMERICA: 1986

A HANDBOOK FOR AMERICANS

By Dwight Bohmbach
with
Michael Bohmbach

BANTAM BOOKS
TORONTO • NEW YORK • LONDON • SYDNEY • AUCKLAND

WHAT'S RIGHT WITH AMERICA: 1986

A Bantam Book / July 1986

ISBN 0-553-25711-0

Published simultaneously in the United States and Canada

Bantam Books are published by Bantam Books, Inc. Its trademark, consisting of the words "Bantam Books" and the por-
trayal of a rooster, is Registered in U.S. Patent and Trademark
Office and in other countries. Marca Registrada. Bantam Books, Inc.,
666 Fifth Avenue, New York, New York 10103.

PRINTED IN THE UNITED STATES OF AMERICA

KR   0 9 8 7 6 5 4 3 2 1

For Anne and Steven Barnier
and
The Future

Thanks to my wife, Ree, for putting up with me and spurring me forward while all this was going on; to Michael for his wide and deep research contributions; to Leo Shapiro and George Rosenbaum for their gift of original survey research; and to my old friend Sol Polk for first turning my thoughts toward what's right with America, so long ago.

D. B.

Contents

★

III. THE WAY WE LIVE

IV. THE WAY WE MAKE OUR LIVING

V. THE WAY WE GOVERN OURSELVES

Before You Go Inside . . .

★

This is the third time I've taken a year off to take an inventory of America. The first *What's Right* book was written in 1972, when the Vietnam War and the opening act of the Watergate tragedy shadowed our view of the nation. That book was written as a kind of therapeutic exercise, a search for solid things in a society uncertain of itself.

The second *What's Right* was written for the nation's Bicentennial year, 1976. That was the year of tall ships parading on a newly unpolluted Hudson River, "streakers" on college campuses, American women winning 13 of 32 Rhodes scholarships the first time they were permitted to enter the competition—and a sense of new opportunities across America.

Chuck Peebler and Alan Jacobs saw the manuscript for *WR76* and immediately decided that their advertising agency, Bozell & Jacobs, Inc., wanted to sponsor and distribute the book as their contribution to an advertisement for America on our nation's 200th birthday.

When Chuck and my longtime friend David Bell asked me if I'd consider setting aside another year to take inventory of America again, this time to celebrate our national "rediscovery" of the Statue of Liberty, I was noncommittal at first. The country has changed tremendously during the first years of the ascendancy of the baby boom generation, as its members took the lead in choosing the course for our government. But now that *What's Right With America: 1986* is done, I realize again how taking the time really to take your own measure of all that's *right* with our country revives your spirit and hopes for the future. With all its faults, there is no better place in the world to live.

Don't expect a whitewash. This is one person's view of our country. It doesn't overlook things I think need changing and fixing. Right things are often shown in context with things that are wrong. You may not agree, but there they are, one American's free opinions.

A word about the format: This probably isn't like most books you've read. You can read it any way you want to—forward, backward, or even from inside out. It's put together like a mosaic. There are literally thousands of up-to-date facts and figures about our country in these pages—all documented, so you can look them up for yourself, as well. Meaty facts need to be well chewed and digested. So instead of a conventional continuous flow, I've broken the book up into almost 50 little "helpings," each looking at our country from a slightly different perspective.

Dip into the book anywhere. Each piece is complete in itself. But if you step back and view the whole, the pieces come together to make a rather surprising picture of the greatest, most complex country in the world.

Dwight Bohmback
Phoenix, 1985

A man full of warm speculative benevolence may wish his society otherwise constituted than he finds it; but a good patriot, and a true politician, always considers how he shall make the most of the existing materials of his country.

Edmund Burke.

Reflections on the Revolution in France, 1790

I

The Land

★

There is not an American on earth but what loves
land.

Sam Houston, speech, 1848

In the United States there is more space where
nobody is than where anybody is. This is what
makes America what it is.

Gertrude Stein,
The Geographical History of America, 1936

The Only Country with a Welcome Sign at Its Door

★

Two out of three Americans say they get "emotional" when they even think about the Statue of Liberty. Almost a third say they get "very emotional" just thinking about this American symbol![1] But what moves them so?

The statue itself is a magnificent symbol, the biggest ever created by one person. The Colossus of Rhodes, erected at the entrance to the harbor on the island of Rhodes in the third century B.C., was one of the Seven Wonders of the ancient world; when Arabs hauled away its fallen metal remains for scrap, 900 years later, it made over 900 camel loads. But the Statue of Liberty is said to be 46 feet higher than even the Colossus of Rhodes. The Statue of Liberty is an enormous and yet delicately, intricately fashioned construct, 151 feet high from base to torch and weighing some 225 tons.

The skin of the statue, 300 copper plates, stitched together with over 300,000 copper rivets, was hand-hammered to a thickness of 96 mils ("just a bit thicker than an American cent," as the statue's sculptor, Frederic Auguste Bartholdi, described it).[2] After almost 100 years of wind and rain—now *acid* rain—the statue's original gleaming skin has only lost about 4 mils of its thickness.[3] The pedestal, 150 feet high, stands on 23,500 tons of concrete for a foundation. It's one of the heaviest pieces of masonry ever built. When you add the height of the pedestal to the height of the statue, you get 300 feet plus a few inches—almost exactly the length of that standard of measurement for almost everything in America, a football field. Even the 300-ton aluminum scaffolding wrapped around Miss Liberty during reconstruction this past year (the scaffolding outweighed the statue itself) was epochal—the largest free-standing scaffold in the world.

Surely you have to be impressed by the enormity, the

gigantic exercise in technological creativity and artistic élan of this artifact. But what on earth makes people so emotional about the Statue of Liberty? A 19-year-old cement-bag loader working on the reconstruction project inched his way out on the scaffolding and while a friend photographed him, "put his lips to the statue's, which are three feet across, and kissed the lady."[4] How on earth can people fall so in love with a hollow copper "lady" whose lips are 1/100th of a football field wide?

It wasn't easy. It took a while for Americans to get to love their Statue of Liberty. How it came about gets to the heart of what moves us so about her today. Originally, when the idea for the statue came up for the first time, it wasn't even conceived as a symbol of liberty so much as *friendship*. During a dinner party of young French artists in 1865 at Glatigny, near Versailles, the host, Edourd de Laboulaye, a journalist and historian, suggested that France and America should share in a memorial of the friendship of the two nations since the American Revolution, "when, supported by the French with sinews of war," that friendship had "helped turn the tide of victory to the side of the Colonies."[5]

But the Franco-Prussian War of 1870–71 came along to shove the idea aside. It wasn't until 10 years later that 200 French and Americans got together over dinner to discuss the idea again and set up the Franco-American Union, with Laboulaye as its president. The union picked an Alsatian sculptor, Bartholdi, to create the memorial because he had an established reputation as a creator of monumental patriotic and symbolic statues to glorify "heroic ideas, personalities, and events." But the first time Bartholdi ever saw America, as his ship moved slowly into New York Harbor, we are told that he was so moved by that sight, he ". . . conceived the idea of a colossal statue to stand at the very gateway of the New World to represent the one thing man finds most precious—Liberty."[6]

He chose the Bedloe's Island (now renamed Liberty Island) site because "he wanted the statue to welcome the immigrants coming here to a new life." And so, on October 23, 1886, ten years after the actual Centennial it had been planned to celebrate, the Statue of Liberty was unveiled on a cold, rainy day veiled with heavy mist. President Grover Cleveland accepted the colossal gift as a "friendship gift to mark the hundredth United States independence anniver-

sary" and added: "We will not forget that liberty has made
here her home."

As a matter of fact, most Americans did seem to forget the
statue during the first decades after it was installed. At first it
served primarily as a lighthouse. In 1901, Miss Liberty was
placed under control of the War Department, which maintained Fort Wood, whose star-shaped wall still surrounds the
base of the statue. Immigrants arriving at the harbor, on their
way to the New World, did certainly see the statue with great
feelings of emotion, but the truth is, most Americans felt no
particular connection with the copper memorial until over 1.3
million of our soldiers, sailors, and marines were shipped
overseas in 1917–18: "The Statue inspired meager emotional
response here until World War I, when doughboys from all
over the country sailed past her, and the 77th Division,
which fought in France as the Statue of Liberty Division,
chose her as their insignia."[7]

That, plus the accumulating memories of millions of immigrants, whose first sight of America was imprinted with the
image of the giant lady, really came together to generate the
emotion Americans feel for their colossus today. For returning sailors, soldiers, and marines, the overwhelming meaning
of the statue was one of *welcome*—welcome to the only nation
in the world with so much open space, so much generosity,
so much freedom, so much security about itself that it puts a
welcoming light to guide you in at its door, day and night,
every day of the year.

"Liberty" is an abstract word with many meanings to many
people. "Welcome" is a warm invitation to join us in the
enjoyment of our many blessings and opportunities. Emma
Lazarus, a young American poet from a family of Spanish
Jews, wrote a sonnet called "The New Colossus," addressed to
the Statue of Liberty in 1881. Most of us know at least a few
lines from it now, but the poem went unnoticed until 1903, a
total of 16 years after Lazarus died at age 38. Then the last
five lines of her poem about the "Mother of Exiles" welcoming the poor and oppressed of the world were cast in bronze
and added to the statue's pedestal, just at the beginning of
the era of heaviest immigration from southern Europe. The
last two of these lines express the idea of welcome, too:

> Send these, the homeless, tempest-tost to me,
> I lift my lamp beside the golden door!

More than 17 million immigrants passed by at the feet of Miss Liberty between 1892, when Ellis Island opened, and 1954, when it closed. They never forgot, and they passed on to their families, their thankfulness for the welcome expressed by her upheld lamp. *That's* what makes two out of three of us feel "emotional" at the very thought of the Statue of Liberty— not the colossal construct of metal and cement, but the welcome to freedom that she symbolizes.

Maintaining even a symbol involves responsibility—responsibility to preserve the symbol itself, and responsibility to preserve what it stands for. You can't have one without the other.

Maintaining the Statue of Liberty has always been a burden to anyone charged with the responsibility, and some have shirked along the way. It's always been a money problem, for one thing. To help finance the original designs and construction, Bartholdi signed 200 small terra-cotta replicas, each four feet high, which were sold to collectors. The French, who had begun the project with the goal of financing it entirely through personal gifts, soon found it was not easy. At first, gifts poured in, many small contributions coming from "workmen, tradesmen, peasants, school-children, scrub-women, and hundreds of persons with limited resources." But then collections slowed. It took 10 years to raise the necessary money for the statue itself.

The same was true in raising money for the statue's pedestal in our country. With "a committee of prominent men" heading the collection effort, enough money was raised to build the first 15 feet of the pedestal. Then (as so often happens with projects like this) they found a lot more money would be needed to finish the job, or Miss Liberty "wouldn't have a leg to stand on." But "there was not too much interest in this undertaking in New York itself . . . elsewhere in the United States most of the people were 'even more apathetic.' "[8]

At that point, Joseph Pulitzer, an immigrant who became one of America's leading publishers, volunteered to raise the necessary money. He staged a vigorous and extensive promotional campaign, selling small replicas of the statue and sheet music about it, and using a steady stream of publicity, cartoons, editorials, and ads in his paper to drum up contributions and get people involved in the product and project. By 1885, some time after the French had finally raised the money to finish the statue and it was in New York waiting to be assembled, Pulitzer could announce that he'd raised enough money to set it up. So *money* was the cause for the statue's being unveiled 10 years late for the nation's Centennial.

Over the years that followed, as the statue was shunted from one set of caretakers to another, it and the grounds around it declined. In 1934 the arm holding the torch began to show signs of drooping; it took three years to get it repaired. And by the time a private commission began discussing restoration for the statue and grounds in 1975, buildings on Ellis Island had deteriorated, and the statue itself was in sorry shape. In 1985 *The Nation* commented that "The history of government neglect of these important landmarks of the American heritage is a national tragedy." A hole the size of a dinner plate had rotted through the tip of Miss Liberty's nose. Her skeleton was so corroded, connecting rivets were pulling through the outer skin of the statue, and the whole structure had twisted from weakness.[9]

After many shifts and changes of responsibility for refurbishing the statue and the grounds and buildings around it, just as an immigrant businessman-salesman, Joseph Pulitzer, had taken over the job in the 1880s to complete the statue's pedestal, now, in the 1980s, a *son* of Italian immigrants, Lee Iacocca, was elected chairman of the Statue of Liberty Foundation in late 1984, with responsibility for raising hundreds of millions of dollars in time to get the statue and its surrounding areas restored by July 1986. As a graduate engineer, Iacocca knew the enormity of the job to be done in less than 24 months; as one of the most successful salesmen-business executives in America and a perpetual optimist, he felt confident that it could be done.

Iacocca promised to invite all Americans to participate in the fund-raising and restoration project, and he did. Just as fund-raising to construct the statue in the 19th century had run short of funds because it cost much more than original estimates, the rebuilding project had also suffered from huge underestimates. Rebuilding the Statue of Liberty and refurbishing buildings and grounds around it had become the largest private-sector financing effort in history. But as work went forward on refurbishing, now it also began to move more quickly on financing. By November 1985, over $170 million of the $230 million needed had been raised, with most of it (54%) coming from "grass roots" contributors. Nineteen corporate sponsors of the project had paid the rest of the money.[10] And by February, 1986, the Statue of Liberty Foundation headed by Iacocca had raised $233 million.

The idea of corporate contributors to the Statue of Liberty restoration being given the right to use what had become a national symbol in their own advertising and sales promotions offended purists. (Joseph Pulitzer's successful promotion efforts to raise the original construction money, which also identified the national symbol with his own newspaper, must have griped a lot of purists in the 19th century, too.) But let's face it: Ours is a capitalist economy; we have private citizens and we also have corporate citizens. Private citizens give, and take a tax deduction. They also get listed in programs and honor rolls. Corporate citizens who contribute $1.5 million to $10 million each as founding or official sponsors also look for ways to benefit through their identification with a worthy national project.

Our symbol of welcome is renewed; her guiding lamp shines brighter than ever. With permanent, corporate-maintained exhibit areas in the island areas, and with museums of the Ellis Island experience and permanent archives clustered around her feet, we can feel more confident now than before that America's symbol of welcome will be maintain for generations to come.

But we will need to remember that the statue is, after all, only an artifact. It symbolizes a far more profound concept—that of a nation not only great in size and wealth and power, but also in humanity; the one nation in the world generous enough in spirit to put a "welcome sign" 300 feet high in its front door, with a lamp that shines day and night to guide the oppressed people of the world in, for sanctuary. The spirit may vary, from place to place: In Arizona, during 1985, a man with a criminal record, who had been hired to spy on clergy and laymen in church meetings, testified for our government against them after they openly declared a sanctuary for political refugees from El Salvador and Guatemala. The government wanted to send the sanctuary-movement members to jail![11] Meanwhile, in California, after similar actions by nearly a dozen other cities, Los Angeles, the second-largest city in America, declared the whole city a "sanctuary for Central American refugees fleeing political persecution and violence in their homelands."[12] The lamp of welcome shines more brightly in some places than in others.

*   *   *

In San Francisco in July 1985, a group of immigrants were gathering for a swearing-in ceremony before a federal district court judge. He was scheduled to administer the oath of American citizenship. An 80-year-old Latvian, who had been imprisoned in Moscow for three years under Stalin and was freed in 1953, was riding up in an elevator, on his way to the swearing-in. He came to America in 1979, and now he was about to become a citizen. But the excitement was too much for him. He collapsed with heart trouble in the elevator.

When he regained consciousness in a chair where he had been propped up, the 80-year-old absolutely refused to be taken to a hospital. He was determined to get the American citizenship he'd come so far to get. A guard hurried to tell the judge about "a man having heart trouble, who needed the oath administered." The judge "told him to relax, he'd be an American citizen in two minutes."

The pale, shaky old man was helped to his feet to take his oath of citizenship. Then, as he shook hands with the judge, he said with a grin, "Now my heart will start beating again, because it's an American heart."[13]

That's what the Statue of Liberty really is all about. The restoration workers and fund-raisers and contributors have done a fabulous job of renewing her on the outside. From now on it's up to us to keep her *heart* beating and the welcome light shining.

NOTES

1. Data from Leo J. Shapiro & Associates survey, 1985.
2. Maymie R. Krythe, *What So Proudly We Hail* (New York: Harper & Row, 1968), p. 173.
3. I. Peterson, "A Statue of a Different Color," *Science News*, Vol. 127, p. 404.
4. Wendy McBane, "Crews Work Feverishly to Finish Liberty Face Lift," Knight-Ridder news service (July 28, 1985).
5. Krythe, op. cit., p. 169.
6. Ibid., p. 171.
7. Ibid., p. 181.
8. Ibid., p. 175.
9. McBane, op. cit.
10. Judann Dagnoli, "Liberty Campaign Not Free of Controversy," *Advertising Age* (November 18, 1985).

11. Garry Wills, "Sanctuary?" Universal Press news service (October 21, 1985). Also, Gene Varn, "Sanctuary Case Was Run from Washington," *Arizona Republic*.

12. *Los Angeles Times* news service, "Council Declares LA Latino-Refugee Haven," *Arizona Republic* (November 28, 1985).

13. "Man Insists on Oath Before Medical Help," *The New York Times* (July 31, 1985).

We Still Have Plenty of Stretching-out Room

★

Is America getting too crowded for comfort? Some people think so. We have added roughly 60 million more people and 41 more cities of over 100,000 in population since 1960.[1] Is that too many?

Most Americans don't think so, and figures say they are right. A nationwide Shapiro Poll during 1985 asked adults if they thought there are "too many people in America today." About seven in ten (68%) said no. And Americans *least* inclined to say we have too many people were living in cities of up to 1 million in size. Fewer than one in five of these urban-dwellers (18%) felt overcrowded.[2]

The fact is, Americans started this country with a whole continent to stretch out in, and we've still got a lot of open space left today. What makes some Americans feel cramped is that they crowd together. Three out of four of us live in a city,[3] close enough to our neighbors to feel the heavy beat of their hi-fi right through our walls, and hear the tinkle of their ice cubes and sizzle of their barbecue at the end of the day. This has been known to bring on a mild twinge of anthropophobia in even the most neighborly of us.

What we may need when we feel that way is to get out into the open more—to Alaska, for example. The Alaska population density averages a lean one person per square mile. Or you can take your pick from nine other states where the population density today is actually lower per square mile than the national average 100 years or more ago.[4] Take Wyoming, for example; Wyoming has an average density of just five people per square mile today—almost as few as our national average density of 4.5 per square mile shortly after the American Revolution, in 1790. North Dakota (10 people per square mile) and South Dakota (9 per square mile) have

10

practically the same number of people per square mile as in 1930—and also in 1940![5] Talk to yourself all you want, nobody will hear a word you say out in the middle of a field in either North or South Dakota.

But to come right down to it, most of us seem to want companions, even if we don't know them. Three out of four Americans live in cities today, compared to only a little more than half of them (56%) in 1930. Even where people have a whole range of environments and climates, and all the land anybody could use to choose from, they cluster in cities. In Arizona, an incredibly varied state, with a statewide population density of 26 per square mile—well below the national average of 65 per square mile—almost eight out of 10 Arizonans (77%) have settled in either the Phoenix or Tucson metropolitan areas.[6] Jobs and services also cluster in the major metropolitan areas, drawing more people.

America's population density of 65 persons per square mile is high compared to that in our good neighbor to the north, Canada. Slightly larger than the United States in terms of land, Canada averages only seven people per square mile, one of the lowest levels of national population density on earth. Mexico, our other good neighbor, to the south, has 102 persons per square mile.[7]

When we take a world view, the United States begins to seem absolutely roomy. The population density per square mile for the whole world is 91. Among 157 countries sharing our world today, 93 nations pack more people into a square mile than we do. In fact, 14 nations (Bahrain, Bangladesh, Barbados, Belgium, Taiwan, Grenada, Japan, Republic of Korea, Maldives, Malta, Mauritius, Netherlands, St. Vincent and Grenadines, and Singapore) have a population density at least 10 times as high as ours.[8]

Compared to nations in Europe and the Mediterranean area, the United States also has far more land space per person than do most of them. Only seven out of 40 nations in Europe and the Mediterranean area (Finland, Libya, Norway, Saudi Arabia, the Soviet Union, Sweden, and the United Arab Emirates) have a lower population density than ours. Taken together, the European countries have four times more people per square mile (261) than we do.[9] Now, doesn't that make you feel more expansive than when you started reading this section?

Looking ahead at world population projections, it doesn't

look like we are going to be much more pinched for living space in this country over the next 20 years. For the first time in modern history, the rate of world population growth has slowed, declining from 2.0% to 1.7% in the past decade.[10] In population, America is one of the 24 slowest-growing nations in the world today, with our 0.9% annual population growth.[11] Our own Census Bureau projects a growth of just 7.3% in our population between now and the new-century year 2000. That will raise our overall American population to 267.5 million.[12] If you live in a city now—the chances are that most of the added millions of Americans also will head for cities—yours will grow, and new cities of over 100,000 in population will be added.

Fortunately, in America we still have a lot of wide-open spaces to fit them into. You're going to have new neighbors, but they won't have to crowd you.

NOTES

1. *Statistical Abstract of the United States 1985*, (Washington, D.C.: U.S. Department of Commerce, Bureau of the Census, 1984). Table 23 shows 132 cities of 100,000 and over population in 1960; 173 in 1983.
2. Data from national poll conducted in June 1985 for this book by Leo J. Shapiro & Associates.
3. *Statistical Abstract, 1985*, table 24.
4. Ibid., table 11 for present population density; and *Historical Statistics of the United States, Colonial Times to 1970* (Washington, D.C.: U.S. Department of Commerce, Bureau of the Census, 1975), part 1, table A-5 for 19th-century data.
5. Ibid.
6. *Statistical Abstract, 1985*, tables 11 and 22.
7. Ibid., table 1475.
8. Ibid.
9. Ibid.
10. See *State of World Population 1984* (United Nations Fund for Population Activities) for full data.
11. Based on 1983 data from U.S. Department of Commerce.
12. *Statistical Abstract, 1985*, table 14.

We're Still Homesteaders at Heart

★

Three hundred fifty-seven years ago, "at Nehumkek, now called Salem," in what we call Massachusetts, a young immigrant preacher named Francis Higginson wrote of the two hundred settlers in *New England's Plantation*: "We that are settled at Salem make what haste we can to build houses, so that within a short time we shall have a fair town."[1]

One hundred thirteen years ago, somewhere outside Beloit, Kansas, the first breakfast Tom and Emma Hill ate at their new homesite was made on their cookstove, set the night before "right down in the dry creek bed," sheltered from blowing snow and gale winds by "horse blankets and old carpet and we did very well." The two had come to Kansas by prairie schooner, to set up homesteading. Two days later, Tom started for town to take out papers on their land, expecting to be gone three days. But because their goods had been delivered to another town, he had to travel on.

> He had no way to let me know, so I had a rather anxious time. But about 3 o'clock one morning I heard our wagon and knew everything was all right. He came bringing our goods and a few pieces of dimension stuff for doors and window frames, and a few boards, and three bushels of potatoes. Now we were ready to start operation on our homestead.[2]

Last night our daughter, Anne, telephoned from Minnesota. Her first words were, "Steve and I have bought a house!" Their first home of their own is a turn-of-the-century stucco-and-shake-shingle house in a culturally mixed part of town, with "solid oak floors, a big basement with separate room for Steve's carving, a huge kitchen, and three beautiful

13

stained glass windows with grapes in them." They bought it from the estate of a 101-year-old woman, who had made it her home since her husband built it—while the world changed around her. Now Anne and Steven are ready to start operations on *their* homestead, too.

Homesteading and homeowning have been a key part of our American tradition since the earliest days of America. "The American never builds himself a house; he builds himself a home," wrote English journalist George Warrington Steevens in the 19th century.[3] This is as true today among the towers of Manhattan, in the suburbs of Chicago, in Nome, Thousand Oaks, or along a beach in Guam: Americans are "homesteaders." The Homestead Act of 1862, which made it possible for more than 1.6 million Americans to claim an average of 169 acres apiece of public lands, in return for clearing the land, building a house, and living there, was a kind of official recognition of the fact, as well as smart policy. It made early settlement of our western states—especially Oklahoma, Kansas, Nebraska, and the Dakotas—a reality. It's been repealed since 1976 for all states but Alaska. Even so, as late as 1983 a thousand acres were granted to a homesteader up there who qualified for it.[4] The law is scheduled to expire in 1986, but the basic tradition that inspired it goes on across America.

In spite of the fact that American families of the 1980s probably spend less time at home than any generation before, because so many of us go out to work, school, and day-care centers every morning, the American yearning for a "home, sweet home" of our own is as strong as ever. In the spring of 1985, one in five young Americans under age 39 said they were planning to buy a home during 1985–86.[5]

This continuity of the American homeowning tradition helps to hold us together today, both culturally and economically. It gives us a solid, shared foundation in a world and an economy that often seems shaky on its pins. In spite of zooming housing prices and interest rates, the percent of homeowners across America has gone up, from 62.9% in 1970 to 64.4% in 1984.[6] The average first-time homebuyer in 1984 was 29 years old, paid $81,500 for a home, had saved for almost two years to accumulate money for the down payment, and would pay out over a third of the family's income (33.7%) in monthly payments. They'd spent an average of four months house-hunting, and looked at 14 different houses before finding the House of Their Dreams.[7] *You bet!* The old magic is still there!

"But what of the walk-aways?" someone asks. What the media have called "an epidemic of mortgage defaults" during 1985 raised the mortgage default rate to nearly 1%—up 63% since 1980.[8] Thousands of Americans who bought homes in the 1970s, when housing prices (and values) were going up like an escalator, year-to-year, "went over their heads" because they felt sure their house would be worth more each year. Many signed up for mortgages that start at a low rate but adjust to market levels after three years. Later they found their incomes hadn't risen enough to meet the increased monthly payments. Meanwhile, housing values were dropping; they could no longer afford even to sell the house they couldn't afford to keep. So they become "walk-aways." And "for the first time, we're seeing a willingness to walk away," says a mortgage company executive.

Sad as this is, it is not new. In the Great Depression and dust-bowl years, whole communities reluctantly walked away, to look for a living elsewhere. Before that, as Americans pushed the frontier west in the 19th century, whole towns sprang up at minesites, railroad heads, and steamboat landings, only to be abandoned when the mine ran out, the railroad moved on, or the river changed course.

On the frontier, houses and housing were built to fill the need of the moment. In Burke, Idaho, for one example, housing sprang up so fast along the main street (which was also the railroad's roadbed) that when the town was completed it was a mile long, only a hundred yards wide, and awnings on the store windows had to be raised to leave room for passing trains![9] When the economy changed, people walked away from their homes, and moved to a place where it was better. And the first thing they did when they got there was build themselves another home.

We're still doing this, on a massive national scale. Between 1970 and 1983 America increased the number of occupied housing units ("homes," that is) from 63,445,000 to 84,638,000. Of these homes, 58,606,000 were "owner-occupied" in 1970, and 72,562,000 in 1983.[10] That's an added 13,956,000 homes in 13 years—a little more than 1 million a year. And it adds up to more new homes built in 13 years than all the owner-occupied housing units there *were* in the United States in 1940.[11] Putting it another way, we added as many new housing units between 1970 and 1983 as all the existing housing in California, Texas, and Nevada in 1980 put together![12]

As I write this, in January 1986, nearly one in six American families (15%) say they plan to buy a new home during the year ahead; one in eleven (9%) is actively shopping for one—studying the ads, comparing prices, and trudging through the rooms of houses and condos in search of the dream house.[13] About a million and three quarter brand-new homes are going up in cities, suburbs, and the countryside. The old American dream of "a home of our own" is as bright as ever!

NOTES

1. Francis Higginson, *New England's Plantation* (1630).
2. Emma Hill, *Autobiography of Emma Hill,* quoted in Joanna L. Stratton, *Pioneer Women: Voices from the Kansas Frontier* (New York: Simon & Schuster, 1982), pp. 48–49.
3. Daniel J. Boorstin, *The Americans: The National Experience* (New York: Vintage Books, 1965), p. 297.
4. *Statistical Abstract of the United States 1985* (Washington, D.C.: U.S. Department of Commerce, Bureau of the Census, 1984), table 535.
5. Leo J. Shapiro & Associates, *Second-Quarter Report* 1985, table 32.
6. *Statistical Abstract, 1985*, table 1315, and National Board of Realtors' 1984 data, *USA Today* (September 5, 1985).
7. Chicago Title Insurance Co. data quoted in *The Wall Street Journal* (April 22, 1985).
8. Patricial M. Scherschel, "As Mortgage Defaults Keep Spreading—," *U.S. News & World Report* (August 26, 1985).
9. Martin F. Schmitt and Dee Brown, *The Settlers West* (New York: Ballantine Books, 1974), p. 59.
10. *Statistical Abstract, 1985*, table 1315.
11. *Historical Statistics of the United States* (Washington, D.C.: U.S. Department of Commerce, Bureau of the Census, 1975), table N–242.
12. *Statistical Abstract, 1985*, table 1312.
13. Leo J. Shapiro & Associates, national poll (January 1986).

The Folks Who Put Food on Our Tables—Farmers

Practically all my life I've felt guilty about farmers. They were always working so hard, feeding us better than any other nation on earth—and practically always in deep trouble. One of my earliest memories is of farmers dumping cans of milk onto country roads in Wisconsin because prices were so low it didn't pay them to sell it. Another early memory is walking to school in St. Paul, past the Minnesota state capitol, and seeing cows grazing on the sculptured lawns out front. Farmers had brought their cattle in and tethered them there because they said they couldn't afford to feed the cows themselves.

The worst part of all this is that a city kid who has never spent overnight on a farm is completely flummoxed by the plight of the farmers; he doesn't know how to help them, and so he is left simply feeling guilty about eating their food every day. After a while you just give up and go back to drinking your morning orange juice (it's probably from Brazilian oranges, anyway) and evening apple juice (knowing that the odds are it's from either Argentine or West German apples).[1]

The Farm Problem has become so complex, so immense, so laden with human emotion, that I think in a nation like ours, where most of us are now city folks, we're *all* itching to help the farmer but don't know where to scratch. In early spring of 1985, when we began to hear about the plight of farmers, especially in Iowa and the other Farm Belt states, there was a genuine outburst of concern across the country. In March, 8% of Americans said "farmers' troubles" were one of the nation's most serious problems; but by November only 4% even mentioned farmers when they talked about national problems. Most people just couldn't figure out what to do about it, so they turned to other worries.

Another thing that makes it hard for us consumers to know how to help farmers is that we get so much conflicting information about their plight. Take, for example, these side-by-side quotes from different authoritative journals, published no more than six months apart:

One Reputable Source

We're losing one American farmer every 2 minutes.[2]

. . . worst agricultural crisis since the 1930s Depression.[4]

The U.S. alone has about one-third more land in food production than it needs to feed U.S. consumers and meet export demand.[6]

. . . big trouble for the banks, because the value of farmland is crashing. The gloomy outlook has kept potential buyers away, fattening an already huge land glut . . .[8]

Another

Farmers are not being driven from the land. From October of 1984 through January of 1985 . . . the Farmers Home Administration actually foreclosed on forty-two farms nationwide. The FmHA provides loans to farmers who can't get credit elsewhere . . . its borrowers who "discontinued farming due to financial difficulties" . . . totaled 1,249, or 0.5 percent of the FmHA's 264,000 clients.[3]

Two of three American farmers have no trouble paying their bills, according to a USDA farm finance survey conducted earlier this year. In the 1930s average farm family income was a third that of the average American family, while in 1983 it was slightly higher.[5]

The U.S. imported 752 million tons of fruits and vegetables last year compared with 591 million tons four years ago. As an inevitable result, the U.S. agricultural trade surplus is slipping. . . . Fully $12.6 billion, or 65% of our 1984 agricultural imports, were what the government calls supplementary products that we produce ourselves.[7]

Who's foolhardy enough to invest in agriculture at a time when farmers are going broke, land prices are declining and farm income is taking a nose dive? . . . Some of the biggest outside investments in

One Reputable Source

Another

agriculture come from insurance companies. . . . Promoters of farmer-investor deals report that cash returns can average anywhere from 5 to 10 percent a year, plus offering current tax write-offs and the potential for long-range appreciation of the land.[9]

Agricultural industries . . . constitute the largest sector of the American economy, accounting for 20 percent of the GNP and employing more people than the steel and automobile industries combined.[10]	Only about one in eight farm families gets most of its income from farming. Those who do make a living from farming are on the largest farms in America.[11]
[We recall that the USDA predicted, only a decade ago, that the way the world population was growing, food production would fall behind world food demand.][12]	Farm exports for 1985 are . . . $2 billion below the estimate only three months ago. Reasons include the strong dollar, *bumper crops* world-wide.[13]
Most farmers don't have burdensome debt.[14]	The interest expense of farmers in constant dollars rose by 60% between 1975–79 and 1980–84, leveling off at $21 billion per year vs. income from assets that averaged only $19 billion.[15]
To some extent, farmers can blame their woes on their own productivity. Massive stockpiles, the product of huge 1984 harvests, overhang all major agricultural markets. This year's harvest promises to be almost as bountiful.[16]	But some U.S. companies are quietly beginning to look for grain abroad. One consultant says two of his clients . . . are exploring European and South American sources of soybean meal, soybean oil, corn and sorghum.[17]

I don't doubt a single one of these statements. Each comes from an unimpeachable source. I *do* confess, however, that read side-by-side, even in their full original context, they make me more and more uncertain about the true plight of the farmer and what our family might be able to do to help. We certainly want the American farmer—that dawn-to-dusk-and-after, hardworking, land-loving, most productive farm family on earth that we all grew up admiring—to survive and prosper. But are they, or aren't they?

If only someone who really knows everything there *is* to know on the subject—a kind of agricultural Peter Drucker—could tell us how to manage the farm crisis, with Walter Cronkite there beside him to interpret, and ask the wise questions we need to have answered but don't know how to ask, I believe Americans would rise right out of the grass roots to help get the farmers back on their feet and their farms again. During harvest time in 1985, consumers around the country were asked if they would be willing to pay an additional 3% for their groceries if they could be sure the extra cost would go to help the farmers.[18] Over a third of the food-shoppers in the country (35%) said, "You bet!" My little calculator estimates that this could generate up to about $3 billion a year for farmers. Not much, as billions go these days, but it certainly shows one thing: Americans want to help the folks who put food on their tables!

NOTES

1. Ellen Benoit, "Coals to Newcastle," *Forbes* (September 9, 1985).
2. Kenneth R. Sheets, Sarah Peterson, Mary Galligan, and Douglas C. Lyons, "America's Farmers Down the Tubes?" *U.S. News & World Report* (February 4, 1985).
3. Gregg Easterbrook, "Making Sense of Agriculture," *The Atlantic Monthly* (July 1985).
4. Sheets, Peterson, Galligan, and Lyons, op. cit.
5. Mike Meyers, "Propping Up the Farm," *Minneapolis Star and Tribune* (August 11, 1985).
6. Marj Charlier, "Fallow Field," *The Wall Street Journal* (April 25, 1985).
7. Benoit, op. cit.
8. Charles F. McCoy and Marj Charlier, "Banks Give Farmers Loans and Pray for Bailout," *The Wall Street Journal* (June 6, 1985).
9. Kenneth R. Sheets, "Now It's City Folks Who Are Pouring Money into Farms," *U.S. News & World Report* (October 7, 1985).
10. Easterbrook, op. cit.
11. Meyers, op cit.
12. See, for example, the USDA book *Famine 1975*.
13. "A Look Ahead from the Nation's Capital," *U.S. News & World Report* (June 10, 1985).
14. Easterbrook, op. cit.

15. Henry F. Myers, "Why the Farm Crisis Is Likely to Worsen," *The Wall Street Journal* (August 26, 1985).
16. John N. Frank with Patrick Houston, Mary J. Pitzer, and Jeffrey Ryser, "The Farm Rut Gets Deeper," *Business Week* (June 17, 1985).
17. Wendy L. Wall, "Sudden Worsening of Nation's $37 Billion Farm-Export Market May Postpone Recovery in the Troubled Agricultural Economy," *The Wall Street Journal* (March 25, 1985.)
18. Leo J. Shapiro & Associates survey (November 1985.)

More Small Towns Than Ever

★

How small is a small town? As our society becomes more complex, it's harder to define "small" when we talk about towns. But the numbers show that we have more small towns in America today than ever. Not only that, we have more Americans living in rural areas than ever before. And more to come.

Before 1950, the Census Bureau simply called any incorporated place with under 2,500 inhabitants "rural" and let it go at that.[1] Today, people living *either* in the countryside or in communities of less than 2,500 are classified as rural. And any "densely populated area" or community of 2,500 or more is "urban."

We now have more "places under 2,500" classified as "urban" (1,016) across America than in 1970 (627), and nearly twice as many as in 1960 (596). The percent of all Americans living in these smallest "urban" areas is tiny (0.6%). Even so, it's larger than in 1960 or 1970 (0.4%).[2] But these are people probably living in the fringes of an extended city—suburbs just waiting for the city to catch up to them.

What's really surprising is that over a fourth of Americans (26.3%) live in a "rural" area. More of us live in rural areas today (59.5 million) than ever before, but because our natural population has increased, they represent a smaller percent of all Americans (26.3%) than in 1970 (26.5%) or 1960 (30.1%).

At the same time, there are more nice, bucolic little *rural* places of under 2,500 souls (13,800) than in 1970 or 1960, and more Americans live in such places (10.9 million) than in those years.[3]

Growth in the percent of Americans who live in urban areas from 73.5% in 1970 to 73.7% in 1980 was the smallest increase since 1820. But something has happened during the

1980s. The trend of the 1970s toward decentralization of the population has reversed, and by 1983 the percent of Americans living in urban areas was up to 76%. Again, metropolitan areas were leading the nation in terms of population growth.[4] Meanwhile, what's happening to those lovely little townlets we were just discussing? Plenty.

In the past century, it became almost a tradition that people left the farm to move into the city to get jobs and make their fortune (or at least a living). Even as late as 1950–70, this migration continued. Moving became easier, urban-metropolitan areas expanded, and more Americans left farming and other rural occupations. The migration into town continued right up to the mid-1970s.[5]

But then a lot of people began to rediscover the traditional advantages of life in a small community. There were some new advantages, too: As small towns were abandoned beginning in the 1950s, their property values and taxes dropped far below those in the cities. This attracted older Americans and retirees, looking around for cheaper living. A lot of them sold houses in the city, where selling prices had gone sky-high. They took their one-time, tax-free capital gain from the sale, bought an inexpensive house in a small town, banked the balance, and added the interest from it to their income.

At the same time, young families, looking for affordable housing and a quiet, safe place to raise children, also settled into small towns. Medical, dental, and legal professionals moved right along with them. After all, with the explosion of communication technology, it was becoming easier than ever to do big-city–type work outside the metropolitan area. With telephones; computers; fast, flexible private mail and package services to any part of the country overnight; satellite TV; and VCR, you can be as close to the midtown office out in the country as if you were in a central-city high-rise.

Many small communities developed industrial parks, offered tax incentives and water and sewer projects, and launched aggressive campaigns to recruit "clean industry" to provide jobs close to home. This not only brought jobs, it also brought the world to many rural American towns.

In Wisconsin, a Finnish company, Fiskar, opened a plant to manufacture scissors in one small town. In another—Lodi, Wisconsin, where harvesting and packing peas and corn has been the big industry—the Alkar Division of DEC International began turning out stainless-steel smokehouses. And in tiny Walworth, Wisconsin, the 348-year-old Japanese Kikkoman Soy Sauce Company established a new plant for their traditional Oriental products. Over the telephone, its general manager, Toyaji Murai, told me how apprehensive seven Japanese families who moved to Walworth to help set up the new plant were when they first arrived. They were delighted with the countryside itself—"no pollution!" Mr. Murai exclaimed. Then they were won over by the warmth of people in the rural area, who welcomed their company and their Japanese families. "No problems at all! Spirit is very good!" Murai exclaimed. Then: "People here are honest . . . steady . . . *hard* workers."

Now, in the mideighties, there is a swing back toward metropolitan living. New housing starts in metropolitan areas have grown by 80% since 1982, compared to 21% in nonmetropolitan or rural areas. But this doesn't necessarily foreshadow a boom in metropolitan growth. The average metropolitan growth rate in the 1980s has been just about what it was in the 1970s: 0.1%. What's changed is a slowing of the annual growth rate in *non*metropolitan areas, from 1.3% to 0.8%.

Unemployment in rural areas (which was lower than in metropolitan areas during the 1970s) has been higher in the 1980s. Farming and the agricultural services that support it; mining; and energy development—all prime sources of jobs in rural areas—have been hard hit during the 1980s. In contrast, the fastest-growing job sector is services. That's concentrated in the cities and their suburbs. So recent growth has been in suburbs rather than in rural areas. For example, within a few years, more prime office space will have been built in what *used* to be open land in northern New Jersey than there is in midtown Manhattan!

Any massive social change is unsettling. When a lot of people begin migrating at the same time, everything is thrown off balance. High-density suburban growth brings noise, pollution, and crime—the very problems people fled to the suburbs to avoid during the 1950s—along with jobs and services. The new wave of suburban growth has created monumental traffic problems in what used to be little crossroads with a general store and a filling station. Take Tyson's Corner, Virginia, as an example: In just 40 years a placid, country-store crossroads has become the site of the largest "downtown" in the state, where just one shopping center and office complex has brought in 70,000 workers and over 400 retail service operators.

But living and working in suburbs didn't reduce commuting time one bit. The 1980 census showed 27 million Americans, roughly one in four in the labor force, commuting from one *suburb* to another to get to work. This is twice as many as commute to work in central cities. And this mass movement can turn the daily "drive in the country" to and from work into a 10-mile-per-hour, start-stop ulcer session.

Even now, almost half of the adults in America say they would move to towns of under 10,000 to live if they could just get work there.[6] And community planners are preparing the way for them. The Washington, D.C.-based National Association of Towns and Townships has established the National Center for Small Communities to help small towns gear up for the next wave of migrants from cities. Funded by companies such as United Parcel Service, Burlington Northern, John Deere, and R. J. Reynolds, with a modest amount of federal grant money, the Center hopes to help them avoid the problems that come, along with growing population, in what used to be "far from the maddening throng."

With all this going on, we can look for more little rural towns to bloom 50 to 60 miles from the nearest city during the next decade. They will become the bedroom suburbs of suburbs of what used to be the outskirts of cities. Already many rural areas are among the fastest-growing job markets in the United States as industry moves outward.

You can find more little rural places of 2,500 population or less to live in than there used to be. You can open your bedroom window at night and hear bullfrogs but no buses. You can even stand on your front steps and hear the wind soughing in the trees and almost hear the flowers growing. But if you want it to *stay* that way for a few years more, you'd better move pretty far out!

NOTES

1. *Statistical Abstract for the United States 1985* (Washington, D.C.: U.S. Department of Commerce, Bureau of the Census, 1984), table 23.
2. Ibid., table 3.
3. Ibid.

4. Richard A. Engels and Richard L. Forstall, "Metropolitan Areas Create Growth Again," *American Demographics* (April 1985).
5. Glen Fuguitt and Harley Johansen, *The Changing Rural Village in America: Demographic and Economic Trends since 1950*, quoted by United Press International (June 22, 1984).
6. "Back to the Small Town," *Forbes* (April 29, 1985).

We're Still Exploring Our Country

★

Socrates is supposed to have remarked: "See one promontory, one mountain, one sea, one river, and see all." But Socrates was not an American. No American would be that easily satisfied. After confronting the Grand Canyon for the first time, an American lady of our acquaintance turned away from its rim, saying, "See it once, and that's enough." She was eager to get to bigger things.

We Americans can't wait to see parts of the world that we've never seen before. If no one *else* has seen them, that's all the better. We inherit a tradition of exploring, frontier-chasing, and pioneering. It "comes with the territory." After all, much of America was still waiting to be settled three or four generations ago.

Today millions of Americans still yearn to turn off the TV, turn back the thermostat, pack the portable cooler, and get out somewhere exploring—in outer space, over or under the waters, on land, and even under the land. Some prefer to explore in smooth-rolling Airstream luxury, but a surprising number of us still explore in the Western frontier style—on "shanks' mare." Here's a sampling of what adventurous Americans have been doing outdoors during the past years—plus a dozen or so expeditions that still have room for incipient explorers like you and me to join up during 1986:

One evidence of our itch to get back closer to nature (but without getting too close for comfort) is the way Americans are investing in serious outdoor vehicles: Over 44,000 new camping trailers and camper trucks hit the trail for the first time in 1983 alone.[1] (Some weekends it has seemed they were all pulling in at the same campgrounds.)

Catching the Big Ones

Almost a fourth of all Americans (23.8%) went camping in
1983.[2] And among all of the 228 million "visitor days" Americans spend in our National Forest Recreation areas during a
single year, almost a fourth (23.6%) of the visitors were
exploring what the Forest Service calls "general undeveloped
country," which is as close to nature in the rough as you can
get in our national forests.[3]

More Americans than ever before are fishing, too—almost
42 million. While you hear some people "bad-mouthing the
smallmouth" by claiming that "fishing isn't what it used to
be," or "they don't come as big as they used to," the official
records say something else. The fact is that almost half of the
world's record-size deep-water fish caught around the world
in latest record-years were landed in American waters—12
out of 25 new world-record fish. These giants included a
78.8-pound striped bass caught off Atlantic City, New Jersey;
a 1,376-pound blue marlin from Kaaiwa Point, Hawaii; and a
991-pound hammerhead shark brought in at Sarasota, Florida.

More than half of the world's record freshwater fish (seven
out of 11) landed in the two latest years were in American waters. This includes a 557.13-pound carp caught in the
Potomac River in Washington, D.C. (!); a 91.4-pound flat-
head catfish caught in Lake Lewisville, Texas; and a 468-pound
sturgeon landed at Benicia, California.[4]

We also have more big- and small-game hunters than ever.
Over 28 million hunting licenses were sold in the latest
reporting years.[5]

For most Americans, "going exploring" probably includes
trekking through one of our 48 national parks, or one of our
286 national monuments, historic sites, seashores, and
battlefields scattered from Maine to Hawaii and Alaska to
Florida. The National Park Service expected 255 million "recreational visits" to the park areas during 1985—and not
without some trepidation. The parks have become so enormously popular that park officials have had to take cautiously
firm steps to control crowds and cut down on motor pollution
in some of the most popular areas.

Shuttle buses chauffeur visitors through such fragile beauty
spots as Yosemite National Park, Grand Canyon National
Park, and Mesa Verde National Park. This is so more of us

can experience these magnificent areas without getting trapped in a traffic jam.[6]

People planning to camp in the most popular national parks must now make an advance reservation for a campsite. An average of over 44,000 campers a night (a camper may be one lone backpacker, or a family tentful!) "sleep over" in national park campsites. That makes them probably the biggest "motel complex" in the country.[7] To take the hassle out of checking in, a computerized nationwide Ticketron system has been installed; you can make your reservation by telephone. The technology involved in ordering a ticket to the great outdoors from a concessioner's computer is a far far cry from the days of Dan'l Boone and even Dan Beard, but as one Sierra Club official explains, without some concessions "people will love the parks to death."

Really Far-out Camping

The farthest-out exploring done by Americans these days is in outer space. Just as the great sea explorations of the 15th century were financed first by nations, later by private capital, and finally opened the way to new lands for individual travelers, so space exploration in our century was first sponsored by governments. Our government has been encouraging other nations, as well as private investors, to share in space exploration by the Space Shuttle. A Houston firm— Space Industries, Inc.—plans to loft two 36-foot factories into orbit around the world in the hold of a 60-foot Space Shuttle in 1989. The project will be entirely paid for with private funding.[8]

Space in the factory will be leased to manufacturers of pharmaceuticals, electronic crystals, metals, and other products that require a gravity-free environment during manufacture. This is true "exploration," in the original spirit of privately sponsored colonization that opened our hemisphere to settlers almost 500 years ago. But while 15th-century investors colonized their new space with people, the new space factories will operate automatically, without human workers and with only occasional periodic maintenance visits by astronauts.

This doesn't mean that space travel is going to be out of bounds for the rest of us, though. Society Expeditions, a specialized travel-tour agency in Seattle, Washington, has planned a mid-1990s civilian space voyage for people who've been everywhere else.[9] If you can afford to spend $1 million a seat for a three-day vacation, now is the time to line up. They anticipate a trip for 24 to 32 passengers in a Space Shuttle-type vehicle. The civilian "space explorers" will spend three days in orbit and will dock with a space station during the flight (where they will probably attend the captain's welcoming cocktail party!). The original per-person ticket price for Project Space Voyage was only $50,000, but this has been raised to over $1 million per passenger (as of 1985). Don't pack until you hear the final price.

Meanwhile, closer to earth, during 1984 a retired U.S. Air Force colonel, Joe W. Kittinger, Jr., completed the longest solo flight in history by a balloonist—3,543 miles, from Caribou, Maine, to Cairo Montenotte, Italy. It was also the first solo transatlantic balloon crossing. Colonel Kittinger already held the world's high-altitude parachute-jump record (from 102,800 feet).[10] How's that for American pioneering spirit?

Seagoing American explorers made news, records, and fabulous discoveries during 1985:

• After 17 frustrating, costly, dedicated years, 62-year-old Mel Fisher's explorations to find and bring up $400 million worth of gold and treasure, long lost in the hulk of a 17th-century Spanish galleon, *Nuestra Señora de Atocha*, paid off when his divers brought up the first bars of gold from under sands and 55 feet of water off Key West, Florida.[11] Once that site has been fully explored, you might expect Fisher to retire "on the beach" for the rest of his days, counting his doubloons. Not a chance. Fisher already is planning to move on to explore waters near Vero Beach for another galleon, the *San Roman*.

• Eleven American scientists and 26 crew members made twice-daily dives into the icy waters of Lake Superior, using a four-person submarine. No human had ever ventured deeper than 200 feet below the world's largest lake's surface. (Anyone who has ever set foot in its bone-chilling waters on the hottest day of the year will know why.) The expedition's scientists penetrated gorges over 1,300 feet down to study the ecology and bring back scientific samples. "It turns out that it was cold, deep and dark, but there's a whole lot of life," reported William Cooper, chief scientist on the final segment of the historic four-week expedition.[12] And so, right spang in the middle of industrial America, explorers have penetrated another new frontier!

• Meanwhile, back on the surface, Sue Connolly, of Mad River, California, and Barbara Hartley, of Indianapolis, became the first women in history to ride the wild rapids of the Colorado River through the Grand Canyon in an open canoe. Connolly is an intensive-care-unit nurse, Hartley a businesswoman, when not pioneering. "We've kind of presented a new opportunity to women canoeists," said Connolly before heading back to her patients.[13]

• Another American sailor, Gene Savoy, of Reno, Nevada, has been exploring in Peru while gearing up for a seven-year sailing voyage around the world in a replica of an ancient twin-hulled wooden boat with cotton sails. Savoy got the design for his ship from pottery fragments thousands of years old, found along the Peruvian coast. He and his crew of 20 volunteer scientists aboard the *Feathered Serpent* hope to prove that primitive cultures could have migrated eastward across the Atlantic Ocean. "I'm sure we're going to find keys to trans-Atlantic and trans-Pacific cultures that will stagger the world," he said. The explorers will sail 2,500 miles down the Amazon River to the Atlantic, across to the Canary Islands, Greece, Egypt, Iran, Saudi Arabia, India, China, Indonesia, Australia, New Zealand, Easter Island, and back to Peru—a 30,000-mile voyage.[14]

Exploring on Foot

• Rob Sweetgall, a 34-year-old chemical engineer from Delaware, spent 1985 exploring America one foot at a time. Rob believes walking is the "perfect" exercise, both healthful and dirt-cheap, and "you can't get hurt unless you step in a hole." He walked 10,600 miles around the perimeter of America in 1982–83. After that warm-up, Sweetgall set off again, in September 1984, to cover 11,600 more miles while visiting all 50 states (flying in to Alaska and Hawaii, hiking through them, then flying back to the rest of the states). He walks solo, and he sleeps where he finds the best lodging along the way, including motels, jails, churches, stores, and private homes.[15] If Johnny Appleseed was a pioneer legend, then Rob Sweetgall might become one today, striding across America, scattering his gospel of walking wherever he goes.

• Another avid "hoofer," 67-year-old Richard Elton, was in the midst of a series of yearly hikes along the Pacific Crest National Scenic Trail from Mexico to Canada. Elton teaches backpacking and walking courses part-time at Rio Salado Community College in Sun City, Arizona. He began his hikes in 1982 and expects to complete the trip in 1988. He plans to cover Oregon and Washington portions of the trail in three 400-mile segments during 1986, 1987, and 1988. Elton welcomes companions on his hikes—if they can keep up with him.[16]

• Other Americans who like to walk on the wild side (but aren't inclined to go to such lengths) have been taking horseback and raft runs in Wyoming, canoe excursions in Pennsylvania, and autumn white-water fishing jaunts on Oregon's Rogue River, with guides and equipment furnished by a company called American Wilderness Experience. To qualify for this more luxurious mode of exploration, "You should be old enough to get on a horse and young enough to stay on," the company advises.[17]

Scientific Expeditions for Amateurs

For those hardy souls among us who would actually like to work side-by-side with scientists and scholars exploring around our world, an Earthwatch exploration during 1986 might be just the ticket. Since 1971 over 14,000 amateurs, ranging in age from 16 to 80, have joined Earthwatch expedition teams working in America and 68 other countries of the world on over 700 different scientific projects. Sponsor of this global program is Earthwatch, a nonprofit American organization with branches in Europe and Australia.

Volunteer amateurs actually fund and staff the Earthwatch field research expeditions they go out on. Their contributions, including expedition costs and transportation to and from the research sites, are fully tax-deductible, since they work with scientists in the field. Contribution for a two-week field expedition may run anywhere from $795 to as much as $2,385, depending upon where the site is located. Food is described as good and plentiful; housing depends upon the locale, and may range from tents and trailers in the field to cottage living in Scotland, modern cabins in America, or bedrooms in estate buildings in the Rhône Valley of southern France. Here are just a few samples of what amateur explorers have in store for them during 1986 Earthwatch explorations:

• *Swaziland:* Two weeks with archaeologists at Early and Late Iron Age excavation sites, studying early man in Africa.

Except for weekends, members of the expedition team live in a fully equipped permanent bush camp overlooking the Mlawula Wildlife Sanctuary, where there are "plentiful white rhinos, baboons, and wildebeests."

• *Ireland:* Two weeks studying origins of ancient Irish agriculture and seeking prehistoric artifacts with archaeologists in County Waterford, along the seacoast of southeastern Ireland.

• *South Dakota:* Two weeks excavating, mapping, recording, and preserving 26,000-year-old mammoth bones and other fossils at a National Natural Landmark site in Hot Springs, South Dakota, working with a paleontologist.

• *France:* Two weeks working with a team of ornithologists in the Camargue, on France's romantic Mediterranean seacoast. Volunteers will join in tracking, recording, collecting prey samples, and monitoring gray herons at the world-famous Tour du Valat research station.

• *North Carolina:* Two weeks studying the behavior of black bears in the Pisgah National Forest, with a zoologist who has been monitoring these beasts for three years. Teams will trap and radio-collar bears, track them by radiotelemetry, and help map the area and collect food samples.

• *Norway and Scotland:* Two- or three-week tours in Spitzbergen and Bear Island, Norway; or Solway Firth, Scotland, working with an ornithologist, observing, counting, rounding up, and banding the magnificent barnacle geese.

• *Spain:* Two weeks as part of an archaeologist's team, excavating one of the richest Bronze Age sites in Spain, at Moncin and Frias, Aragon. Since 1979, teams here have recovered thousands of Bronze Age artifacts in a "vast El Greco landscape steeped in history." This year's volunteers will help excavate, survey, draw, and record artifacts as well as process finds.

• *Australia:* Two weeks radio-tracking red kangaroos, helping to capture them and surgically implant radiotelemetry devices for monitoring, working with a zoologist at the Fowlers Gap Arid Zone Research Station in New South Wales, Australia. This is the final year of an extended study of these fascinating animals.[18]

These are just a few of many ongoing Earthwatch projects available to American amateurs. If you're eager to explore the world we live in close-up while also making an historic contribution to understanding it better, then one of these expeditions could be your opportunity.

Samuel Johnson (who had something wise to say about practically everything under the sun) divided knowledge into two kinds: "We know a subject ourselves, or we know where we can find information about it." One of the true sources of America's leadership has been our endless quest for more information about the world around us. We "know where we can find information"— and we go there to get it. All of our explorations are part of this process—whether they involve a family jaunt to Yellowstone, digging for Bronze Age artifacts in Aragon, or space-walking over Africa. We never stop exploring, testing ourselves and our environment. And that's why we'll never stop *growing*.

NOTES

1. *Statistical Abstract of the United States 1985* (Washington, D.C.: U.S. Department of Commerce, Bureau of the Census, 1984), table 1040.
2. Ibid., table 374.
3. Ibid.
4. International Game Fish Association, 1982–83 figures, confirmed to June 1984.
5. *Statistical Abstract, 1985,* table 387.
6. Linda Werfelman, "Popularity Alters Character of U.S. Parks," United Press International (August 18, 1985).
7. *Statistical Abstract, 1985,* table 371. Figure for 1983 is latest available.
8. Associated Press, "Firm Wins Bid to Operate First U.S. Space Factory" (August 2, 1985).
9. Bill Johnson, "Deluxe Travel Tours Offer Vacationers a Taste of the Exotic . . ." *The Wall Street Journal* (July 22, 1985).
10. Joe W. Kittinger, Jr., "The Long, Lonely Flight," *National Geographic* (February 1985), pp. 270–76.
11. *U.S. News & World Report,* "Treasure Hunter Who Went for the Gold" (August 5, 1985). Also Associated Press, Knight-Ridder, and United Press International stories published during July 1985.
12. Associated Press, "First Trip to Bottom of Lake Superior Set" (July 21, 1985), and "Sub Ends Study in Lake Superior" (August 21, 1985).
13. Dirk Beveridge, "River Record," Associated Press (July 25, 1985).
14. Sarah Graham, " 'Primitive' Global Sail," Associated Press (May 23, 1985).
15. Frederick C. Klein, "When Sweetgall Walks, People Listen," *The Wall Street Journal* (April 26, 1985).
16. National Retired Teachers Association *News Bulletin* (July 1985).

17. *Changing Times Magazine* (July 1985), p. 28.
18. Information excerpted from project descriptions published in *Earthwatch News* (May, August, 1985).

Where to Write for More Information

Ticketron national park campsite reservations: Telephone your local National Park Service office for nearest number.

Project Space Voyage: Telephone Society Expeditions, Seattle, Washington.

Richard Elton: 9802 Balboa Drive, Sun City, AZ 85351; telephone 602-933-9573.

American Wilderness Experience: P.O. Box 1486 Boulder, CO 80306; telephone 303-444-2632.

Earthwatch: 10 Juniper Road, P.O. Box 127, Belmont, MA 02178; telephone 617-489-3030.

You've Never Had Safer Driving

★

"It just isn't safe to drive anymore," my friend lamented, shaking his head as we tooled through Friday afternoon traffic on the freeway. "Too many cars. Too many fool drivers!"

It certainly seems that way some days. But the fact is, driving in America is safer than it's been in over 60 years. In 1984 we had 18.4 traffic fatalities per 100,000 population,[1] compared to 25.8 in 1970 and 23.3 in 1950.[2]

Today you're a lot safer on the road in your car than you are at home or at work. Twelve out of 100 Americans are laid up or need medical attention during the year because of household accidents. Five out of 100 get hurt at work. But only 2.2 per 100 are injured in automobile accidents. Incidentally, *men* are more accident-prone than are women, both at home and at work. Men and women are equally likely to be injured in an automobile during the year.[3]

We must be doing something *right* about driving: As our safety record on the road has improved, we've been adding more and more cars, trucks, and buses. Today we have more than three times as many vehicles on the road as in 1950, and more than twice as many as in 1960.[4] In fact, we have the highest level of car ownership in the world—one automobile per 1.9 Americans[5]—even more motor vehicles than telephones![6] (Could that be why so many people are installing telephones in their cars?)

We're doing a *lot* of things right to increase safety for American drivers; all these things contribute to the fact that fewer Americans are dying in motor vehicle accidents today than in 1970:

1. *Cars are built safer than they used to be.* We get

better brakes, more effective seat belts, and better-engineered designs, based on manufacturers' ongoing safety research.

2. *The federal Department of Transportation monitors safety for us*. This is one government agency that's been doing a superb job in our behalf, especially under the direction of Philip Davis, a physicist who was chosen specifically "because he's a good administrator." Any make of car, truck, or bus with a safety defect will almost certainly be spotted by this department, which is in daily contact by its "hot line" with consumers. The department has an outstanding record for getting defects corrected.

3. *The 55-mph federal speed limit saves lives*. In 1970, before the 55-mile-per-hour speed limit went into effect, 44% of drivers were clocked at over 65 mph. In 1975, after the Arab oil embargo cut driving, and the Speed Limit Monitoring Program helped to cut driving speeds, only 7% of drivers exceeded 65 mph. Now, in a more permissive environment of "deregulating everything" in the 1980s, more drivers are speeding again: A total of 14% are clocked at over 65 mph.[7] And the average speed of *all* highway vehicles has crept up to 59 mph. However, that's still below the 64 mph average in 1970—and our motor-vehicle death rate is 29% *lower*[8] than it was then.

4. *Accident victims get quicker help*. With today's electronic communications equipment, paramedics, and helicopter ambulances, when there is an accident the victims get the medical care they need a lot faster than before.

5. *We Americans are learning to be better drivers*. Much of the thanks for this should go to the many thousands of brave (though often shaken) driving instructors in schools across the country. They've taught millions of us to drive defensively. Few of us would have either the courage or the patience to take their jobs, but they truly are lifesavers.

There are a lot of people working together to keep you safe every time you get into your car. So "Buckle up and have a safe trip!"

NOTES

1. Department of Transportation estimated 43,800 traffic deaths in 1984, reported in "Traffic Deaths Creep Up Again," *U.S. News & World Report* (February 11, 1985), the first increase since 1979.

2. *Statistical Abstract of the United States 1985* (Washington, D.C.: U.S. Department of Commerce, Bureau of the Census, 1984), table 1041 for 1984 and 1970 figures; *Historical Statistics of the United States*, vol. 2 (Washington, D.C.: U.S. Department of Commerce, Bureau of the Census, 1975), table Q-208 for 1950 figure, and figures in previous years. Last year's traffic death ratio, lower than 1984's per 100,000 population, was the same as the 1918–22 average ratio of 12.3.

3. *Statistical Abstract, 1985*, table 179.

4. Ibid., table 1036.

5. *The London Economist* (March 2, 1985), "Diminishing Expectations," p. 4 of Motor Industry Survey 3.

6. *Statistical Abstract, 1985*, table 925, shows 151 million telephones in the United States, Puerto Rico, and the Virgin Islands as of 1982. It excludes intercompany duplications: one company equals one telephone.

7. *Statistical Abstract, 1985*, table 1046.

8. Ibid.

For Driving Safety Information

To find out about a safety problem on your car, to get immediate information about safety recalls, or to get answers to questions about federal safety standards and regulations: Auto Safety Hot Line. Toll-free call: 1-800-424-9393; also 202-426-0123 in the District of Columbia.

For child-restraint–system information: Write for free publications, *The Early Rider* and *Early Rider Fact Book*, to: National Highway Traffic Safety Administration, Public Affairs, DOT, 400 7th Street, SW, Room 5232, Washington, DC 20590; telephone 202-426-9550.

For safety information on tires: Write for free publications to National Highway Traffic Safety Administration, 400 7th Street, SW, Washington, DC 20590; telephone 202-426-2768.

For safety information on brakes: Write for free publications to National Highway Traffic Safety Administration, 400 7th Street, SW, Washington, DC 20590.

Freedom to Go When and Where We Please

★

Our ship moved quietly toward Haifa after sailing all night from Port Said. Now, Haifa lay just ahead in the early-morning light, and everyone aboard was eager to go ashore. But we dropped anchor well offshore, outside the actual harbor. Engines silent, our ship swayed gently while we waited for something to happen. But what?

An Israeli patrol boat approached gingerly, but stopped at a cautious distance. More waiting. Nothing was happening that we could see. Finally, after some time, our ship came alive again. The anchor came up, engines throbbed, and the *Golden Odyssey* moved gently into dock while the Israeli patrol boat turned and went on about its business. Only then did we learn that before we could enter the Israeli harbor, frogmen from the patrol boat slipped overboard (on the offside, where we couldn't see them), swam under our ship, and examined the hull, foot-by-foot, for bombs.

When we stopped our little rented sedan at the barrier in front of the border station between the Republic of Ireland and Northern Ireland, the beefy-faced young guards were polite. But they surprised and impressed us with the thoroughness of their search as they went over our car. They recorded the serial numbers of each tire. Then the serial number of the engine (we had not even looked under the hood!). Meanwhile, they inspected the car inside and out, from top to underside-bottom. When we were finally permitted to drive into Fermanagh, we were somberly aware of sidelong suspicious glances from women walking along the way. And at the police station, where we stopped to check an address, we zigzagged through a maze of sandbags as we walked to the door. That was bolted, and only opened after the officer inside had time to look us over through a tiny hole.

At the border between Portugal and Spain we were directed to stop, leave our car, and enter a little guardhouse standing alone in the bleak Extremadura countryside. In the shabby, cold little room inside, I had to bow low to hand our passports to a military functionary for inspection. He sat inside a window in the wall that must have been installed by a midget carpenter; its top was no more than four feet off the floor. "Why are you here? Where did you come from? Where are you going?" the man on the other side of the wall asked in *rápido* Spanish. We answered the questions while bowing low toward the invisible armed man who held our passports inside.

How strange it seems to Americans—being searched, recorded, and questioned at borders we cross overseas! With our 220 different borders between and around our individual states, America has about twice as many border-crossing points as in all of Europe. Yet at only 15 of our state borders (all international) must we even pause to identify ourselves. Imagine how it would be if we had to carry a passport in America to be checked at each state border, and left at the desk of our hotel or motel whenever we were out-of-state visitors for the night!

Europeans accept border searches as a matter of course. They've been accustomed to passports since the 16th century. We didn't even need a passport to go into or out of the United States until World War I. The traditional American official attitude has been that our passport is issued simply as identification for American citizens when they are overseas, never as a means of controlling our movements. Now, in a world where terror may be traveling with you, our State Department has added precautions but few outright prohibitions when we travel.

Since 1977 Americans have been free to travel to any country in the world that is not at war with us. However, our State Department does issue two kinds of cautions to Americans going abroad: warnings and advisories. The warning is issued only when there have been openly unfriendly acts by an unfriendly government, authenticated reports of harm to Americans, or when there is acute civil unrest in the area we're planning to visit. The advisory may tell us of hotel shortages in the area we plan to be in, outbreaks of disease, changes in visa requirements, or political developments that may be threatening. (After the 1985 hostage incident in which terrorists boarded the hijacked flight in Athens, a State Department advisory suggested that American travelers avoid the Athens international airport. This was lifted when the Greeks seemed to have tightened security there.) A State Department advisory may also include prohibitions. For example, Americans visiting Cuba are prohibited by the Treasury Department from using credit cards, or engaging in commerce—including stocking up on Havana cigars. (¡Qué lástima!)

At the same time, our government has made it easier than ever before to travel outside the country. You can now pick up a passport application at your neighborhood travel agent's office, fill it out, and mail it in to have your passport mailed to your home. And in an emergency, you can even get a passport within 24 hours or less. All that's necessary is to show your travel tickets and other identifying documents at any State Department office; they can issue your passport on the spot. You certainly wouldn't get fast service like that in the USSR—unless you were booked for Siberia.

Whether it's the lack of travel red tape, general affluence, bargain air fares, or a combination of all three, Americans have been traveling overseas in record numbers. During 1984 there were 4.6 million new passports issued—more than twice as many as in 1970.[1] The year before that, nearly 20 million people took off from American airports bound for foreign countries around the world, compared to only 12 million in 1975. We not only travel a lot, we also travel *far*. More of these jet-setters took off for various points in the United Kingdom, overseas, than to Mexico, just next door. And more headed for Japan than hopped to the Bahamas![2]

This business of traveling far and fast is part of the American tradition. Europeans have always been both amused and bemused at the casual way we approach distance. "You Americans think nothing of flying across the continent," a young Irish engineer told me during a flight from Boston to Phoenix recently, "as for me—this is the first time I've been outside Ireland, and I'd not be here if I weren't working for an American company!" In the 19th century, practically every European who came to our shores seems to have written home about the American predilection for traveling light, fast, and far.

When the international legal authority Francis Lieber came here from Germany in 1826, he wrote, ". . . a lady in New York thinks no more of going to Havre or Liverpool than a lady in London of going to Paris," and he suggested, "the vast unsettled continent before them induced Americans to push on and settle at great distances, especially as the life of the early colonists was such as to develop a daring spirit of enterprise, which gradually has settled down into a fixed trait of American character."[3] Lieber added, "Not distances alone are measured here by a standard different from that of other countries; time, too, receives a different value, but it is measured by a smaller standard than in Europe. An American wants to perform within a year what others do within a much longer period." Lieber was so impressed by this American trait that he stayed here the rest of his life.

We're still covering more ground and traveling more freely than any other people on earth. Here in this country during the 1980s our 144 million cars and trucks cover 1,592 *billion* miles a year—most of it probably to our corner convenience stores. We traveled another 300 million miles on trains— nearly half of it commuting to and from work.[4] Amtrak alone served 19 million passengers a year—17,500 a day just between Washington, D.C., and New York City.[5] And in a single year our certificated air carriers serve 318 million passengers, flying 281 billion miles in the process.[6]

To put all these billions of miles into family-sized perspective, this past summer of 1985, Americans planned to take 282 million trips of 100 miles or more—a little more than three per household.[7] Just for summer jaunts!

When you think about all those grimly guarded checkpoints crisscrossing other parts of the world; all the barbed wire; all those gates, and long lines of citizens waiting to be let in and out—isn't it great to be a "footloose and free" American?

NOTES

1. *Business Week* (May 6, 1985), p. 142.
2. *Statistical Abstract of the United States 1985* (Washington, D.C.: U.S. Department of Commerce, Bureau of the Census, 1984), table 400.

3. Francis Lieber, *Letters to a Gentleman in Germany*, ed. Francis Lieber. (Philadelphia, 1834), quoted in *America in Perspective*, ed. Henry Steele Commager: (New York: The New American Library, 1948), pp. 51–52.

4. *Statistical Abstract, 1985*, table 1027.

5. James Kilpatrick, "Amtrak: It's at the End of the Line," Universal Press Syndicate (May 9, 1985).

6. *Statistical Abstract, 1985*, table 1074.

7. *Forbes* (July 1, 1985), p. 8.

II

The People

★

Don't put no constrictions on da people. Leave 'em ta hell alone.

Jimmy Durante (attributed)

All his life [the American] jumps into the train after it has started and jumps out before it has stopped; and he never once gets left behind, or breaks a leg.

George Santayana,
Character and Opinion in the United States, 1920

The More We Know America,
The More We Care

★

Getting into the wrong elevator in the morning could spoil
your whole day. That almost happened to me the other day. I
had just punched the button for my floor when a man reading
the *Times* opposite me in the elevator shot me a glance over
the top of page 39, shook his head somberly, and grumbled:
"I dunno about people these days. They care about football
. . . the market . . . what happens to J.R. But they don't give
a *damn* anymore about America, right?"

Just as I opened my mouth to answer, the elevator doors
opened, too. "My floor," the Prophet of Doom muttered,
crumpling his paper under one arm as he stepped out. "Have
a good day," he ordered me over his shoulder as the doors
closed.

Any one person who makes a blanket charge like that
against the rest of us deserves a far better answer than you can
give on an elevator. It may be too late—but I'd like to give it
now, just in case he's with us on this page.

It's true that all too few of us take an active part in our
community, at any level. I live in a small section of our town
with just 117 homes, and it's always disappointing to see how
few people are willing to give some of their spare time to
serve on the homeowners' committee. There are a handful or
so of solid citizens, but most neighbors don't even show up
for the annual meeting, where the coffee and cookies are
fresh and free.

It's like that in the national community, too. Only 38% of
us even voted in the 1982 congressional elections, and in
some states fewer than one in four citizens turned out to vote
that year.[1] But it's *not* true that most Americans don't care
about the country. Young and old, Americans today care very

much about their country—and the more they know America, the more they care.

During 1985 we asked hundreds of people across the country, "Do you feel that Americans don't seem to care about the country anymore?" More than six in 10 said people *do* care.[2] But the most interesting thing of all was this: The people who felt the *most* sure about America were baby boomers, age 30 to 39, busy raising families, starting homes and businesses. Also the oldest Americans, age 60 and over. About seven in 10 people in each of these two groups rejected the very idea that Americans wouldn't care about their country.

What makes baby boomers so high on the country? They're from the generation born to understaffed hospitals, overcrowded schools, job shortages when they graduated, and housing they couldn't afford—and yet a big majority of them are enthusiastic about America. I suppose you might say much of this is the sort of high hope and enthusiasm the young always have.

But how about all those elders, age 60 and over? What makes them so sure that Americans generally are high on the country? Think for a minute of all the hard things these 38 million or more elders have been through with their country since they were children. America's elders lived through the great 1929 stock market crash that ruined many of their families; the Depression years; the Bonus March on Washington, when veterans were dispersed by Army troops; the New Deal years; Pearl Harbor; the loss of the Philippines; years of long days and nights in defense plants in the 1940s; fighting in Europe and the Pacific; D-Day; the Battle of the Bulge; V-E day; the hope-filled beginning of the United Nations in America; the A-bomb; V-J Day; the Marshall Plan in Europe; the Berlin airlift; war in Korea; the disillusioning U-2 incidents; the Bay of Pigs invasion; the Cuban missile crisis; the killings of President Kennedy, Bobby Kennedy, and Martin Luther King; the civil rights struggle; the long, miserable Vietnam War; Americans on the moon; Watergate and the resignation of a president and vice president; the energy crisis; Three-Mile Island; Iranian hostages; a new president shot in 1981; the bombing of our embassy and hundreds of Marines in Lebanon; becoming a debtor nation, with the highest budget deficit in history. What a lifetime!

Over 38 million of us who are 60 or over have lived through all these troubles and triumphs together, as Americans. We've seen the United States grow from a mostly rural nation of 123 million people and 45 million jobs to a mostly urban nation of nearly twice as many people and more than twice as many jobs. And these people who have been through the *most* with America, as well as the ones who are really only getting their lives well under way, are the ones most confident about America and Americans!

That's the answer to anyone who says, "Americans don't seem to care much about the country anymore."

The more you *know* about America, the more you *care*.

NOTES

1. *Statistical Abstract of the United States 1985* (Washington, D.C.: U.S. Department of Commerce, Bureau of the Census, 1984), table 425.
2. Leo J. Shapiro & Associates national poll (1985) conducted for this book.

Minority-Group Americans Have Shown
What They Can Do

★

Ten years ago I wrote these paragraphs about a young
Hispanic couple whose story I knew firsthand:

"Burgie and I met in the carrots." Rose Burguan's dark
eyes flash and her face glows, recalling how she and her
husband, Rosario, met while picking carrots, as young
migrant field workers in California. "We were picking
field crops with our parents. For months they wouldn't
let us actually speak to each other—our parents were
that strict. But we smiled a lot, across the rows!"

After this rigidly supervised courtship, when Rose and
"Burgie" Burguan married, they continued working in
the fields. "We had no real home," Rose recalls. "For the
first two years we lived in our car, sleeping there at
night, and eating in the ditches."

The Burguans are still in their early 30's, but they now
own a charming home in a tree-shaded residential neighborhood in Phoenix. They have their own truck, gardening equipment, and family car. As operators of their own
landscaping service, the Burguans are such fierce gardening perfectionists that their fame has spread. They
have a waiting list of prospective customers.

"Burgie" doesn't read English, but Rose Burguan has
completed two years of college. A bright, extremely literate woman, she chose to work as a gardener rather than
in an office when their son Enrique was born: "I wanted
Enrique with me during the day— and I could have him
with me while I did gardening work," she explains. Now
Enrique is in school; Rose and "Burgie" work together
from early morning until dark, six days a week. . . .

Everything the Burguans have has come by their own efforts. But in the Anglo neighborhood where they work, the Burguan family has earned admiration and friendship.[1]

That was in 1976. The world has changed a lot in 10 years, and not all for the better. But today the Burguans remain shining examples of what *can* happen in America. Today the family landscaping business continues to flourish, but with Burgie doing most of the work and Enrique pitching in to help whenever he's not in school. Enrique is now a tall, handsome high-school star athlete who not only hits the ball and hits the line on the sports field, but who also is hitting the books harder than ever before in preparation for college. He has his heart set on a career as a psychologist and has already done "apprentice counseling" as a volunteer aide in summer camp.

Rose Burguan went back to college with the full and enthusiastic support of both her husband and son—who took over her part of the landscaping chores so she could drive 40 miles a day to and from classes at the state university. She graduated with a degree in special education two years ago and immediately set out to apply for a teaching job in the city school system. "'I was so scared when I went out," she recalls now, "because, you know, I was *older* than most new graduates. I didn't know what to expect when I went for interviews."

The first school Rose went to "just to pick up an application blank to fill out and mail in" hired Rose on the spot! The combination of her bilingual fluency, her special training and interest in teaching disadvantaged youngsters, and her enthusiasm and intelligence was irresistible to the school principal. The second day after she started looking, she had a teaching contract.

In the two years since she started teaching, Rose has been voted "Teacher of the Year" by her peers and has been urged to continue her education and move into administrative work. "But I love teaching—I love the children and the school too much . . ." was her first reaction; now she plans to take graduate work so she can become a better educator, a better contributor. There may be better teachers than Rose somewhere, but none is more enthusiastic, none more dedicated to giving children what they need to grow in America. Having come "from the carrots," she's determined to help others up the same path.

* * *

This true story of Rose, "Burgie," and Enrique is an example of what's *right* in America for many minority-group citizens in 1986. Many who got their "leg up" toward affluence and careers in the mainstream during the 1960s and 1970s are showing the full range of their potential in our society. And more are on their way.

But the 1980s, years of growing affluence for whites, have been hard on minorities. It's as if the hopes for growth among blacks, Hispanics, native Americans, and other non-Anglo Americans that were just beginning to come into full bloom have been cut back. National employment and education statistics document the results:

In employment. Black unemployment in September 1985 was 15.3% or 2.5 times the white rate. Hispanic unemployment was 10.4%, or 1.7 times the white rate. Both of these multiples were higher than in 1980. In 1980, the black unemployment rate was just two times that for whites; the Hispanic rate, just 1.4 times that for whites.[2] As *Business Week* commented about this difference in job opportunity between white and minority-group workers earlier in 1985, "The conventional wisdom is that minority unemployment is a fact of life that no one can do much about. But it doesn't have to be."[3]

In education. Although more black and Hispanic students are graduating from high school than did a decade ago, a smaller proportion of them are going on to college. And findings by two authoritative education groups suggest that the reason many young minority-group adults are dropping plans for college is that student financial aid hasn't gone up as fast as college costs. "Their college-entrance rate is declining," a spokesperson for the American Association of State Colleges and Universities said, adding, "The major factors in that decline are economic."[4]

The AASCU findings showed more blacks and Hispanics on college campuses in the 1980s than in the 1970s. But the percent of those eligible for college actually attending was down 11% for blacks and 18% for Hispanics. The high rates of unemployment among blacks and Hispanics, relative to those of whites, may be one contributing factor; in low-income families, when you have someone unemployed, the young have to forgo their chances for higher education. Another factor: The share of federal financial aid for education going to

white students increased by 8% between 1978 and 1983; but
the share for blacks went *down* by almost 5%.[5]

In 1975, when I first wrote about the Burguans, the doors
to education were opening wider and wider for American
minorities. A Rand Corporation study showed that the proportion of black high-school graduates enrolling in college
then matched the proportion of whites. But cutbacks in federal
aid to students since have closed the doors to college for
many minority students. Their numbers have fallen, while
the percent of whites going on to college edged upward to
almost one in three since 1975. The president of the National
Association for Equal Opportunity in Higher Education has
predicted that if this trend continues, minority-group Americans denied education "will lose purchasing power, be sicker
and poorer."[6] If that is so, we'll all lose.

One of the most heartening things about Americans and
our government is that when change becomes necessary, the
people seem to sense it all across the country, as if a wide
wind began to blow and move them. We shift to correct the
course of government. There are two thirds more black elected
officials in America now than there were in 1975; a third
more in state and United States legislatures. Black members
of Congress, who had little influence until recent years, have
been adding seniority, and with seniority in Congress comes
power. The 20 black members of the House of Representatives now chair five of the House's 22 standing committees,
plus several important subcommittees. They have heavy clout
on the Budget Committee, Education and Labor, Ways and
Means, the Armed Services Subcommittee on Military Instal-
lations and Facilities, and other key legislative groups that
control the flow of laws and of funds. Norman Ormstein,
resident scholar in political science at the American Enterprise Institute, has called the growing power of black congressmen "a coming of age for a group of people who were in
many ways disenfranchised but who have now worked their way
up through the system."[7]

While black power is growing at the top of the political
ladder, support for it is growing at the bottom. More than
half of all black adults voted in the 1984 national election—
the highest proportion in 16 years. And the biggest increase
in black votes, as well as the biggest increase in registrations,
was among *young* adults. Meanwhile, there was little or no

difference in voter registration and turnout among white voters between presidential elections in 1980 and 1984.

I think the doors to equal opportunity are going to blow open again. America's minority groups will not be denied their equal chance to contribute to society. Just as the immigrant ethnic minorities of the 19th century worked their way up through the system by adding vote power, 20th century minorities will also come up in that same American way.

NOTES

1. *What's Right With America: 1976*, p. 62.

2. *Statistical Abstract of the United States 1985* (Washington, D.C.: U.S. Department of Commerce, Bureau of the Census, 1984), table 654 for 1980 data; U.S. Department of Labor *News*, "The Employment Situation: September 1985" (October 4, 1985), for most current data.

3. Aaron Bernstein with Lois Therrien, Pete Engardio, Deborah C. Wise, and Michael A. Pollock, "The Forgotten Americans," *Business Week* (September 2, 1985).

4. Mary Margaret Walker, quoted by Washington *Post* news service, "Colleges Get Low Portion of Minorities" (March 31, 1985).

5. Data from American Association of State Colleges and Universities study conducted by human-resources division of Applied Systems Institute, Inc., reported ibid.

6. Samuel Myers, quoted in Linda M. Watkins's, "Losing Ground: Minorities' Enrollment in College Retreats After Its Surge in '70s," *The Wall Street Journal* (May 29, 1985).

7. Norman Ornstein, quoted by Kenneth T. Walsh in "Black Leaders Move up the Power Ladder," *U.S. News & World Report* (April 1, 1985).

The American Family Is Changing— for the Better

★

After getting shaken up in the 1960s and 1970s, by 1985 the American family was getting its act together again. The good news came to us during the year in a series of announcements brought to us by the media:

The wedding announcement. The number of married-couple households rose 2% between 1980 and 1984, to a cozy 50.1 million.[1] That may not seem like a big upward leap, and it isn't. But for millions of parents from a more traditional generation, who never could feel casual about explaining an offspring's informal live-in arrangement, the increase in married-couple relationships was a great turn for the better. The number of unmarried couples living together had exploded from 523,000 in 1970 to 1.988 million in 1984—the most ever. But after growing steadily for over a decade, the number of "live-in" couples ticked downward by 5,000 in 1985, to 1.983 million.[2] It was a small move, but at least it was in the right direction—toward the altar.

The birth announcement. The birth rate rose in 1984 by 1%, and so did the fertility rate—the number of births among women of childbearing age. It also rose 1%, to 66 births per thousand women aged 15 to 44.[3]

The divorce announcement. The announcement that the number of divorces in America had dipped for the first time in 20 years was the most hopeful family news of all when it arrived during 1985. The number of divorces in 1982 (the latest year for which detailed information was available) had dropped by 43,000 after two decades of steady increases since 1962. At the same time, the divorce rate per 1,000 people also fell, to five in 1982, from 5.3 in 1981.[4] The average duration of marriages in the United States during 1982 was 9.4 years, the same as in 1972.

Some experts suggested that the decrease in divorce came because couples have been marrying later in life. (The younger the couple at marriage, the less likely they are to stay married.) Others suggested that since employment had gone down between 1980 and 1982, probably divorces fell because couples couldn't afford to break up. (Two can live more cheaply than one if there are no lawyer's fees and court costs.)

The family-reunion announcement. A final piece of good news for families during 1985 came in a large national study that found that "the three-generation family may never have been stronger or closer than it is today."[5] The study found strong ties between grown children and their parents and siblings. Women with parents or a parent living see them an average of about 62 times a year; men see them about 47 times. These frequent family reunions are possible because almost half of all adult Americans (45%) live within 50 miles of their hometowns, and two out of three live within a two-hour drive of a parent. (This makes it easy to "reach out and clutch someone.")

This finding that three-generation American families are more closely knit than we used to assume confirms what sociologist Theodore Caplow wrote earlier, on the basis of a 1979 study in Middletown (Muncie, Indiana):

> The single most important fact about the nuclear family in contemporary Middletown is that it is *not* isolated. Most people have relatives in other households nearby with whom they sustain close, continuous, and easy interaction. Indeed, it is the presence of those relatives that accounts for their own presence in the community and keeps them from moving away.[6]

So the good news about the American family is that more people are married, fewer are "living in sin," babies are up, divorces are down, and the nuclear family is not fragmenting after all.

But It's Not the Same Family

The makeup of the American family is flexing, and in some ways changing shape, to fit the requirements of our rapidly changing economic and social environment. As we noted earlier, Americans are waiting longer to marry these days. The median age at marriage during 1985 was 25.5 years for men and 23.3 for women. That's over two years older than the average couple married in 1970, and the highest median age at marriage ever recorded in America for women. More young people are putting off marriage while they finish education, or get firmly launched in careers. And that means they're going into marriage better equipped for it than in previous generations.

On the other hand, many of the young Americans who are putting off marriage while they pursue careers may decide *never* to marry. The proportion of women aged 30 to 34 who have never married more than doubled between 1970 and 1983, from 6.2% to 13%.[8] Young women who are as well educated as men no longer need to "find a man to support them," thank you. At the same time, more young men *and* women are staying at home with their parents, apparently because of the high cost of living alone. In fact, young *men* in their 20s are more likely to be still at home with parents these days (one in three) than are young women the same age (one in four).[9]

So, since Americans are marrying later in life, American households today are smaller than they used to be, even a few years ago. The average number of individuals per family fell from 3.58 in 1970 to 3.23 in 1985.[10] This is becoming "a worrisome demographic situation" in Europe, according to French demographer Alain Girard, because of what he characterized as "the collapse of fertility since 1965" in the developed world.[11] Girard added, "The key problem to think about is this: Will the prevalence of individual aspirations in our social behavior rule out the reproduction of our kind? The prevailing values are anti-family and anti-lineage."

Girard speaks, I think, for the traditional French view of family and "lineage." In America, baby boomer couples, with their one or (at most) two boomlets, are going to be more divorce-resistant than young couples in the past. Nowadays, having children together need not be a "little accident." Couples wait until they're ready and plan for children. So they are agreed in advance that they want them. Children make a marriage that is much more likely to endure. As Victor Fuchs has put it, "The number and ages of children are systematically related to divorce . . . the more young children present, the less likely the marriage is to dissolve."[12]

Even during the socially unstable years of the 1960s and 1970s, when many baby boomers were sampling various life-styles and household-styles, children were the bond that strengthened marriages. A 13-year Rand Corporation study of 10,000 households between 1968 and 1981 found that even though marriages were of shorter duration then than now, a married-couple family with children could be expected to stay together for almost seven years, compared to just a bit over four years for a childless marriage, and 1.8 years for an unmarried cohabitation.[13] Now, in the more stable society of "aging baby boomers" in the mid-1980s, the odds for families with children will be much better—as we're already beginning to see.

In their relatively small household, with more than one income, and grown-up, well-educated parents who have waited and planned for both marriage and family, children of the boomlet generation should have a great head start on the future. And so should their families.

But while those fortunate children of comparatively afflu-ent couples are off to a good start, the number of single-family households headed by women continues to grow, and is expected to grow as rapidly as two-parent families for the rest of this century. The Ford Foundation has reported that more than half of the children in single-family households live in poverty, an entirely different kind of head start. A March 1985 Census Bureau report showed that over one in five of all American children live in poverty. That's a shameful thing for our government to admit; but here's another: One authority has estimated that a third of the children living in the United States today will be on welfare themselves by the time they are 18.[14] Most of these poor or almost-poor children are *not* the offspring of unwed mothers, but of divorced mothers who were once in better financial circumstances.

These are American families, too, and the children of Amer-ican families. In spite of the overall figures that show us a favorable progress report on the American family generally, these poorest children and their mothers remain in their desolate and threatened position. Even the most conservative studies document the fact that they, and other low- and middle-income family groups, have been placed at increasing risk. An American Enterprise Institute study showed that during the past 30 years, the average effective tax rate on middle-income married couples with two children nearly tripled; that for single people and married childless couples increased by only one sixth.[15]

Our dynamic, affluent, and family-oriented Judeo-Christian society has these least-favored of its families and children on its social conscience.

NOTES

1. Census Bureau figures quoted in "Married Couples," *The Wall Street Journal* (May 7, 1985).
2. Census Bureau figures quoted in Associated Press news service "Unmarried Couples Are Fewer" (November 20, 1985).
3. Preliminary National Center for Health Statistics report quoted in United Press International news report "Birth-Rate Rose, Divorces Dipped in '84" (March 30, 1985).
4. National Center for Health Statistics report quoted in Associated Press report, "Divorce Falls for First Time Since 1962" (March 7, 1985).
5. The Family Life Survey, conducted by National Opinion Research Center of the University of Chicago for *Family Circle* magazine, reported by Associated Press news service, "American Family is Doing Fine" (September 26, 1985).
6. Theodore Caplow, Howard M. Bahr, Bruce A. Chadwick, Reuben Hill, and Margaret Holmes Williamson, *Middletown Families: Fifty Years of Change and Continuity* (Minneapolis: University of Minnesota Press, 1982), p. 340.
7. Census Bureau figures quoted in Associated Press news service "Unmarried Couples are Fewer" (November 20, 1985).
8. U.S. Dept. of Commerce data quoted in "Marriage, Young-American Style," *U.S. News & World Report* (July 30, 1984).
9. Peter Francese, "Growing Number of Men Elect to Shun Fatherhood," Cowles Syndicate news service (June 16, 1985).
10. *American Demographics* study, "Households, Families, Marital Status and Living Arrangements: March 1985," reported in Associated Press service "Unmarried Couples are Fewer" (November 20, 1985).
11. Alain Girard, quoted in interview for the conservative *Magazine Hebdo* (Paris, October 5, 1985).
12. Victor R. Fuchs, *How We Live* (Cambridge, Mass.: Harvard University Press, 1983), p. 148.
13. Rand Corporation data quoted by Peter Francese, "Cureall for 7-Year Itch Eludes Researchers of Family Change," Cowles Syndicate news service (August 25, 1985).
14. Daniel Patrick Moynihan, quoted by David Gergen, "Restoring the American Family," *U.S. News & World Report* (April 22, 1985).
15. Douglas J. Besharov and John C. Weicher, "Return the Family to 1954," *The Wall Street Journal* (July 8, 1985).

An Instinct for Simplicity

★

When some animals and insects feel insecure they become "flashers." Birds who think their territory is being invaded flash a panoply of brilliant feathers and puff up their breasts to frighten the invader away. Dogs flash their teeth and raise their hackles. Insects flash strips of color they don't normally display. These are all inherited rituals of insecurity.

Human heads of state greet other heads of state who enter their territory by flashing a bristling line of brightly feathered ceremonial warriors. What could be sillier, when you stop to think about it, than a president of the United States in our nuclear era leading a lady head of another presumably friendly state in a ritual march past a chorus line of matching warriors, all clutching unloaded guns in a rose garden? He should know better.

Ordinary citizens display better manners. When visitors arrive at your house, how do you welcome them? Do you take them to view the family gun collection? Display your American defense and marksman medals from World War II? Demonstrate the family's electronic alarm system? I hope not. Most of us ordinary folk invite guests to take a seat—any seat. We ask, "What can I get for you?" Then we all settle down to the pleasant human business of sharing experiences and friendship.

Why can't heads of state be more like us?

Why must generals and admirals be flashers? When they are insecure they display a glittering chestful of medals and campaign ribbons. The ribbons are meant to flash a signal that this human being has been present at great scenes of mass killing, and *he* survived. They also signal that after all that killing, this person and the forces he represents are still

59

going through the same old stratagems of the past, still flashing threats. Don't we all deserve something better?

What we need is more Samantha Smiths. I think this is
why people around the world felt a surprised pang of personal loss when young Samantha died. Almost none of us
actually knew this American child. But I believe we all felt
proud of her because she spoke for something hidden in us.
We've grown up among the old tribal rituals, but we still have
an instinct for simplicity, too, that makes us hope for something cleaner and more direct.

Samantha worried about nuclear war, as we all do. She
followed her instincts, and simply wrote to the head of
another great state, asking him how *he* felt and what he
thought we ought to do about it. It was a disarming gesture
that no nonhuman creature, locked into genetic patterns of
behavior, is capable of making. Samantha gave us a little
momentary feeling that perhaps we might all act that human.

When Samantha died we were reminded again how much
we all yearn for the open honesty of shared fears and shared
hopes. We go along with the ancient failed rituals because we
have inherited them. But our continuing hope is that somewhere among the new generation there may be young leaders
with that instinct for simplicity that could disarm us all.

Americans Are Good Sports

★

A Chinese writer educated in a Buddhist monastery and in American universities, No Yong-park, wrote this about us in his book *Oriental View of American Civilization:*

> Another thing which impresses me most about the American is his spirit of sportsmanship. Of course, there are a lot of unfair people in every country, but the representative [American] is a good sport. In play or in work, he follows the rules of the game. He is willing to let his opponent have a fair chance. If he is defeated, he is a good loser; he does not cherish any animosities. He congratulates the victor cheerfully and consoles himself with being a good sport.[1]

No nation is more competitive than ours; we play "hardball" in every arena of activity: sports, business, the courts, even in our schools. But it is true, as No Yong-park noted: Americans are "good sports." We play hard, we play to win, we hate to lose, but we play by the rules.

Remember the fifth-inning brouhaha in the last game of the 1985 World Series? Cardinal pitcher Joaquin Andujar charged toward umpire Don Denkinger (who had just called two of his pitches balls) like a raging bull. Cardinal manager Whitey Herzog, usually a model of pensive restraint during games, had already gone jaw to jaw with Denkinger after the first call and been ejected from the field by the umpire. When Andujar went for Denkinger after the second pitch, his teammates charged toward him, too—but only to physically restrain the *pitcher*.

In the midst of all this fury, what were the tens of thousands of rabid fans at the game doing? Were they storming the

barricades? Thronging onto the field to tromp the ump? Not a
bit of it. Not a single fan hit the field—much less the officials.
The only blow struck was John Tudor's frustrated haymaker
in the locker room, at an electric fan. Even pitcher Andujar
sounded like a model of self-restraint when a reporter asked
him later if he would have physically accosted the umpire had
he not been pinned by his teammates: "I have to be a
dumb—to hit an umpire."

What happened in Kansas City that October night was high
drama and will be remembered and debated in the Hot Stove
League on winter nights for years to come. But it was a
shining moment of sportsmanship compared to the way fans
reacted at sporting matches elsewhere around the world during the same season:

> *In Buenos Aires*, on April 7: "A teen-ager was killed, 50
> persons were injured, and 100 others were arrested in a
> brawl between fans at a soccer game. . . ."

> *In Bradford, England*, on May 13: "The police said today
> that smoke bombs were thrown at the Bradford soccer
> stadium on Saturday, before a fire swept through the
> main grandstand, killing 53 people."

> *In Birmingham, England*, on May 13: "Nearly eclipsed
> by the Bradford fire was a riot in Birmingham the same
> day in which police officers tried to separate hundreds of
> fighting fans on the field. . . . Eighty spectators and 96
> police officers were injured and 125 people were arrested."

> *In Peking*, on May 19: "Thousands of Chinese soccer fans
> went on a rampage outside a Peking stadium tonight
> after China lost a match to Hong Kong. Much of their
> wrath was directed at foreigners. . . ."

> *In Mexico City*, on May 27: "Ten people were trampled
> to death and 30 were injured today when fans tried to
> force their way into a Mexican soccer championship
> match. . . ."

> *In Brussels, Belgium*, on May 29: ". . . 38 people were
> killed and more than 200 injured before the start of a
> soccer match here between British and Italian teams."[2]

I am not trying to suggest that foreign sports fans are a
bunch of ravening animals, and Americans a troop of Goody-

Twoshoes. Not for a moment. We have incidents of sports violence here, too. An American sociologist, J. M. Lewis, recorded 312 different reports of riots at baseball, football, and basketball games in our country between 1960 and 1972. What I am suggesting is that Americans are generally inclined to honor the rules of every game they play or watch. Our differences are often about whether or not the *rules* were followed. And we celebrate winners but also honor any honest, hardfighting loser who has gone by the rules.

This carries over into all areas of our national life, including business. The competition is fierce for our business dollars; it's a no-holds-barred game sometimes. But the final rules of business play in America are the law, and those who step over the line of the law know the penalties. We are "good sports"—or else.

Nowhere else in American life is the "good sports" rule more more evident than in our major-league politics. The campaigning may be vicious—but as we've seen, we draw the line at "dirty tricks" that overstep the law. And when the campaigning is over and the scrupulously guarded and counted secret ballots are all in, both our winners and our losers go forward like "good sports."

On election night in 1984, after a long and brutally competitive campaign, the Democratic vice-presidential candidate expressed her congratulations to the Republican winners and reminded us:

Tonight the campaign ends. This is not a moment for partisan statements. It is a moment to celebrate our democracy and to think of our country. . . . I ask all Americans to join together and pledge our support for our president in the search for a more just society, a strong America, and a world at peace.

Her fellow candidate, who had just lost his bid for the highest office in the land, also personally congratulated the winner, and then said, of the voters who had taken part in the contest by voting:

Their choice was made peacefully, with dignity and with majesty, and although I would have rather won, tonight we rejoice in our democracy, we rejoice in the freedom of a wonderful people, and we accept their verdict.

After that, the losers in the World Series of American politics were free to go home and write their books, give their interviews, and return peaceably to their lives as citizens. *That* sets our country apart, too, from many in the world today, where only the winners survive.

We are, as our Chinese observer No Yong-park said, "good sports." And as long as our competitors at the very *top* are that way, the fans in the stands also feel free to abide by the rules. I know it's been said that "Nice guys finish last." But it hasn't worked that way for America, and for Americans generally.

NOTES

1. No Yong-park, quoted by Henry Commager, *America in Perspective* (New York: New American Library, 1948), p. 294.
2. All of these news excerpts come from extended reports in *The New York Times* (April 8, April 14, May 20, May 27, May 30, and May 31, 1985).

We're Getting Fitter All the Time

★

Avoid running at all times.
Satchel Paige

A lot of us still subscribe to Satchel Paige's advice for staying fit. It must have worked for him. Satchel Paige was indisputably the most durable baseball pitcher who ever walked the bases. And one of the best. On one historic afternoon in the 1930s, Satchel struck out Rogers Hornsby—then the mightiest right-handed hitter in baseball history—five times in a single game. Paige was still playing big-league ball in 1953, at the venerable but vital age of 54.

But there's also increasing evidence that jangling your frame around, working up sweats, and even running a bit may actually be beneficial for you. All around us Americans are "into fitness" these days, and going at it with vigor.

Just to give you a glimpse of how serious we've become about the strenuous life: In 1984 Americans spent over $4 billion to buy 207 million pairs of athletic footwear![1] That's an average of about 1.2 pairs of athletic shoes per American adult. Any nation where every adult has a pair of athletic shoes has got to be doing something more strenuous than watching Sergeant Slaughter pounding on the fearsome Ugandan Giant Kamala in cable wrestling.

We even feel fitter these days than we used to. In a 1985 survey, adults across the country were asked if they "ever felt Americans are getting fat and soft." Six in 10 said yes, they had. "How about now?" they were asked. "Do you feel Americans are getting fat and soft now?" Fewer than *five* out of 10 Americans said they think we're out of shape now.[2] So you see? All this jogging, bench-pressing, and general Jane Fonda-ing has even *us* admitting that we look better to ourselves than we used to.

It's true that we're eating more—49 pounds of food per person more per year than we ate 20 years ago. We're also averaging 270 calories more per day per person. But the good part is, we're eating more fish, poultry, vegetables, fruits, cereals—the stuff of champions.[3] More than half our families say they're "concerned about good nutrition" these days; 35% are even doing something about it.[4] One other positive thing: We have cut back on our smoking: 15% fewer cigarettes per capita, and 33% fewer cigars.[5]

But that's just "the spinach." The big difference in how we're staying fit these days is exercise. We are exercise-mad. Six out of 10 American adults say they exercise every day—more than twice as high a percent as in 1961.[6] Almost half of us swim; about a third bicycle; roughly 40 million bowl; 34 million jog; 30 million roller-skate; 28 million play softball; and 25 million play tennis.[7] Twenty million kids are involved in some kind of organized sports.[8]

Dad and the kids used to be the ones who got sweaty and bruised while playing. Now one of the most intriguing new developments is the way women have joined in the games. A 1984 survey of 11 different sports found that in eight of the 11, more than half of the new participants were women. Seven in 10 new participants in bicycling are women; about two out of three new participants in physical conditioning with aerobic equipment, or in weight training, are women.[9]

"*Weight* training?" Yes, weight training. Did you ever in your born days think you'd live to see "the little woman" pumping iron? Maybe that's one reason why no wise man would dare call her "the little woman" nowadays. She'd bust your arm. In a suburban Detroit body-building center for women (aptly called "Spunky's"), the proprietor, a 41-year-old mother of three who tips the scales at just 100 pounds, can bench-press 130 pounds! That is *fit*.

Jogging, a sport known to so few Americans 20 years ago that surveys didn't even ask about it, is now commonplace; 26% of Americans over age 12 claim to have run or jogged during the past year—23% of them women.[10]

Where Did All This Start?

There's speculation about what is driving us to all this physical-culture stuff. Some social scientists think worries about health and diet have even replaced sex as the primary source of guilt feelings in America. One writer, who points out that our new passion for exercise is "age-irrelevant and gender-indifferent," speculated, "It's motivated by the all-American desire to improve oneself—to be better, to be healthier—as opposed to, say, just trying to look sexy."[11]

I think our new fitness drive has more profound sources. Americans have always had a self-improvement streak. We were raised on an ethic of "bettering oneself." I think our fitness kick today is part of an instinctual drive for survival in an increasingly threatening environment.

Since the 1960s, a whole series of events have reminded us again and again how vulnerable our bodies and our ecological envelope are to a lot of invisible dangers that we didn't even suspect existed before. Consider just a few examples: The surgeon general's bombshell report on smoking in 1964; the Truth in Packaging law, which rubbed our noses in all the unpronounceable chemicals listed on food packages in 1966; Earth Day in 1970, with 20 million Americans out demonstrating for a clean environment; a whole series of discoveries of deadly substances lurking in the walls of our homes and schools; and detergents, insect sprays, deodorant soaps, product containers, foods, drinking water, air, medications—even in the little stream that sparkled beside the country road and alongside the suburban schoolyard.

Is it any wonder that we've become a nation of people trying to protect our vulnerable bodies, trying to erect a shield around ourselves, each with a heightened desire to relish the life that's threatened in so many new ways every day? That is the need, I think, out of which today's fitness culture emerged.

Media, book publishers, manufacturers—all suppliers of our daily needs and wants—are acutely tuned to consumers' needs. They sensed and responded to our concern for our well-being. They flooded us with information, products, and programs created to feed our hunger for what soon became a program in itself: "wellness." We yearned to stay well, even as the world around us seemed to turn sick. The whole concept of "wellness" as it has evolved combines exercise, healthful diet, rest, and control of stress. Whether we buy the entire "wellness" concept as individuals or not, we're caught up in a kind of nationwide multifaceted movement aimed at self-preservation, and self-enjoyment of feeling alive—even if it takes extra effort, and if stiff, sore muscles are one of the necessary components. "No gain without pain" replaced the playboy hedonism of earlier, more carefree and juvenile decades.

Fitness Made Fun

In response to America's social change of mind since the sixties or so, wellness has become a huge convenience market for fitness consumers filled with new and better products and ways to (1) stay alive and (2) enjoy it. In earlier years, exercise was once calisthentics: "one-two-three, up-down-up-down . . ." Calisthenics were very dull long before they became rewarding. And they required not one shiny stick of equipment. In earlier years, healthful diet was a lot of raw stuff, every raw mouthful chewed 40 times before swallowing, because we had been taught that

> Nature will castigate
> Those who don't masticate[12]

Today we've streamlined both diet and exercise, as Americans streamline everything. We've also made them a lot more fun. Now you can get 100% of your U.S. recommended daily allowances of 100 vital nutrients in one breakfast cereal bowl. Add milk, wait five minutes, and you won't even have to chew at all. As for exercising—we can get all the physical benefits of old-fashioned calisthenics and more during aerobic dancing. It's still hard work, but *fun*, and you're interrelating in a support group of other flab fighters, all "dancing with sweat in their eyes." If you don't like to interrelate under bright lights while flapping your pectorals and varicosities publicly, then there's an infinite range of elegantly shiny, efficient-looking personal exercise devices for what they call "shaping up at home."

One issue of *Runner's World* (a sort of *Better Homes and Gardens* for joggers and marathon runners) lists over 100 different "top training aids." All have come to market during the 1980s, to serve the needs of a huge and growing number of Americans on a nationwide fitness kick. Ranging from a reflective headband for roadside running in the dark ($1.59) to a "state-of-the-art" computerized Exercycle from an aerospace manufacturer ($3,995), there's gear to make exertion more comfortable, and more productive, too, from the ground up: socks designed to keep rocks from getting into runners' shoes; a special leash for runners and dogs who jog together; for carrying things, a pocket that you attach to the shoelaces of your running shoes; a jump rope with a digital counter built into its handle to keep track of calories while you skip along; a "snugly fitting fanny pack to carry snacks while on road or mountain"; water-filled vests to vary your weight; a video cassette that takes you on an hour-long bicycling tour of Yellowstone National Park while you pump along on your stationary home Exercycle; a whole host of home gym equipment, ranging from a complete exerciser that folds into an attaché case or under the bed, to an adult jungle gym too big for the average living room.[13]

For hacker-joggers, there are even athletic shoes with a built-in microchip that measures the distance you run and the calories you burn on the road. The shoes come with software, so when you get home from your run, you simply plug one end of a cable into the heel of your shoe (first removing from the foot), and the other end into your Apple IIe or Commodore 64 computer. The software instantly transfers the data from your heel to your computer. "What hath God wrought now!"[14]

Some 30 million Americans now say they use exercise equipment of some sort at home.[15] This might be called the "home stretch" phase of a fitness trip that began when millions of us started jogging back in the 1970s. Next, more of us flocked into health clubs and spas to tone up muscles jogging missed. After that came our cardiovascular period, with the pulsing fitness disco beat of aerobics. And now we find we didn't even have to leave home to find fitness. Home exercise equipment is where it's at. We pump iron in the bedroom to the easy rock of morning FM radio, while coffee maker and microwave oven make breakfast just down the hall from our folding spa.

More Fit

And it's working. We feel fitter. We are living longer. Americans males' average life expectancy at birth climbed from 67.1 years in 1970 to 71.0 years by 1983, women's from 74.7 years in 1970 to 78.3 years in 1983.[16] Exercise is even improving our mental condition: New public-health studies suggest that all this physical activity we're into can make our heads work better, "improve self-image, social skills, and cognitive functioning; reduce the symptoms of anxiety; and alter aspects of coronary-prone (Type A) behavior and physiological response to stressors."[17] We are healthier: Heart-disease deaths went down 36% nationally between 1978 and 1983 "probably due to reduced smoking, dietary changes, increased physical activity and improved medical care . . ." and stroke deaths went down 51% in the same period.[18]

More Gold

Not only is America's fitness drive paying off for those of us at the grass roots of physical culture, it's also paying off in gold at the Olympics. In 1984 Olympic Games track and field competition at Los Angeles, American men and women ran off with 14 gold medals compared to just six in 1976 (the last time we competed). In swimming competition our men and women took 21 gold medals, compared to only 15 in 1976.

Most Soviet bloc nations boycotted the Olympic Games at Los Angeles in 1984, as we boycotted the Olympic Games at Moscow in 1980. Still, in the 1984 Olympic Games Americans set eight new all-time, all-nation Olympic records in track and field, and 11 new all-time, all-nation records in swimming. Compare these with just two new Olympic records set by us in 1976 Olympics track and field, and only one in 1976 Olympics swimming competition. We've made enormous progress in international sports competition during a decade.

More Women Winners

Since the federal government began leaning on colleges and universities to put more of their athletic program funding into women's sports, which had historically been shorted in favor of men's athletics, American women have come into their own in sports. Take our 1984 Olympics track and field women athletes, for example: Evelyn Ashford, who won the gold for us in 1984 in the 100-meter run, did it in over a second less time than our *male* Olympic champion's time over the same distance in 1896. Valerie Brisco-Hooks, who won the gold for both the 200- and 400-meter runs, ran both events faster than did four different American male winners in the 1896, 1900, and 1904 Olympics. Joan Benoit won the gold for us in the marathon in 1984 in 2:24.52, a new Olympic women's record. Her time was an hour faster than that of the American male winner in 1908. "They were giants in those days," but American women are catching up to them today.

The performances of our modern women Olympic swimmers are coming very close to the best men did in recent times. Take the gold-medal–winning time set by both Carrie Steinseifer and Nancy Hogshead in 1984 in the 100-meter freestyle swimming competition (55.92): That's faster than any male Olympic winner ever achieved until 1956. (Johnny Weismuller—Tarzan of the films—won the gold in 1928 with a time of 58.6, almost three seconds slower than what our women Olympians now clock.)

Tiffany Cohen's 4:07.10 time for the gold in the 400-meter freestyle competition in 1984 was faster than any male Olympians ever achieved until 1972. Buster Crabbe—the other famous film Tarzan—won the gold in 1932 in 4:45.4, some 38 seconds slower than Tiffany's time.

Theresa Andrews won the gold for us in 1984 with 1:02.55 in the 100-meter backstroke, faster than any male Olympian up to 1956. And Mary T. Meager's 2:06.90 record time in the 1984 competition for the 200-meter butterfly stroke gold was faster than that of any male Olympian until 1964.

"Sure, sure, sure . . ." you may say, "but you're talking about the youngest, best-trained Olympians in the world! What does this have to do with fitness down at the neighborhood sandlot level?" Okay, let me give you one more truly sandlot sample of how fit Americans can be at *any* age today. Would you believe a baseball team that plays three days a week, year-round, and even the batboy is at least 75 years old?

Down in fountain of youth country, at St. Petersburg, Florida, there's a softball league known as Kids & Kubs. It's made up entirely of players who have to be at least age 75 even to qualify. The two teams are competitive as cats and dogs, but they are gentlemanly about it. Rules specify that if either team falls four games behind, the captains get together and swap a few players to beef up the losing side. (If only heads of state could be so gentlemanly. All they trade is spies!) As a result of this sensible agreement, after 38 games played in 1985 they were all tied up at 19 games each.

The heaviest hitter in the Kids & Kubs league had already

hit 16 home runs in the first 38 games. Four years earlier, after a triple-bypass when his pacemaker was installed, doctors thought he might die in his sleep. Now he's a league-leading slugger at age 77. But then, maybe that's not so surprising. He's one of the youngest players in the league. The Kubs' lead-off batter, just recovering from throat surgery, was age 100.

Woman and girl, man and boy, we Americans probably are fitter today than any other generation of Americans before us. It's because we're taking better care of ourselves and know more ways to do it. They didn't know as much about wellness and fitness in earlier years. One elderly American, Charley Smith, told reporters who asked him his secret for longevity, "I smoked, I drank, I chased women. If I'd have known I was going to live so long, I'd have taken better care of myself." Charley Smith was age 138 when he died.

We're smarter these days. So keep watching your diet and your weight. Pump that iron. And when you turn 75 you could be playing baseball three days a week in St. Petersburg.

NOTES

1. American Sports Data, Inc., figures, in "On the Run," *The Wall Street Journal* (August 29, 1985). The shoes included 75 million running and jogging shoes, 50 million sneakers, 29 million tennis shoes, 16 million basketball shoes, and 7 million hiking boots.
2. National telephone survey conducted for this book in July 1985 by Leo J. Shapiro & Associates; 48.6% of all adults did not think we are currently getting fat and soft.
3. Basic data from U.S. Department of Agriculture.
4. NPD Group nutrition survey 1985, quoted in "The Nutrition Gap Quiz," *Health Magazine* (January 1985).
5. *Statistical Abstract of the United States 1985* (Washington, D.C.: U.S. Department of Commerce, Bureau of the Census, 1984), table 1366.
6. Gallup Poll data quoted in Steve Huntley with Ronald A. Taylor, "Keeping in Shape—Everybody's Doing It," *U.S. News & World Report* (August 13, 1984).
7. A.C. Nielsen Company 1982 figures used as base for rounding off.
8. Data reported by Youth Sports Institute, Michigan State University.
9. American Sports Data, Inc., figures quoted in "Women Athletes," *The Wall Street Journal* (September 5, 1985).
10. *Statistical Abstract, 1985*, table 384.
11. Owen Lipstein, quoted in "Ain't Sexy Healthy?," *Forbes* (July 1, 1985).

12. This was the rhyming slogan of Horace Fletcher, who won thousands (some say hundreds of thousands) of disciples in the United States early in this century. One of Fletcher's basic nutritional principles was that each mouthful of food must be chewed 40 times before swallowing, so "the main part of its flavor has been set free and appreciated." In those days, of course, people didn't "eat and run"; but how could they with all this long-term chomping going in?

13. "Charting the Top Training Aids on the Market," *Runner's World* (August 1984).

14. Puma RS Computer Shoe and Software Package described in *Fortune* (May 13, 1985).

15. John P. Tarpey, "Home Exercise Gear: Another Industry Gets Fat on Fitness," *Business Week* (January 28, 1985).

16. National Center for Health Statistics, preliminary 1983 data available in 1985.

17. *Public Health Reports* (March–April 1985).

18. *Nutrition Action* (September 1984).

19. All of these Olympics records came from *The World Almanac & Book of Facts 1985*, published by Newspaper Enterprise Association, Inc. (New York, 1984), pp. 833–39. The type is mouse-size, but you're invited to check my historical comparisons between women's and men's Olympic performances and see if you can catch me "off the mark."

A Genius for Organizing to Get
Things Done Together

★

"I believe that for every problem there is a solution," said Candy Lightner. Five years earlier, as Lightner's 13-year-old daughter walked to a church carnival, a car swerved out of control, hit and killed her. The man arrested for the accident had been bailed out of a hit-and-run drunk-driving charge less than a week earlier. But a police officer told Lightner that even though the man charged with her daughter's death had a long record of arrests for intoxication, he would probably never be jailed.

The night before the funeral, Candy Lightner announced to friends: "I'm going to start an organization." Less than five years later, the organization Candy Lightner launched single-handedly was a nationwide force, with 320 chapters and 600,000 volunteer members and donors. As a result of Mothers Against Drunk Driving (MADD), all 50 states have introduced tighter drunk-driving laws, and a new federal law reduces highway grants to any state not raising its drinking age to 21. "If you believe in something badly enough, you can make a difference," said Candy Lightner.[1]

Americans are born organizers. It's in our genes and in our traditions. When something needs doing, we organize. And then we do it together.

You can see this trait in our national games. We have great individual stars, but baseball, football, and basketball are all essentially games of organized skill and effort. Leaders organize; the *team* wins.

You can also see it in our national history. In the 18th century, Americans organized 13 wildly different, fiercely independent, sovereign and separate little colonies to create the United States of America. The Constitution is not so much a great piece of writing as it is a superbly organized structure of law to build on.

In the 19th century, Americans organized wagon trains to cross the vast and alien lands westward, opening a continent. No single settler could have made the trip alone.

In our own century Americans organized 20,000 independent contractors and 400,000 individual workers to fit together over 3 million separate parts to build and launch a new kind of ship that set the first human being on the moon.

Nowhere is our native organizing ability put to wiser or better use than in American social services. Americans lead the world in organized volunteer efforts to solve human problems. Candy Lightner, and the national volunteer social service organization she created, are inspiring examples of this, but there are many others, serving human needs daily on international, national, and neighborhood levels.

Following are just a few examples of how Americans are organizing and volunteering to help solve problems because they "believe in something badly enough" and want to make a difference.

Feeding Hunger in America

"Right now, in this land of plenty, about 20 million Americans don't have enough to eat. Not for lack of food, but for lack of information," said John Driggs. He, too, believed the problem must have a solution. For Driggs, the solution was to *reach* the 40% of Americans who were actually eligible for federal food stamps but not participating. Driggs was convinced that most people who were going hungry without food stamps simply needed to be informed: "They don't know they're eligible, they don't know the rules, they don't know how."

Driggs went out and got support for his idea from the National Governors' Association, the National League of Cities, the United Way, the Salvation Army, the American Association of Retired Persons, the National Council of Churches, and others. Then he went to the Advertising Council for more volunteers—volunteer specialists who could create a national advertising campaign to inform people about available food and how to get it, if they were hungry. Members of the Advertising Council are America's leading advertising agencies and media representatives. They donate creative help and media space and time to worthy causes. The Council liked John Driggs's idea and volunteered to take it on as a public-service project.

All he needed then was to raise half a million dollars to cover actual production and printing costs for the national public-service campaign. "I'll get it," John Driggs promised. "It's just a matter of ringing enough doorbells."[2] And he did.

John Driggs's idea is now a national campaign, created by a big-league New York advertising agency as a volunteer project, running on television and radio stations and in publications across the country in space and time also donated on a volunteer basis.

Feeding Starving People in Africa

In Ireland, a singer had an idea to help raise money to feed millions of people starving in Africa. The idea was to bring together the world's top pop music talents performing free, as volunteers, in a spectacular fund-raiser for African relief.

When entertainment impresario Michael Mitchell heard about singer Bob Geldorf's idea, he was equally enthusiastic about it. He and his organization, World-wide Sports & Entertainment, specialize in creating and staging large-scale events. The end result was "Live Aid," the spectacular, star-studded, 16-hour telethon last July that used 14 satellites to join people together in 150 countries around the world and raised an estimated $50 million for African relief. It was "the most visible charity effort in history," bringing together 1.5 billion participants, not to mention all its volunteer superstars and corporate sponsors such as Eastman Kodak Co.; PepsiCo, Inc.; American Telephone & Telegraph Co.; and General Motors Corporation.[3] And it all started with a single human idea; a single human being who saw a problem, knew there must be a solution—and found volunteers to bring it to life!

Beauty and Pride for Neighborhoods

Alex Alvarado and James Inghram saw a problem all around them: low-income youngsters, looking for work, and graffiti everywhere in their inner-city neighborhood. Both Alvarado and Inghram work for a silk-screening company. They got the idea that neighborhoods littered with graffiti could be beautified, and community pride revived, if the scrawls and spray-painted threats were replaced by murals.

The two 23-year-olds talked their idea over with area businesspeople, whose walls had been literally smeared with graffiti. Business owners agreed to supply paint if Alvarado and Inghram would find a way to supply mural-painting talent. The two took their idea to the city councilwoman representing their area, Mary Rose Wilcox. She was enthusiastic about it and got start-up funding of $3,600 in city money to be used in hiring mural painters for the project. "We thought we'd try this as a pilot project for our teens," Wilcox said. "Maybe if we got the same kids who graffiti the walls now to paint the new murals, they wouldn't do it again."

All through a long, hot summer, with scorching temperatures nearly every day, Alvarado, Inghram, and artist Martin Moreno worked with two teams of teen-age youths, "brightening up the corners where they were." Handsome, imaginative, highly colorful murals were painted over the old graffiti. Three city social-service agencies handled distributing the funding. The youthful brush-wielders (who were also paid for their work) were supplied by other city programs.

By the end of the summer, 13 huge murals were up in the area. Some were simply designed to beautify. Others, including a powerful allegorical mural warning about the dangers of paint-sniffing, deliver messages. "We are utilizing murals as an instrument of education," said artist Martin Moreno. "Murals should get people in the community involved, excited, and reinforce culture." Not everybody in the neighborhood agrees about the content, but everybody certainly agrees that the murals are a great improvement over the graffiti they replaced. And, as councilwoman Wilcox points out proudly, "So far, nobody has graffitied over the murals!"[4]

Neighbors Helping Neighbors

It has been traditional in America that problems too big for any individual can be solved by bringing in volunteers—neighbors helping neighbors. The first settlers at Plymouth helped each other raise log walls and roofs against the winter weather. Later, in frontier days in the Midwest, "the construction of the new cabin became a festive affair for the entire neighborhood. Always ready to assist one another, the local settlers would join together to help their newest neighbors. While the men set to work building the house, the women gathered to brew hot coffee and bake special breads or cakes for the occasion. For the grateful newcomer, this house-raising party was a warm introduction to the frontier's brand of hospitality."[5]

Nowadays, that kind of amateur house-raising would also draw city building inspectors; citations for code violations; pickets from several building trades unions; a vice president from a savings and loan concerned that its mortgage money might be misused; and an insurance man recommending more personal-injury coverage in case one of the volunteer house-raisers fell off the roof during the festivities. Life has gotten a lot more complex than it was in frontier days. But the good old volunteer spirit is still in place all across America, working to solve all kinds of problems in a thousand different innovative new ways, as well as through long-established agencies. We still work out our problems together.

An international Gallup Poll conducted in the United States and 13 nations throughout Europe found that Americans are much more likely to do voluntary work for their churches and other religious organizations than are people in any of the foreign nations. About one in four Americans (23%) are volunteers. The only other nationality groups that come even close to that are in Northern Ireland (14%) and Spain (10%). In contrast, fewer than one in 20 people in Finland, France, or Denmark say they volunteer help for religious groups or church.[6]

Still another Gallup Poll, conducted only in America, found more Americans doing volunteer work in 1983 than in 1981. More than half of us (55% in 1983 vs. 52% in 1981) were doing some kind of volunteer work in both years.[7]

Volunteering Money

Volunteering "by remote control," by contributing money that can be used to hire for the job to be done, makes it possible for millions of us to help individuals through giant funds. Individual Americans contributed $61.6 billion to charity in 1984—11.1% more than in the year before.[8] We're certainly not pikers: That works out to $359 apiece for each individual American aged 18 or over. Our overall contributions to major fund-raising organizations have increased enough to more than keep pace with the rising cost of living since

1975 and 1976, even through high-inflation years. For example, while the cost of living rose 65% between 1976 and
1983,[9] our contributions to the United Way rose 77%—from
$1.104 billion to $1.95 billion in the same period.[10] In fact,
Americans' total private philanthropic contributions rose from
$32.5 billion in 1976 to $64 billion in 1983—a healthy 100%
increase.[11]

Just a few examples of the hundreds of different ways in
which individuals contribute to charitable organizations will
show how diversely we contribute. We give not only to
various charities for religious, educational, health and medical care, social welfare, arts and humanities, civic and public
purposes.

• Over 100 screen, sports, stage, and television stars took
turns on the air to raise money for National Public Radio in
its first coordinated national fund-raising effort, in 1985. Over
$1 million was pledged in listener contributions by halfway
through the first day of a six-day campaign.[12] Public Radio,
which carries no advertising, gets only 15% of its funding
from the federal government. Federal funds for both Public
Radio and Public Television have been cut drastically, since
reaching a high of 27% in 1980.[13] Now audiences are "taking
up the federal slack" in cultural and public-service programming.

• To help fellow citizens in the economically depressed Iron
Range mining and forest region of northern Minnesota, people of the state rallied 'round, dug down, and contributed $88
million out of their own pockets.[14]

• Individual citizens donated $1.9 million to the IRS in 1984
"to help pay off the national debt." This just about doubled
the amount contributed by public-spirited citizens the year
before. It wasn't enough to keep up with the increase in the
federal debt over the same period, unfortunately. Interest on
it alone was costing over $3.5 million a day.[15]

Volunteering Themselves

• In the Peace Corps, some 5,500 volunteers are serving in
60 developing nations around the world. When the Peace
Corps sent out a call to recruit an additional 600 agricultural
specialists to help increase food production in Africa at the
beginning of 1985, it got 10,000 replies![16]

• In VISTA, thousands of Americans are serving as volunteer workers with rural and urban poor throughout America, helping them find solutions to community problems.

• In the Older American Volunteer Program, low-income volunteers serve 20 hours a week for a small stipend as members of the Foster Grandparents Program or the Senior Companion Program. Other volunteers serve in various capacities as members of the Retired Senior Volunteer Program. This sets no limits on income or the number of hours a week its volunteers may work. RSVP members receive no compensation. Over 350,000 Americans 60 years of age or older are involved in these government-sponsored volunteer programs.[17]

• Through 460 local agencies across America, adults volunteer to spend four to six hours a week for at least a year as Big Brother or Big Sister to one child who needs companionship, and the stability of a continuing relationship. The children are of school age. Most are living with a single parent. Great care goes into recruitment, screening, and matching Big Brothers and Big Sisters with the children so the new friendship will become enriching for everybody involved.[18]

• Over 272,000 members of the American Association of Retired Persons (AARP) are serving as volunteers for worthy causes, doing everything from tax counseling to community work.[19]

• Some 1,500 teenage volunteers every summer are working, living, and learning with professionals in 225 federally administered conservation and resource management areas around the country as part of the Student Conservation Association's Park, Forest, and Resource Assistant (PFRA) program and in high-school programs. The young volunteers help maintain and construct trails, build bridges and shelters, and replant heavily used areas.[20]

• Nearly 600,000 Americans are currently serving as volunteers with police or sheriff's departments around the country. They save their communities tens of thousands of dollars a year. On average, four volunteers furnish the equivalent in personnel of one extra police officer. At the same time, volunteers have the satisfaction of doing immensely useful and satisfying work. As one woman volunteer explained it: "If you haven't worked with arrest sheets, types of crimes, and that sort of thing, you have no idea what goes on in your city. It's made me much more aware." About half of the volunteers working in police and sheriff's departments are age 55 or older.[21]

• An estimated 10 million Americans are involved in 20,000 volunteer neighborhood patrols against crime. They also help to take the pressure off overloaded and often underfinanced police departments. "There's no better way of curbing crime than to have citizens looking out for each other," in the opinion of a big-city police lieutenant. "We can't have a cop on every block."[22]

• Other neighborhood volunteer groups are getting together to maintain property values. Each member agrees to put in front-yard flower beds, trim hedges, clean part of the street and alley (a service some cities can no longer afford to provide), and even scrub their front steps. Others are joining together to install yard lights, and to set up telephone or walkie-talkie programs between neighbors, to watch each other's houses for signs of crime. By getting together to accomplish these small joint efforts, citizens learn that they can make real changes in their neighborhood once they get together. The next step is that they get together to become active in city politics. There they apply group pressure to get major improvements for their area—better streets and other city services.[23]

• Conservative Christian families nationwide are establishing what they call "shepherding homes" for pregnant teenagers who have been rejected by their own families. In over 300 homes nationally, volunteer couples take girls in to live with them. The girls help with family chores while continuing their high-school work and preparing for the birth of their child.[24]

• In a desert-area training ranch, volunteers from throughout the United States live in a tiny "Third World" village. The village was built to help train the volunteers in what life will be like when they go overseas to work with locals, in arid Third World countries. After 10 days of living in the arid desert without plumbing or electricity, cooking on mud stoves and solar ovens outdoors, eating food of Third World countries and sleeping in mud huts or plastic 12-by-12–foot "Hope houses," volunteers "graduate" to a similar camp in Florida. There the climate is like that in tropical Third World countries. Volunteers are mostly in their 20s, but some are in their 50s. The training program costs volunteers $150. They must raise their own $950 a month support money to fund two-year assignments overseas as members of the Christian-oriented Food for the Hungry movement. The still-small but growing group has members serving throughout the world. Most raise the money they need for their volunteer service through pledges from church groups.[25]

• Professional psychotherapists, counselors, psychologists, and psychiatrists from various religious groups have volunteered to provide therapy for individuals and families in a program developed by a large Catholic retreat center run by the Franciscan order. People who can't afford to pay for their therapy sessions help out around the sprawling center as volunteers. Those who can pay make a donation of any amount—"whatever you can afford."

• At one state university, retired professors and other professionals have formed a Retired Volunteer Service Corps group. Members volunteer to work six to 10 hours a week at the university. They provide all sorts of services in the school, from tutoring undergraduates to collecting statistics for varsity teams. "These are things that often are in very short supply on college campuses," according to a dean at the school. The coordinator of the program estimated that volunteers provide "in the neighborhood of a half million dollars in services to the university each year." The average volunteer in the program "keeps on giving" for three years.[26] Why? *They love the work!*

• Helping to save land, restore landmarks, build parks, and grow food for the needy has become a volunteer project for local groups all over the country, with guidance and help from the America the Beautiful fund.

• Thousands of volunteers who love to read and are good at it are helping others learn to read. They tutor illiterate adults through their local Coalition for Literacy agency. Some 27 million adults in America are functionally illiterate. The volunteers who help unlock a whole new world for these people and make them more self-sufficient than ever before.[27] The volunteers are given training in tutoring.

• Crafts workers are building housing for the poor in their communities, using volunteer labor, donated materials, and contributions as part of the Habitat for Humanity movement.

• Women volunteers all over the country are giving support services to battered women and their children at some 700 shelter centers. Women are referred to the centers by the volunteer-staffed National Coalition Against Domestic Violence.

• Men and women are working with handicapped and disabled children as volunteer helpers in arts programs at institutions, schools, and other locations in their communities. The programs are coordinated and promoted by the National Committee, Arts with the Handicapped.

• Others provide companionship, personal care, and homemaking services for terminally ill patients at their homes or in homelike hospice facilities as part of the 1,200 hospice programs around the country.

• People who like to read, record textbooks and other educational material for blind students and professionals at 28 local locations around the country. Readers have at least two years of college, and clear speaking voices; knowledge of a technical subject also helps, since much of what is to be recorded is technical material. Volunteers are auditioned. Then they are trained either to read or to help with taping, as part of the famous Recording for the Blind project.

• Others help out as part of office staffs and household services at one of 63 Ronald McDonald houses across the country, where parents can stay while their children are being treated in hospitals nearby.[28]

• In community food banks, hospitals, nursing homes, the Salvation Army, the St. Vincent de Paul Society, Goodwill, and the Volunteers of America, the hours of service are long, the money is short, and the need for help is endless, but our neighbors are pitching in today as volunteers. You may not even know they're doing it; volunteers don't brag much— they just get out and get the job done.

"Three C's" Volunteering Help

Where the need is too large or complicated for individuals to get it organized, or to deal with the finances, the "three c's" are joining hands as volunteers: citizens, communities, and companies. A dozen brief examples will show how varied the means and the approaches are in this combined volunteering. All provide dramatic examples of Americans finding new ways to lend a helping hand to others who need it.

• *Giving a secure home and professional counseling to troubled teenagers.* A nonprofit organization with houses in four cities takes abandoned or abused girls with enormous

problems, and girls aged seven to 18 from broken homes, and
provides them with a residence and professional counseling
for up to 18 months. Support for the homes comes from
whatever parents of the girls can pay, plus state agency
funds, donations from individuals, and fund-raising. Sponsors
of the project also give volunteer worker assistance. There is
no federal funding involved.[29]

• *Winterizing senior citizens' homes.* Simple energy-saving
measures such as weatherstripping can cut heating and cool-
ing bills by as much as a fifth—a saving that means more food
on the table for elderly low-income people. A public utility,
the state planning office, a governor's advisory council on
aging, and volunteer senior-citizen energy consultants worked
together to send trained two-person teams into the homes of
over 1,200 senior citizens in a southwestern state to provide a
free energy audit. Then they installed weatherstripping, caulk-
ing, water-heater blankets, and pipe insulation, all without
charge, at an average cost to the public utility of $10 to $12.
The company estimates that this kind of proper weatherizing
can save the elderly customers $120 to $240 a year on utility
bills.[30]

• *A program to help find missing children* that began as
the idea of one dairyman has become a nationwide multime-
dia volunteer crusade. And it's getting results. One midwestern
dairy began putting photos of missing children on its milk
cartons. Soon more than 400 dairies across the country were
doing it. Then pictures began to appear on paper plates;
sports scoreboards; moving vans; cereal boxes; on posters in
aircraft, subway cars, and commuter buses; film envelopes;
and on bags and displays at 13,000 supermarkets. A TV
network showed photographs of 51 missing children; 11 were
found. "We now know . . . the display of missing children in
public is successful in the return of some children safely to
their homes," said Jay Howell of the National Center for
Missing and Exploited Children.[31] All because of one volunteer effort that grew into a national volunteer crusade!

• *Teenagers gathering oral histories of elderly* are creating
a valuable permanent record of what life was like in the past
100 years. They're also learning firsthand about the process of
aging and how other people have lived their lives. And they're
learning how to relate to old people. The New York project
was sponsored by a college institute on humanities, arts, and
aging and financed by a $244,791 grant from a private founda-

tion. College students videotaped the project. Each interview was audiotaped, and the tape-recorded interviews will be printed in a book, which will make it accessible to historians in the future. More than 500 homebound and frail people are expected to be interviewed, with 53 teenagers doing the questioning.[32]

• *Helping unemployed workers prepare for jobs, and helping them find the jobs by watching cable television programs*. At a time when the unemployment rate in Detroit was 12.7%, Otto Feinstein had an idea for helping unemployed people. He went on the air with it. Feinstein launched Working Channel, the first 24-hour cable TV channel in America dedicated exclusively to the unemployed. He also became executive director of the Communication/Information System for the Unemployed. This nonprofit organization combines Working Channel with Working Circles, support groups in which people discuss their job-seeking problems. The channel has aired programs on how to do your best in the high-school equivalency exam, on making a good impression when interviewing for jobs, and on labor organizations and vocational training that might benefit an unemployed person. It also aired three daily half-hour listings of latest job openings in the area. Other stations in other cities have also become interested in the effort. Funding for Working Channel was provided mostly by federal funding and local philanthropies.[33]

• *Providing a temporary home for elderly and handicapped* who have neither money nor a place to stay. Worn-out, unemployable workers in Phoenix who have no pension or family have a home until they can obtain entitlements for general assistance, S.S.I. disability, or other financial aid, thanks to a combination effort of the Department of Economic Security, Metropolitan Phoenix Commission of the United Methodist Church, the St. Vincent de Paul Society, the city of Phoenix, and individual donors.

The residents themselves contribute whatever they can toward rent, if they have any income at all; the city provides the house and a major part of utilities costs; and staff, food, furniture, and clothing, as well as "going money" to keep the facility open and care for its residents, comes from its sponsors and donations from individuals.[34]

• *Cleaning up a city by providing jobs for youngsters*. A public-service grant from the Gannett Foundation has made possible a project in El Paso to refresh city parks and remove graffiti throughout the city. The grant was made to a private nonprofit organization, which administers the program. The program, called Trash Busters, hires a cross section of city youngsters to work full-time during the summer and on weekends during the school year. Volunteer retirees serve as advisers. The youngsters are paid for their work; they also become eligible for scholarship grants based on year-long projects. Mayor Jonathan Rogers of El Paso was enthusiastic about the prospects for Trash Busters: "It will be a fantastic benefit to the city, and more importantly, it will clean up the city."[35]

• *Turning unused public buildings into housing.* A nonprofit foundation set up in 1982 has been helping to turn an old Philadelphia school building into a 55-unit housing project for elderly poor. The Enterprise Foundation, established by community developer James W. Rouse, contributed a $20,000 planning grant for the project, then lent $200,000 at 5% interest and helped to create further financing as well as furnish technical advice. The project is being sponsored by a citizens' group in Philadelphia.

• *Creating and donating $800 million worth of public-service ads a year to raise funds and awareness for good causes.* Because of massive cuts in government funding for social-service programs, there's more need than ever to involve public support for such programs. Every year, dozens of America's top advertising agencies turn teams of their best creative people loose, developing advertising campaigns for such public-service programs as the National Crime Prevention Council, Smokey the Bear, the United Negro College Fund, the campaign against drunk driving, and over two dozen other worthy causes.

The campaigns are created as a volunteer contribution by the agencies. The ads appear in $600 million worth of magazine and newspaper space, and during television and radio time also donated by the media as a volunteer contribution. Are they effective? Enormously—and the Advertising Council (which has been coordinating public-service campaigns of this sort as a volunteer effort ever since the war-bond campaign of 1942) monitors its campaigns every year to be sure they're doing a good job. Take just one shining example: Since volunteer Ad Council campaigns for the United Negro College Fund began in 1972, annual contributions to the fund have increased from $11 million to $30 million a year. Think

how many more young men and women that's helping to get
education that can bring out the best in them![36]

• *Helping struggling women to support themselves and
their children by getting a better job.* In the four years since
it was founded in 1981, Arizona Women's Employment and
Education, Inc., has trained 2,500 women so they could get
into (and ahead in) the work force. About half of the trainees
were on welfare when they came to AWEE. Close to nine
out of 10 (86%) were working in 1985, or training for jobs.
Women not only learn job skills in the program, they are also
helped to develop self-esteem and discover talents and capa-
bilities they may not have known they had. Funding of
$332,000 a year for the program comes largely from state and
county governments. However, Carol Hebert, director of
AWEE, said "firms want to work as partners" in the program;
the group aims to raise $85,000 in corporate contributions in
1986.[37]

What a tiny amount that is, against the enormous sums
spent by departments of the federal government these days—
and how much human meaning this has for taxpayers it
benefits directly.

• *Giant companies volunteering to help public-school kids
become engineers.* "Increasingly companies around the country are pitching in to help educate public-school students,"
wrote Joe Davidson in *The Wall Street Journal.* And that's
not all. At one high school in Washington, D.C., students use
computers donated by IBM; and they are taught by teachers
trained by General Motors Corporation. In more than 20% of
the nation's school districts, according to one U.S. Department of Education survey, one in five schools already has
some kind of "partnership" with a company, in which schools
receive resources for programs, and the company gets to help
educate potential workers while they are still students (thus
cutting future on-the-job training costs for itself). Another
25% of the schools don't have such a "partnership" arrangement with a company, but they say they would like to have
one. Interestingly, the survey also found that "inner-city
schools seem to be corporate favorites."

Other giant companies helping schools and students by
donating money or equipment, lending personnel for instruction, or training teachers include Atlantic Richfield Co., Burger
King outlets, Potomac Electric, and literally hundreds of
other corporate and nonprofit agencies around the nation. It's

a quid pro quo deal, with companies donating teaching needs that schools no longer can afford, and getting pretrained, favorably inclined future workers in return when the kids graduate.[38]

Although most students, educators, and business leaders are said to praise these partnerships, it must be recognized that the companies involved have a very big ax to grind. Partnership arrangements virtually give them the pick of the best-prepared graduates when they come into the job market. But isn't that the heart of neighbors helping neighbors, after all? "One hand washes the other."

• *A pioneering volunteer "partnership" to make the community a better place in which to live* has been going on among large corporations and segments of the community in the Twin Cities of St. Paul and Minneapolis, Minnesota. It combines a number of America's biggest and most innovative corporations, their retired employees, and what normally would be classified as a "society luncheon club" in a remarkably effective group of programs aimed at giving a hand to some of the most needy citizens in the state.

The corporations include Honeywell, First Bank System, International Multifoods, Cargill, General Mills, Soo Line Railroad, Sperry, 3M, and the St. Paul Companies. The social group serving as prime mover is the 1,000-member Twin City Junior League. The third key group involved, known as VIE, is made up primarily of retirees past 55 and eager to be of help in the community.

Together these three groups have created many different volunteer community-service projects, including clothing and food drives for the poor, and working with inmates at the women's prison in Minnesota. At monthly meetings, volunteers and corporate sponsors share experiences and ideas for ways to be of service to the community, with some 20 Twin Cities corporations participating, and literally thousands of potential individual volunteers also contributing expertise and enthusiasm.[39]

We can't all be great organizers. But we can all be contributors, one way or another. It takes both to make an organization effective. We are all surrounded today by human problems, but as Candy Lightner said, "For every problem, there is a solution." One at a time, we solve them together.

NOTES

1. "You Can Make a Difference," *Time* (January 8, 1985).
2. Alan Thurbur, "U.S. Hunger Ills Haunt Executive," *Arizona Republic* (July 5, 1985).
3. Jeffery Zaslow, "Next from the Live-Aid Team . . . ," *The Wall Street Journal* (August 9, 1985).
4. Julia Lobaco, "Teens Cease the Writing on the Wall," *Arizona Republic* (August 18, 1985).
5. Joanna L. Stratton, *Pioneer Women: Voices from the Kansas Frontier* (New York: Simon & Schuster, 1982), pp. 50–51.
6. "23% of Americans Are Volunteers," *The Case Spirit* (Scottsdale, Ariz., August 11–24, 1985), quoting surveys conducted by The Gallup Organization and Gallup International Research Institutes (GIRI) for the Center for Applied Research in the Apostolate (CARA), Washington, D.C., and the European Values System Study Group (1981).
7. *Statistical Abstract of the United States 1985*, (Washington, D.C.: U.S. Department of Commerce, Bureau of the Census, 1984), table 647.
8. American Association of Fund-Raising Counsel, Inc., data, quoted in "Charities Count Their Blessings," *U.S. News & World Report* (May 27, 1985).
9. *Statistical Abstract, 1985*, table 792.
10. Ibid., table 649.
11. Ibid., table 650. Figure includes individuals, foundations, corporations, and charitable groups.
12. *Arizona Republic* (April 23, 1985).
13. *Statistical Abstract 1985*, table 931.
14. R. L. Anderson, S.J., "The Economy Pastoral: A View from Minnesota," *Catholic Week* (February 15, 1985).
15. *Statistical Abstract, 1985*, table 496.
16. Jacob V. Lamar, Jr., "New Spirit in the Peace Corps.," *Time* (February 11, 1985).
17. Dan Hurley, "The Call to Care," *50 Plus* (July 1985).
18. " 'Big Sisters' Help Kids," *Essence* (February 1985).
19. "At Your Service," *Modern Maturity* (February–March 1985).
20. Kimber Craine, "Environmental Jobs Available for Summer," *National Parks* (January/February 1985).
21. *Modern Maturity*, op. cit.
22. Ted Gest, "Street Crime: People Fight Back," *U.S. News & World Report* (April 15, 1985).
23. "Block Clubs," *The New York Times* news service (August 3, 1985).
24. Margery Rose-Clapp, "Sharing a Burden," *Arizona Republic* (July 4, 1985).
25. Walter Mattern, *Arizona Republic* (July 11, 1985).
26. "Retirees Find Role on Campus," *Modern Maturity* (June–July 1985).

27. Alvin P. Sanoff and Lucia Solorzano, "It's at Home Where Our Language Is in Distress," *U.S. News & World Report* (February 18, 1985).
28. "10 Volunteer Jobs That Rate a 10," *Good Housekeeping* (January 1985).
29. Dorothee Polson, "Residential Treatment Center," *Arizona Republic* (May 1, 1985).
30. "Homes of 438 Senior Citizens Weatherized," *Arizona Republic* (May 1, 1985).
31. "Milk-Carton Hunt for Lost Children," *U.S. News & World Report* (February 11, 1985).
32. Glenn Collins, "Teens Record Oral Histories of New York Elderly," *The New York Times* news service (June 2, 1985).
33. Catalina Camia, "Cable-TV Programs Assist Unemployed," *The Wall Street Journal* (July 8, 1985).
34. "Home Rescued from Closure," *The Vincentian*, St. Vincent de Paul Society of Phoenix (July 1985).
35. "Gannett Funds 'Trash Busters' in El Paso, Texas," *NRTA News Bulletin* (March 1985).
36. Ronald Alsop, "These Ads Sell Food Stamps and Sobriety—and with Style," *The Wall Street Journal* (January 31, 1985).
37. John Tighe, "Agency Helps Struggling Women Get on Feet and into Work Force," *Arizona Republic*, (June 16, 1985).
38. Joe Davidson, "Partners or P.R.? U.S. Firms Help Public Schools," *The Wall Street Journal* (April 30, 1985).
39. Leonard Inskip, "Retirees: An Untapped Resource," *Minneapolis Tribune* (April 17, 1985).

Want to Volunteer? Here's Where to Get Information

MADD (Mothers Against Drunk Driving): 669 Airport Freeway, Suite 310, Hurst, TX 76053.

Peace Corps: Telephone 1-800-425-8580.

VISTA: Telephone your state VISTA headquarters.

Older American Volunteer Program: Telephone 1-800-424-8580.

Big Brothers/Big Sisters: 230 North 13th Street, Philadelphia, PA 19107; telephone 215-567-2748, or your local unit.

Volunteers in Parks (VIP): Write to superintendent of national park area that interests you. For paid and volunteer seasonal jobs, contact: National Park Service, Seasonal Employment Unit, 18th and C Streets, NW, Room 2227, Washington, DC 20240, or telephone 202-343-6901.

Police and sheriff's department volunteers: Contact your local police or sheriff's department.

America the Beautiful Fund: 219 Shoreham Building, NW, Washington, DC 20005.

Literacy Center: P.O. Box 81826, Lincoln, NE 68501; telephone 1-800-228-8813.

Habitat for Humanity: 419 West Church Street, Americus, GA 31709.

National Coalition Against Domestic Violence: 1500 Massachusetts Avenue, NW, Room 35, Washington, DC 20005.

National Committee, Arts with the Handicapped: NCH Education Office, John F. Kennedy Center for the Performing Arts, Washington, DC 20566.

National Hospice Organization: 1901 North Fort Myer Drive, Suite 402, Arlington, VA 22209.

Recording for the Blind: 20 Roszel Road, Princeton, NJ 08540.

Ronald McDonald Houses: 500 North Michigan Avenue, Chicago IL 60611.

Americans Are "Peculiarsome" About Books

★

Remember that illustration of young Abe Lincoln lying on his stomach in front of the fireplace, reading by firelight? It was in schoolbooks to inspire us back in my primary-grade years at school.

The picture itself was romanticized, but the situation was real. Abe was a bookworm. "The things I want to know are in books; my best friend is the man who'll git me a book I ain't read," he told his half brother Dennis Hanks. His other half brother, John, said, "Whenever Abe had a chance in the field while at work, or at the house, he would stop and read."[1]

I must confess that when I look at that picture of young Abe today, I can't help wondering: "If Abe had a television set there instead of the fireplace . . . would he have been reading?"

When radio first moved in with American families, in the 1920s, some authorities predicted that it would "be the death of books, and reading." Again when television took over living rooms across the country in the 1950s, the *next* generation of authorities wagged their heads sadly and predicted that books were "on their way out." But, as often happens with authorities, they turned out to be wrong. Americans are reading more today than we did in prebroadcast days of the 1930s, the 1920s, and before that. (That may be hard to believe, but read on. . . .)

During the 1920s and again in the 1930s, sociologists Robert and Helen Lynd conducted two monumental surveys of everyday life in "Middletown," a typical American city. In the 1920s the Lynds commented that book-reading in Middletown then meant ". . . the reading of public library books."[2] A total of 48% of the population in Middletown had a public-library card in 1925 and checked out an average of 15 books a year per capita. In the 1930s most of the books Middletown read still came from the public library. The Lynds said, "Middletown is not a book-buying city."

In the mid-1970s, when Middletown was again studied by teams of sociologists, they found more reading going on than ever. There were about as many books per capita circulating from the public library as in 1925. But as people became more affluent, "by 1977, Middletown was emphatically a book-buying city," with 13 retail bookstores, including two specializing in religious literature and two in pornography. "There is much more recreational reading in Middletown today than in 1925, and its content is not noticeably less serious," sociologist Theodore Caplow concluded.[3]

What was true in Middletown between 1925 and 1975 was true even more so across the whole country. The number of new books and new editions published in America each year more than quadrupled between 1925 (9,574) and 1975 (39,372).[4] Not only were people reading more, they also were reading more *different* books.

Book Burners

Of course, not everybody wants us to buy and read a wide range of literature. We've always had a few commissar types around who would like to censor our reading, to protect us against learning things they don't want us to learn. Nothing would warm their hearts like books burning.

In the 19th century there was fat, fishy-eyed old Anthony Comstock, a self-styled "reformer" who crusaded back and forth across the country against what *he* considered obscene literature. Comstock took misdirected aim not only at modern works of literature but also at classics, in the interests of "morals, not art or literature."[5] In 40 self-righteous years he was responsible for the destruction of 160 tons of literature and art and is said to have bragged about the number of persons he had driven to suicide!

On the brighter side, Comstock stirred up such a noisy fuss about "improper" books, he undoubtedly drove people into bookstores who might not have been there otherwise, in search of whatever Comstock had found they were missing!

We have latter-day Comstockers among us today. Like him, they yearn to tell you and me what we may and may not read and know, in the interests of "accuracy," or whatnot. As one of them put it, "We essentially think that we have an information duty to the nation to tell the people what's going on."[7] (As if we didn't know at least as much as they do.)

One small-town library in New York had been doing its best to fulfill its "information duty" when this sort of Comstockery reared its head: The library made it a policy that if anyone demanded to have a book withdrawn from circulation on moral, political, or religious grounds, the librarian should assume that the book was "of more than routine interest" and take steps to make sure that plenty of copies would be on the shelves for its patrons. *That's* the American free-enterprise way![8]

Just as books survived competition for people's leisure time from radio in the 1920s and television in the 1950s, they seem also to be flourishing in the computer age. Recently an authority predicted that the personal computer will lure us away from printed literature.[9] The good news is that he's wrong. If anything, peering at a pale, shimmering monitor for any length of time may drive people away from screen-imprinted material and to the crisp, clear pages of books. A glance at the facts bears this out:

In 1963 publishers issued nearly half again as many different new books and new editions (53,400) as they did in 1970 (36,100).[10] "Heavy readers" of books (who have read more than 26 books in the past six months) doubled between 1978 and 1983, from 18% to 35% of all book readers. At the same time, library visitation increased, and more books were being taken out per visit: 3.2 books in 1983 vs. 1.8 books in 1978.

Abe Lincoln's friends and kin recalled how when "fodder-pulling time" came in Indiana, young Abe "shucked corn from early daylight till sundown along with his father and Dennis Hanks and John Hanks, but after supper he read a book till midnight, and at noon he hardly knew the taste of his cornbread because he had the book in front of him." Abe was such a bookworm, they did say there was "suthin' peculiarsome" about him.[12]

What was "peculiarsome" about Abraham Lincoln is still there in Americans today, in the age of electronic communications. "The things we want to know are in books." And we have more books to choose from than ever before.

NOTES

1. Carl Sandburg, *Abraham Lincoln: The Prairie Years* (New York: Harcourt, Brace & Company, 1926), p. 42.
2. Theodore Caplow, Howard M. Bahr, Bruce A. Chadwick, Reuben Hill, and Margaret Holmes Williamson, *Middletown Families: Fifty Years of Change and Continuity* (Minneapolis: University of Minnesota Press, 1982), pp. 24–25. "Middletown" was a real American city (Muncie, Indiana).
3. Ibid.
4. *Historical Statistics of the United States: Colonial Times to 1970* (Washington, D.C.: U.S. Department of Commerce, Bureau of the Census, 1975).
5. *Encyclopaedia Britannica* (Chicago: Encyclopaedia Britannica, 1974), Micropaedia, vol. 3, p. 59.
6. *The New Columbia Encyclopedia* (New York: Columbia University Press, 1975), p. 629.
7. Ernst Lawrence, "Testing for Bias," *MacNeil/Lehrer News Hour*, National Public Television (August 23, 1985), Transcript 2585, p. 8.
8. Aryeh Neier, *Defending My Enemy* (New York: E.P. Dutton, 1979), p. 103.
9. Oxford University futurist Anthony Smith, *Goodbye Gutenberg* (New York, Oxford University Press, 1980).
10. *Statistical Abstract of the United States 1985* (Washington, D.C.: U.S. Department of Commerce, Bureau of the Census, 1984), table 379.
11. Travis Charbeneau, "The book Is Back," *Esquire* (March 1985).
12. Sandburg, op. cit., p. 43.

We Are Not Warlike People

★

"Why does your big country make war on little countries?" The question hit us unexpectedly. My wife and our daughter Anne stood with me at a roadside pottery outside Lorca, Spain, talking with the young proprietor and his wife. They made lovely Spanish plates in their own kiln, and we had just bought six to take home with us. He was wrapping the plates very carefully, one at a time, in newspaper. He didn't even look up as he asked the question. His voice was conversational, but the question seemed accusatory, and it came like a sudden slap.

We explained that not all Americans agreed with administration policies. Many were opposed, and they made their opposition openly known, and felt at the very top of government. "That's part of the whole process of American freedom," we added. The young man said no more on the subject, but we went away from Lorca feeling less welcome as Americans than when we came there. That was in the summer of 1971. The war was in Vietnam.

Fourteen years later, I sat next to another young European on an airplane. I asked how he was enjoying his visit to our country. He said he was "very impressed" with America, and he had liked the Americans he met along the way. "But . . . you know, the *impression* we get is that seventy-five percent of you Americans are working on military projects." This was in the summer of 1985.

What's going on here? Did I just happen to run into a couple of "Commie dupes"? Or does the world actually see us Americans as a nation of warlovers? Frankly, if you see the major overseas newspapers, we don't exactly come off as peacemakers, and that's a fact. Take what they were saying about us during a single week or so in May 1985:

In London on May 23, the staunchly conservative *Times* told Britons that one in 10 jobs in America is now "related to defense spending." It called the Pentagon our "largest single purchaser" of goods and services and pointed out that war materials account for a tenth of all U.S. manufacturing, with the Pentagon spending at an average rate of $28 million per hour, 24 hours a day, every day of the year. Millions of British readers (who were paying much higher individual tax rates than we do) were told that taxpayers here are often "also picking up the tax bill for defense contractors." General Dynamics was singled out for not having paid federal taxes since 1972, and having "even claimed a tax refund."[1]

In London on May 26, the weekly *Observer* zeroed in on America's Star Wars project with a story about the "bidding game" among defense contractors competing to share a "feast to come" in orders. The *Observer* predicted that "the future—not just of the Pentagon's share of the pie but of the national economy—was gradually being mortgaged to the weapons manufacturers."[2]

In Sydney, Australia, on May 27, the *Morning Herald* raked through the list of exotic coffeepots, hammers, flashlights, diodes, pliers, washers, and other miscellaneous overpriced Pentagon hardware already uncovered in our papers, as examples of "technical obfuscation" associated with American arms procurement.[3]

In Dusseldorf, West Germany, on May 31, the influential business publication *Wirtschafts Woche* reported to German readers that about a third of the $70 billion a year paid out to Pentagon contractors goes to just four companies; the rest is "spread among 20,000 other contractors and 150,000 subcontractors." That's not bad, but *Wirtschafts Woche* went on to comment that members of Congress had predicted that a third of the entire military procurement budget "will be lost this year through errors and fraud."[4] How does that make you and me look to the world community?

In Cairo, Egypt, on May 31, a story in the semi-official publication *Al-Ahram* revealed "glaring defense establishment abuses" in America. It went on to raise a "larger, moral problem: the tremendous influence weapons firms have come to exercise—directly and indirectly, legally and illegally—on the U.S. government." The *Al-Ahram* writer added: "This insatiable complex has created a cultural, political, and economic network that no American can escape."[5] "No American?" That's *us*!

A natural question somes to mind: How did all these less-than-flattering stories pop up in Britain, Australia, West Germany, and Egypt within a few days of one another? Was some cunning conspirator plotting to make us look bad all over? Not necessarily. Word gets around the world as fast as you can say "wire service" these days. America and its military establishment are vitally interesting in all of these countries at all reader levels. Reporters around the world see the same wire service stories almost simultaneously. They simply reshape the news to fit their own papers and audiences.

But when you see us through the eyes of the world like this, some self-doubts begin to take shape. *Are* we the sort of willing dupes of our own military merchants that stories like these make us appear to be? And are we, as people, *warlike*? The historical record of over 200 years shows that we have never been a militaristic people. In fact, until the First World War and our first "universal" draft, America always found it difficult to raise an army. And in every single one of our nine major wars there has been popular opposition to the war. A look at the current record shows 19 other nations spending a higher percent of GNP for military purposes than we do.

A History of Peaceable People

Let's look at the historical facts about Americans in our own 37 years of wars during the past 210: In the *American Revolution*, large numbers of Americans opposed the war to the bitter end. John Adams estimated that a third of Americans were against the war "at any time" during its progress.[6] The *War of 1812* was stubbornly opposed by "individuals, the press, town meetings, and state legislatures" throughout New England, and New Englanders even provided supplies for the British fleet off our coast, as well as for British armies in Canada. The *Mexican War* was dubbed "Mr. Polk's War" by New Englanders and was resisted by thousands of American opponents of slavery because they believed it was started to benefit "Land-Jobbers and Slave-Jobbers."[7] The *Civil War* was opposed by Americans both in the North and in the South. In the North, "opposition to the war was open, organized, and active," and over 13,000 persons were arrested and confined by military authority because of their opposition.[8] In the South, poor whites called it "a rich man's war and a poor man's fight"; by June 1863, almost a third of the Confederate army was said to be "absent."[9] The *Spanish-American War* (that "splendid little war," as John Hay called it) was heavily promoted by the biggest American newspapers, as well as most of the country's clergy; it was over before opposition could gather momentum, but there *was* powerful resistance nevertheless.[10]

World War I was so vigorously opposed that "to convert Americans from their traditional isolationism, the President condoned a terrific propaganda drive to make people love the war and hate the enemy," according to historian Samuel Eliot Morison.[11] Over 1,500 Americans who opposed entry into the war were sent to jail under the Espionage Act and the Sedition Act—among them a presidential candidate and a United States congressman.[12] All through *World War II*, in spite of the fact that it was probably the one American war in which men and women literally "flocked to the colors," there was a strange assortment of groups, ranging from far left to far right in politics, who opposed our getting involved, for isolationist reasons.[13] The *Korean War* (which took 58% as many American lives in three years as the Vietnam War did in 16) was generally unpopular with the American people; General Eisenhower's preelection campaign promise that he would "bring the Korean War to an early and honorable end" cinched his landslide victory in the presidential election of 1952. And during the *Vietnam War*, students across the country burned their draft cards, and on a single day, a quarter of a million protesting marchers showed up at barricades surrounding the White House—the largest mass demonstration ever held in the national capital.

Now, does that sound like the historical record of a nation of goose-stepping jingoists? No, by jingo, it does not. Americans differ on the subject of what some folks call "preparedness" and others call "war preparations," just as we differ heartily on just about everything else. We get the chills when we hear Bruce Springsteen chant "Born in America," whether we're rock fans or not, but we don't all hear it as a call to the recruiting office. Let's take a different look at how Americans and America stack up *today* among the world's nations in a warring world:

Compared to Other Nations . . .

America has been involved in nine "major" wars in the past 210 years, plus two brief but bloody Indian wars: the Black Hawk War of 1832, and the Sioux Indian War of 1876. Compared to that, during just the past 40 years, there have been over 130 wars here and there in the world. Thus in the lifetimes of some 85 million of us who are here in America today, more than 16 million people have died in wars. During 1985 alone there were 41 wars, rebellions, and uprisings going on in our world. That includes one of the most brutal wars of the past century—one whose deaths are so numerous they can't even be calculated yet, the Iraq–Iran War.[14] Seen in this bloody context, America's history is not unusually belligerent.

We have been spending more for military purposes lately than at any time since 1975, measured in constant 1981 dollars. But when you take that in an international context it also looks—well, at least more understandable. When you measure U.S. military expenditures as a proportion of our gross national product, using constant 1981 dollars, in 1982 they amounted to 6.4% of the gross national product. That is a *smaller* proportion of the GNP than is spent for military purposes in 19 other nations of the world: Bulgaria, China, Taiwan, Egypt, Greece, Iran, Iraq, Israel, North Korea, South Korea, Morocco, Nicaragua, Oman, Poland, Qatar, Saudi Arabia, the Soviet Union, Syria, and the United Arab Emirates.[15]

One of America's 17 Nobel Peace Prize winners, the great Ralph J. Bunche, said, "There are no warlike peoples—just warlike leaders." In a world full of war, and with all too many warlike leaders, Americans in the past and Americans today should be counted as peacelovers.

NOTES

1. Nicholas Ashford, "The Awesome Power of Military Contractors," *The Times* of London (May 23, 1985).
2. Robert Chesshyre, "The 'Star Wars' Stampede," the *Observer* of London (May 26, 1985).
3. Jenni Hewett, "Behind the 'Spare Parts Horror Stories,'" the Sydney *Morning Herald* (May 27, 1985).

4. "The 'Toilet Seat Syndrome,' " *Wirtschafts Woche*, Dusseldorf, West Germany (May 31, 1985).

5. Sajeni Dularmani, "An Inexorable Web," *Al-Ahram*, Cairo, Egypt (May 31, 1985). (It should be noted that all five of these quotations are taken from excerpted portions of the original news articles published in that most valuable magazine *World Press Review* (August 1985). You are urged to read their entire "World Press Report" in that issue.

6. Harry J. Carman, Harold C. Syrett, and Bernard W. Wishy, *A History of the American People* (New York: Alfred A. Knopf, 1967), vol. 1, p. 197.

7. Michael Kraus, *The United States to 1865* (Ann Arbor: University of Michigan Press, 1959), p. 431.

8. Samuel Eliot Morison, *The Oxford History of the American People* (New York: Oxford University Press, 1965), p. 659.

9. Ibid., p. 667.

10. Carman, Syrett, and Wishy, op. cit., vol. 2, pp. 288–89.

11. Morison, op. cit., p. 873.

12. Ibid., p. 874.

13. Carman, Syrett, and Wishy, op. cit., vol. 2, p. 677.

14. James Reston, *The New York Times* (May 5, 1985), quotes figures from the Center for Defense Information, Washington, D.C.

15. *Statistical Abstract of the United States 1985* (Washington, D.C.: U.S. Department of Commerce, Bureau of the Census, 1984), table 1513.

For More Information

On this whole life-and-death issue, I commend to your attention a superb new overview: *World Military and Social Expenditures 1985* by Ruth Leger Sivard, published by World Priorities, Inc., P.O. Box 25140, Washington, DC 20007. It costs $5 by mail. It should be in every home. Even the *Congressional Record* calls it "a real eye-opener."

We've Stopped Taking Education for Granted

★

For the first time in years, American adults are really beginning to be concerned about what's happening at school. Some would just as soon close their eyes to the whole education problem and not get involved. But most are really concerned for America's schools and are willing to help improve them—if someone will just tell them how.

This reawakened concern about the state of our educational system is the best thing that's happened to it in a long time.

The last time most of us really looked into America's schools and their needs was almost 30 years ago, in 1957. It's worthwhile taking a backward look at what drew our attention then, because what happened in 1957 was a forecast of what's happening to us today.

In 1957 the USSR launched *Sputnik I*, the first artificial earth satellite. A month later they launched *Sputnik 2*, carrying a dog as passenger. (At our house out in the country in Illinois, we got up at three in the morning and shuffled out into the chilly yard to see the Soviet Union's twinkling symbol of the future arc overhead. "I can hear the little dog barking," said our smallest daughter, Anne.)

In that same year, the United States Office of Education published a survey of education in the Soviet Union.[1] It showed that the emphasis on scientific and technical education in the USSR was far ahead of that in America. Soviet fourth-graders were studying calculus and heroically turning out heavy loads of homework, while our kids were watching *Robin Hood, Sergeant Preston of the Yukon*, and *Leave It to Beaver*. No wonder the Soviets had beaten us into orbit! We needed to jack up our educational standards and produce more engineers and scientists.

Suddenly, in America everybody was concerned that our

school system must become the best in the world, for our own good. Rudolf Flesch's book *Why Johnny Can't Read and What You Can Do About It*,[2] quietly published in 1955, suddenly became a best seller in a new edition. Educational gurus such as James B. Conant, and general-purpose gurus such as Vice Admiral Hyman G. Rickover warned us that we were weakening our American know-how, and the schools were to blame. *Life* magazine warned of overcrowded schools "wild with elective courses" in which "geniuses of the next decade are even now being allowed to slip back into mediocrity."[3]

Reform in the '50s and '60s

Seeing the blinking extraterrestrial symbol of Soviet leadership into space crossing right over our homes was shocking to Americans. A lot of us began looking for the quickest possible answers to America's educational problems. Politicians demanded more appropriations for space research, reorganization of the American military, more money for scientists—and a complete overhaul and refurbishing of our schools and school system. With *Life* predicting that "the outcome of the arms race will depend eventually on our schools and those of the Russians," we saw there was no time to be lost. Teachers churned out new curricula. Students began cramming for science classes. Many of us began breathing a little easier.

A year later, in 1958, America launched its own first satellite, *Explorer I*. It was followed by *Vanguard I* and, under Project Score, *Surveyor*, an unmanned probe, sent the reassuring voice of President Eisenhower back to us from space. By the end of 1958 we had the good news that Project Mercury was underway and would put an American man in space. The National Defense Education Act of 1958 was launched, loaded with dollars; educators, presidential study commissions, and various interest groups took over the discussion of where our "investments in quality education" should be aimed.

Encouraged by all the unaccustomed attention being paid to teaching and the challenge to deliver better-prepared students, educators went to work with a will. In the field of English, for example, the 1960s became a time of great creative ferment as educators looked for better ways to teach rhetoric, syntax, language, and composition. The revolutionary new Transformational Grammar proposed by Noam Chomsky (Cambridge, Mass.: *Aspects of the Theory of Syntax*, 1965) and other new theories and systems were debated, studied, and tried; teachers spent off-hours and vacations in workshops and special courses; spirit ran high in the school system for somehow "doing the job better" in teaching English as well as other disciplines.

It should be noted that the enthusiastic search for finding new ways to do the job better in school was not without a necessary element of risk, which always accompanies enthusiastic experimentation. And it didn't result in success in every area: "The New Math" was a two-decade great experiment crowned with failure. But what was really memorable and exciting about all this educational ferment was the enthusiasm it generated among teachers all over America.

In 1958 alone we built 62,000 new classrooms across the country, at an average cost of $60,000 apiece.[4] Most were undoubtedly necessary; the baby boom was in full force, and America's future was flooding into the schools. But too many of us became satisfied that efficient new classrooms—with green blackboards and carpeting, and streamlined desks and curricula—had our national educational problems on the way to being solved. As Americans often do, we believed enough money applied with vigor and good intentions would fix everything. We turned back to our day-to-day problems and turned off our concern about the schools. After all, wasn't that what we paid teachers for—to keep things under control and get the kids ready for society?

Alarm in the '80s

That's how we got where we are today.

In 1983 the National Commission on Excellence in Education's report *A Nation at Risk: The Imperative for Educational Reform* broke in on our complacency like a school alarm bell.[5] It told us flatly that America had been "committing an act of unilateral educational disarmament" and was now threatened by "a rising tide of mediocrity." Sure enough: The scores of our college-bound high-school students taking the Scholastic Aptitude Test (SAT) had been dropping like spent rockets ever since 1963. Verbal scores had slid from an average of 466 in 1967 to only 421 in 1981 and showed little sign of improving.[6] After years of thinking of America as the land where *everyone* could learn to read and write, we were shaken to discover that 27 million of us—one in seven Americans over age 18—were functionally illiterate, unable to read a newspaper, a product label, or a military manual on how to take care of a rifle.

Not only did we discover that grown-up Johnny and Jane couldn't read; we also found that 1 million American youngsters in the coming generation, age 12–17, could not read above third-grade level.[7] In fact, our general ability to use American language has been declining steadily since the 1950s.

How could this happen here, in the land of universal free education? We had lubricated the system well with plenty of money (at least we thought we had), and yet something had obviously slipped out of gear. What had slipped? The answer appeared to be educational standards. *A Nation at Risk* told us that "secondary-school curricula have been homogenized, diluted and diffused to the point that they no longer have a central purpose." One example: Back in the late 1960s, nearly nine out of 10 high-school graduates (85%) had completed four solid years of English; a decade later only four in ten (41%) had done so.[8] To reduce the number of papers they had to read and correct in overcrowded classes, many teachers cut back on classwork in the principles of composition— how to organize your thoughts and put them down clearly on a blank piece of paper. As a direct result, colleges were being flooded with freshmen who couldn't spell, or write an intelligible paragraph!

With college enrollments double what they had been in 1965 and no sign of their abating in the near future, by the 1980s,[9] colleges were inclined to shuttle illiterate freshmen into "bonehead English" remedial courses and hope for the best; then shunt them out into the business world after graduation—or worst yet, into teaching. And so, all too many students who couldn't read turned up in our school system as teachers who couldn't teach. As word got around, the process accelerated, and now, as *A Nation at Risk* spelled it out, "Too many teachers are being drawn from the bottom quarter of graduating high school and college students."

In the 1950 Americans were shaken by the realization that because we were falling behind in school, America could also fall behind in developing space technology and lose our place as a leader in the world community. Now, in the 1980s, we're again worried about international implications of growing

American illiteracy. Lack of well-educated workers, managers, and professionals can cost us the leadership in a world dominated by high technology and superscience. How can a nation of semi-illiterates, who can hardly read what it says on a monitor, much less decipher the documentation in manuals, compete in a computerized industrial world? Could this be one reason for our lopsided balance of international trade? These are the kinds of gut questions that have us worrying about America's schools again.

Things Are Looking Up Again

The fact that we *are* worried is the first of several hopeful signs for American education today. We face massive problems in finding ways to raise the performance and quality of both teachers and students at every level in our schools. Just throwing money at the problem isn't going to solve it. Money must be paid, but so must attention be paid and commitment made, even by those of us who have no youngsters of our own in school. The kids who *are* there are ours, too. The people trying to teach them need to know we want to help them.

Another helpful sign for American education is that we are already making some progress in dealing with the heaviest problems in our schools: illiteracy, poor educational performance, student dropouts, and teacher shortages.

We're making progress against illiteracy. Illiteracy condemns adults to a lifetime of low-paying jobs and uncertain employment. It not only penalizes the individual; it also penalizes all of us. America spends as much as $6 billion a year on welfare and jobless aid for illiterates, according to one estimate; as many as three out of four unemployed Americans are illiterate.[10]

We stated earlier that 27 million Americans have been estimated to be functionally illiterate. A far higher estimate of 60 million illiterates has been arrived at by Jonathan Kozol (*Illiterate America* [Garden City, N.Y.: Anchor Press/Doubleday & Company, 1985]). Kozol says there are 25 million Americans who can't read at all, or read at below fifth-grade level, and another 35 million reading at below ninth-grade level, which he considers illiterate in contemporary society. There is some argument about Kozol's latter assumption; Thomas Sticht, chairman of the Adult Literacy Committee of the

International Reading Association, argues that people who can read at fifth- through eighth-grade level are not illiterate. I agree with Sticht, but adults with such limited reading ability certainly are disadvantaged in our society and are part of our problem.

SAT Scores Up

The hopeful news is that there are now real signs of progress in raising the learning level, at least among college-bound high-school students. Scores of the 1985 Scholastic Aptitude Test (SAT) taken by almost 1 million youngsters took the biggest upward leap in 21 years. For almost a decade, SAT scores have been rising bit by bit. After settling to an all-time-low combined score of 890 in 1980 and 1981, the scores edged up three points in 1982, stood still in 1983, and gained a healthy four points in 1984. This latest 9-point jump in 1985 carried the combined SAT average for American college applicants to 906 out of a possible 1,600 points. The highest score ever was 980, among the Class of 1963—but we're at least heading that way again.

The combined SAT score includes a math aptitude score and a verbal aptitude score. The math average for American high schoolers rose four points in 1985, to 475, and the verbal average rose five points, to 431. After the long, hard, upward pull, this was enough to make Education Secretary William Bennett issue a cautious "Bravo!" and call the scores "further evidence that American secondary education is on the mend."[11] And so it is.

There was more evidence of improvement in fighting illiteracy, in a September 1985 report by the National Assessment of Educational Progress, a federally funded testing agency. The report found that reading ability among all 9-, 13-, and 17-year-old American students had improved since 1981.

The best news of all is that state legislatures, school administrators, teachers, and parents are working together to raise learning levels among high-school graduates and are getting more done than they have in years. Politicians are famous for establishing "task forces" to get heavy problems off their backs, but this time there are solid signs that something is being accomplished. Some 275 state task forces were set up in the first year after A Nation at Risk rang the alarm bell about education. There have been legislative reforms on all sides, aimed at upgrading schools and education. Almost every state raised high-school graduation requirements, increasing the amounts of math and science classwork during high school.

English Is Essential

The danger is that in the rush to create a generation of scientifically literate graduates, social sciences may be lost in the shuffle. English is every bit as essential as math or the sciences to any American who hopes to survive in the modern world. Teachers know this, and so do parents. The 1984 Gallup Poll, conducted nationally among teachers and parents, found that nine out of 10 parents *and* teachers agreed that both English and mathematics should be required subjects, not only for students planning to go on to college, but also for those planning no further formal education. [12]

If we really hope to raise the level of literacy in this country in years ahead, at least two full years of English, including composition, must be required for graduation from high school. Mathematics and science are important in our era, but this is not *only* the age of technology; it's also the age of communications. In our country that means English. Any young engineer or scientist who can't spell or write a clear paragraph may perform routine tasks in the real world but will be confined to that level if he or she can't even write a simple report.

We're expecting more, and getting more educational performance from students. Across the country, students now get the message that they are *expected* to learn and do well in school. In an increasing number of schools, the student who doesn't do at least average-grade academic work in all subjects must drop sports and other extracurricular treats. The state of Texas (where football is a secular religion) has made it a law that students must pass all courses with a grade of 70 or better, or they're "off the team." In California, after more than a decade of local-option education in which school districts set their own academic standards, new statewide graduation requirements have been established.

New leaner but tougher curriculums, longer school days, harder-nosed testing, and increased homework will produce better-informed graduates. Another thing that will help to raise education levels is the way teachers themselves are responding to the challenge and to the newly awakened interest of parents. But the job is being complicated by tighter operating budgets.

At the beginning of this decade, the federal share of public-school budgets was 9.2%; this was cut by over a third—to 6.2%—during the past five years. As more of the cost load for education was shifted to state and local governments, educators found themselves in a double bind: Funds for education were becoming tighter at the very time when they were asked to raise the quality of education and SAT scores of students. Necessity does give birth to invention; educators have developed many new and productive ways to get "more learning out of less money."

Teachers Are Innovating

Teachers are finding new ways to help students learn, despite federal funding cutbacks. They're developing innovative ways to give needed individual help to students—help there isn't time to give in a crowded classroom. In Mill Creek, Pennsylvania, teachers send students to a computer lab to take math quizzes; this frees the teacher to give individual help in the classroom to those students who still need it.

In Albuquerque, New Mexico, veteran teachers have set up a Dial-A-Teacher Homework Hotline. Students who get hung up on something in their homework call in and get instant help from a teacher on the telephone. In Tacoma, Washington, Los Angeles, and Medford, Oregon, the Homework Hotline concept has gone on the air, using a cablevision public-access channel. In Medford, four English teachers and three math teachers take turns as the "tutoring talent" on a weekly TV call-in show. The one-hour show gives extra help to students in grades one through nine. Students phone in their math or English questions; these are taken down by student workers, who pass the question on to two teachers, on-camera. Total cost of this hour-long show is only $80, of which the teachers each get $25, and three student helpers each get $10. On pleasant days, when kids would rather be outside, the show receives an average of 20 calls an hour; on rainy days this average doubles. Since whether they phone in or not, every youngster watching the show learns from seeing and hearing questions being answered, Homework Hotline is a great low-budget teaching-expander.

A spokeswoman for the National Education Association in Washington reported that Homework Hotline shows "have been gaining in popularity for the past three or four years." The association has promoted the concept. "It's a real nice way to give [students] help, but it also has good public-relations value," she added. "It shows teachers are willing to take the time to help students out."[13] Teachers have *always* been willing to take their time to help students; now they've found new technology to help them.

Cutbacks in funding for public-school education have hit some states particularly hard, and they have found it difficult, or even impossible, to fund their schools' efforts to raise the level of education.

A national government that chokes off funds for education and preparation of its future generation of citizens is borrowing from tomorrow's generation to pay for today's extravagances. It depends on state and local government to provide equal educational opportunity to its youngest citizens, knowing that some states and local governments can't do the job adequately, and some may not even be inclined to do it. For example, a 1973 U.S. Supreme Court decision ruled that Texas didn't have to equalize spending on education among its school districts. As a result, in some Texas school districts—where most students are Mexican-American—as little as $1,800 a year was spent per student, compared to more than $5,000 in more favored districts. New Hampshire is another state that "starved" students in its poor school districts, according to a two-year study of U.S. Schools by the National Coalition of Advocates for Students. In farming states, the will to improve education is there, but the money is absent. Farm income has fallen disastrously low, and the tax base has shrunk, making it especially difficult to provide extra funds for education. "We have to do more—and do it with less," commented one Nebraska high-school principal.

What About the Teacher Shortage?

Attention finally is being paid to "teacher dropouts." Everybody has been concerned about the problem of *student* dropouts since the 1970s. Meanwhile, an even more serious problem was growing and not getting much attention: *teacher* dropouts, and a growing teacher shortage. Now attention is being paid. A former federal secretary of education, Terrel

Bell, and the author of a recent report, *The Coming Crisis in Teaching*, Linda Darling-Hammond, commented on this oversight. Darling-Hammond said that as late as 1983, not much attention had been paid ". . . at all to the situation regarding teachers, the supply of teachers, or the quality of teachers." Bell replied that the teacher crisis is now finally recognized in America, but "We're noting a larger attrition than we anticipated . . . even over the last couple of years the situation has worsened."[14]

Just as there was teacher attrition, so there was also pupil attrition. Between 1972 and 1983, private- and parochial-school enrollment increased 3.6%, while public-school enrollment declined 12%. There were fewer children going to school in those years, and many of those who were, went into alternate schools if their parents could afford it.

From an oversupply of teachers across America in the early 1970s, we've plunged into a teacher shortage, especially in some subject areas and in certain parts of the country. Shortages are most acute in science, mathematics, foreign languages, and special education for handicapped children.

How threatening is the shortage of teachers? Very threatening. Just as "you can't make bricks without straw," you can't turn out well-educated, productive citizens without well-qualified, dedicated teachers. A report on the shortage of qualified math and science teachers in California by a statewide Math Science Task Force put this bluntly: "Many of today's students won't be able to compete for jobs of the future, unless the teacher shortage is checked."

The Shortage Is Growing

This is a problem that's not going to go away in a year or two. It's going to get worse before it gets better. And it's not going to be solved simply by dedicated teachers "doubling up" and working overtime, or by plugging untrained volunteers into gaps in the educational system. A spokesperson for the National Education Association warned that the overall teacher shortage ". . . will be exacerbated over the next few years as many teachers retire and fewer young people come into the profession due to low salary and status, and dismal work conditions."[15] An additional drain comes from industry, which draws people with training and skills in sciences and mathematics away from teaching by paying far better than schools do.

According to the National Center for Educational Statistics, a unit of the U.S. Department of Education, there were 4,000 teaching jobs open in 1983–84 with no one available to fill them. This may not seem like a lot compared to the total of 2.6 million teachers working across the country, but look at it this way: The unfilled jobs were most likely to be in the fields of sciences and mathematics, and in big-city or rural areas. (Suburbs are likely to pay better and have better-equipped schools and a more congenial location, especially for young teachers.) This creates pockets of severe need, where young people are being denied the learning they will need to succeed in today's world.

The shortage is growing: NCES has projected shortages of 12,000 teachers by 1986, and by 1996 the center expects a teacher shortage of 78,000. Multiply that number of missing teachers by the number of students one teacher usually instructs in a day and you get a really disastrous number of young Americans "shorted" on their education, despite all the extra efforts by teachers still in the system. But this is not just a future possibility—it's already happening. *A Nation at Risk* pointed out that fewer than a third of American high schools have a qualified instructor teaching physics. Half of the most recently installed teachers in mathematics, science, and English were not qualified in those subjects. And the National Science Teachers Association has estimated that four out of 10 American science classes are being taught by unqualified instructors. What does this portend for the future of America in the space age?

Where Have All the Teachers Gone?

Many of our best teachers are leaving education. These are professionals who entered teaching a generation ago, full of idealism; now they're showing disillusionment by retiring early, or taking other jobs. If they could choose a career again, more than half say they would not go into teaching. In 1961, eight out of 10 teachers told a National Education Association survey they *would* become teachers again if they were starting over. Twenty years later, in 1981, fewer than half said they would choose teaching as a career again.[16] The new Phi Delta Kappa Gallup Poll found that 46% of teachers wouldn't want their daughters to go into teaching; 59% wouldn't want their sons to do so. Members of the general public share this feeling. Four out of 10 among the general public would not want either a daughter or a son in the teaching profession. Even among college and university faculty members, a poll conducted by the Carnegie Foundation for the Advancement of Teaching found nearly 40% considering new careers.

Why Do They Quit?

Teachers are not simply suffering from low self-esteem or low opinion of their profession. When the Phi Delta Kappa Gallup Poll asked teachers to rate each of 12 different professions according to its contribution to society, they rated theirs the greatest profession—well ahead of physicians, clergy, school principals, judges, lawyers, and other professionals. However, when the same teachers were asked to rate the prestige or status of their profession in their community, they rated teaching at the very bottom of the 12 professions. Teachers feel that their work and *profession* are undervalued.

In a society where how much a man or woman earns is often accepted as a measure of his or her value as a person, teachers feel their relatively low pay is a sign of how little they are valued by the community they serve. Again, in the Phi Delta Kappa Gallup Poll, at both elementary- and high-school levels, nine out of 10 teachers said teachers' salaries are too low. In contrast, fewer than four in 10 people in the general population believe teachers' pay is too low; 7% even said they think teachers are overpaid. An Oregon teacher expressed his feeling that

> I have a lot of expertise, but I'm not being paid for it, and it makes me feel badly because I am not doing what a normal male in America is supposed to be doing: supplying his family with all the things they should have.

The same teacher also commented that

> We have a tradition in the United States of expecting teachers to be sort of missionaries . . . the payment is supposed to come from within; feeling good. You see this in the newspapers all the time when teachers are asking for raises: Well, teachers simply aren't supposed to make money.[17]

The teacher who said this is not a newcomer. He has over 20 years of experience in his field. Even so, to make ends meet for his family, he has to work at part-time jobs after school hours—as a meat cutter, house painter, and gravedigger. He worries about the fact that part-time jobs leave him with less energy to give to students as a teacher during the day. And—although he would "stay a classroom teacher until they threw me out, if I could afford it,"—he is ready to quit teaching for something that pays better. We'll always need meat cutters and gravediggers. But can we afford to use professional teachers like this to do their work?

Educational researcher Darling-Hammond has found that "what causes people to leave the profession is not only salaries but the set of conditions under which they work."[18] In a recent national survey among teachers, conducted for the Metropolitan Life Insurance Company, 36% said they are under "great stress" at least several days a week at work. In contrast, another recent national survey found only 27% of American adults generally feel stress that often.[19]

Teachers are being burned out, especially in urban public schools, by what sociologist-educator Jackson Toby characterized as "the bored, disrespectful attitude of so many students" who "say by their manner, 'Learn me if you can, you jerk.' "[20]

Even 10 years ago, the National Institute of Education reported that two thirds of the teachers in public secondary schools across the country had been sworn at or been given obscene gestures by students in the preceding month. Little wonder that Albert Shanker, president of the 600,000-member American Federation of Teachers, has said that disruptive students do not belong in public high schools and that more security personnel are needed in schools. And little wonder that a majority of new teachers recruited for inner-city schools quit within five years. Professional dedication to teaching is one thing, and there is still an enormous and precious reserve of that all across America. But the reality of spending your every working day in a potential dangerous and uncooperative environment is something else. There are not enough martyrs to go around for schools like that, and they burn out fast.

Where Are the Replacements?

The teacher pool is shrinking just as a new generation of "baby boomlet" students is ready to troop into the schools.

For the first time in 14 years, elementary-school enrollment went up, by 54,000 during the 1984–85 school year. The number of new students will continue to mount every year from now until the 1990s. More teachers are needed and will be needed. But so far, few are coming from college graduating classes. Young women have more career areas open to them now than they used to have; fewer are going into teaching. The number of young men and women earning degrees in education has dropped steadily, from 167,000 nationally in 1975 to 101,000 in 1982. A decade ago, about one college student in five chose the field of education; today only one in 20 does so.

Asked if she would like to become a teacher, a young high-school senior shook her head and said, "Teaching is a lousy job." Another said, "I believe they should be paid more and respected more." If the pay is poor and the respect level low, would *you* spend four years in college to qualify for that job?

Now Help Is on the Way

In some countries, when government leaders make up their minds, the people jump and change. In a democracy it's the other way around. During the 1980s, and especially since publication of *A Nation at Risk* in 1983, the American people have become increasingly aware of and even involved in the need to improve our educational system and product. Public concern has helped to generate and encourage action by governmental agencies and legislatures, as well as in the schools themselves. Already things are changing for the better.

Teacher salaries are rising toward professional and business levels.

"A professional is permitted to operate independently, make decisions, is not tightly supervised, is trusted, and is well compensated."[21] This is how Albert Shanker, a "professional's professional" in education, has described a set of measurements into which our school teachers should be able to fit themselves. Teachers have been a long way from such standards in recent years. But now, there are signs of progress and improvements.

Former Education Secretary Bell called teachers' salaries "a nationwide disgrace, and we need from 30% to 50% increase in the salaries of our teacher. . . ."[22] He suggested that entry-level teachers be paid commensurate with the pay offered beginning baccalaureate-degree engineering and business graduates. Actually, total expenditures for elementary and secondary education went up over 10% between 1970 and 1980, but none of the increase was invested in instruction. In 1970, school boards across the country spent 48 cents out of each dollar in their budgets for teacher salaries; by 1980, while consumer living costs went higher and higher, school-board teacher salaries went *down*, to just 38.5 cents per dollar. In fact, a Rand Corporation study showed that teachers' salaries actually fell 15% in real dollars during the decade.[23]

Average annual starting salaries of teachers across the country in 1984–85 were $15,460,[24] but in many states they were considerably less than that. In Oklahoma, beginning pay was $12,060. In New York City, beginning teachers got only $14,500 in 1983.

Decent Pay

By the closing months of 1985, however, teachers' salaries were already up, and on their way up across the country. In New York City, beginning salaries jumped to $18,500, and they were expected to rise to $20,000 in 1986. Twenty-seven state legislatures raised teachers' salaries, and more were getting ready to raise them. Nevada raised teacher pay by 11% and added a one-time bonus—5% of 1984 salary—in an effort to hang on to teachers it already had. Texas installed a new tax to raise some $3 billion for public education, including teachers' salaries, in the next three years. Teachers' salaries nationally climbed 7.3% on average from 1983–84 to 1985. The best part of that good news was that they went up most in states where teacher pay had been lowest on the national scale: Alabama, Arkansas, Florida, Georgia, Idaho, Kansas, North Carolina, South Carolina, Tennessee, Texas, Vermont, and West Virginia.[25]

College teacher salaries, which lost ground to inflation every year from 1972 to 1980, also have risen again during the 1980s and went up another 6.5% in 1985, "the most encouraging news we have been able to report for many, many years," according to the American Association of University Professors.[26] In real dollars, after figuring in inflation, this brings the college pay level back to 84% of where it was in 1970–71. There's still room for improvement, but at least they're on their way up.

Besides raises across the board, schools are paying extra

stipends to teachers in hard-to-fill jobs, such as bilingual kindergarten or preschool classes. Career ladder, or "master teacher" programs that pay incentives to teachers based on performance and subject knowledge are under way in 25 states. And in at least one state (Washington), the state university is using a legislature-mandated formula to raise salaries of teachers who are considered most vulnerable to job offers from industry and competitive schools—primarily engineering, business, and medical school faculty.

New ways are being found to recruit more teachers. "Wherever teaching is a lousy job, schools will have trouble recruiting good teachers and keeping those who are recruited," predicted the authority on problems of school disorder, Jackson Toby. We have seen how the percent of college education-degree candidates declined in recent years. But that's only part of the problem. The other part is the loss of fine teachers we already have. Margaret Valdez, a 23-year veteran of teaching grade-school students in inner-city schools of Phoenix, is just such a dedicated, talented, and loving teacher who soon may be lost to the school system and children who need her.

Valdez would like to see better teacher salaries so her peers will be rewarded for their work in proportion to "other people of equal educational background." But teaching inner-city poor children has given her another, even deeper wish. She knows that most of her little pupils probably will never see the inside of a college classroom. Surrounded by scrawled classwork papers waiting to be corrected, she leans back wearily from her desk and takes the time to dream a little: "It's too bad I can't take five kids out of the classroom . . . and just let them blossom and get them away from the ones that just don't give a damn." But Valdez plans to take early retirement in five years. "It's not that I don't enjoy teaching," she says. "I'm just getting burned out. I don't enjoy it the way I used to."[27]

Efforts are being made now to recruit more good beginning teachers and also to make teaching more rewarding for those who are already in the profession. Recruitment methods have been borrowed from industry, and some new twists have been added.

Magnets to Attract Good Teachers

Dartmouth College offers teaching-bound students a tuition-free term at school worth about $4,500. The state of Florida offers $4,000 scholarships to college students who promise to teach for four years in the state's public schools once they graduate. And to help college graduates interested in teaching get jobs, the University of Northern Colorado retrains any graduate free of charge if a school employer judges him or her underskilled. The University of Arkansas at Pine Bluff gives its in-state teacher graduates a "three-year warranty" as assurance of quality to prospective employers. (Ever hear of an engineering school that sure of its graduates?)

The city of Chicago is using television commercials to entice teacher substitutes; it has 4,700 substitute vacancies. To fill vacancies in specialty subjects, many systems now recruit out-of-state. One county held a three-day recruitment session in which potential teachers were given sales pitches by local businesspeople on why they would enjoy being part of the community; the session was advertised in areas where teaching staffs were being reduced. Houston, with 1,500 vacancies looming, has been recruiting Americans with teaching certificates in Mexico City and Toronto.

A more rewarding teaching environment is making many teachers think twice before they consider dropping out of the profession. Better textbooks and more of them; more supplies and equipment for teaching; more in-school security; and higher academic demands on students all help to make teaching more satisfying again. But one of the most effective means of all is drawing and holding top-quality teachers by challenging them with roomsful of eager-to-learn, bright students: *magnet schools*.

The magnet-school program allows specific schools in the system to offer specialized and advanced courses that are not offered at any other high schools in the system. City buses are used to transport any students in the city who want to take such a curriculum to the school and back to their own neighborhoods. Programs offered include classes in performing arts, economics, and computer operation, as well as other advanced or specialized fields of study. Education writer Jacquee G. Petchel of the *Arizona Republic* has written of the magnet-school program in Phoenix: "For computer-science teachers, the program offers an opportunity to develop a sophisticated computer-science curriculum at a time when student interest in high technology is soaring."[28]

A computer teacher in the Phoenix system, Rob Forrest, called the magnet-school program "the prize of the district

. . . a chance to teach good classes, all elective. It just sounded so enticing. It's a chance to get in on the ground floor." More than 400 students have enrolled in the program at one school in Phoenix. About 125 live outside the school's attendance boundary; 80% of those are white, in a school where 80% were black or Hispanic before the program began. This is school busing that's welcomed by parents and students because it's voluntary. It draws good students and it holds good teachers, precisely what educators have said the country needs.

New ways are being tried to "grow" more teachers. One of the most controversial new means being tried by state school systems to fill vacancies in their teaching staffs is *emergency certification.* In New Jersey, 100 applicants who never had the college education courses that traditionally have been required for teaching were given 80 hours of training during the summer and then assigned to teaching positions in the school system as of September 1985. They teach under supervision of experienced teachers, but to many educators emergency certification is like giving prospective pilots who have never been to flying school 80 hours of training and then turning them loose with a Boeing 727 and a cabinful of passengers to fly a regular schedule. Others, however, question whether the traditional required courses in education made anyone a better teacher. The first flights of students are off the ground with their emergency-certified teachers in several states; we don't know how the new program will come down yet. But my own hunch is that if school administrators start with smart, articulate people who really want to teach, and give them a decent chance to show what they can do, the old "how to teach" courses and required courses in the history of education in the state will never be missed.

Taxpayers seem ready to invest more in children. With Uncle Sam trying to abolish the U.S. Department of Education and cut federal spending in the schools, who is ready to volunteer to take his place at the pay window? Not everybody steps forward. But in one 1985 Gallup Poll at least, 38% of Americans said they would vote for a raise in taxes if schools needed the extra money.[29] In another recent national poll, more than two thirds of the respondents said they'd be willing to pay an additional $200 a year in taxes to provide better pay for teachers, more teacher training, and smaller classes.[30]

Corporate America also is showing signs of being willing to contribute help and even cash, equipment, and instructors to help beef up America's educational curriculum. Industry leaders are painfully aware that Japanese and European schools are turning out graduates who are better equipped for working in a high-tech world than ours are.

Investing in America's Future

One problem in finding a majority of Americans willing to dig down in their pockets for extra tax dollars is that almost two out of three households in the country are childless (63%) compared to only one in twenty in 1970.[31] These childless households include those of individuals, an increasing number of childless young couples, and a growing number of elderly couples. The presumption has been that they will have "little personal interest in the local school system" and be reluctant to pay more taxes to improve it. But the most powerful group of elder citizens in the country, the combined forces of NRTA (National Retired Teachers Association) and AARP (American Association of Retired Persons), have demonstrated enlightened and lively interest in the need for educating the coming generation, whether some of us will be around to cash in on the benefits of their higher education or not. If corporate America, and especially the communications industry, also gets behind selling education to everybody, the funds will be found, even in a nationful of empty nests.

Meanwhile, the other good news is: Fewer kids are dropping out of school. One out of four high-school students drops out of school. The president wants us to cut that to one in 10, nationally. We're still a long way from such a goal. But the good news is that we have come a little closer each year since 1980, and some states are already there. It can be done. North Dakota, Minnesota, Delaware, Iowa already have done it. In 1980, just eight in 10 high-school freshmen in North Dakota, Minnesota, and Iowa stayed through to graduation; in Delaware, just seven in 10. But in 1983 (the latest year for which data were available), *nine* out of 10 high schoolers in these four states stayed through the four years to graduate.[32]

Perhaps the most encouraging part of this achievement is this: It wasn't all done with money. North Dakota, the state with the highest high-school graduation rate in America (94.8%), ranks 30th in average teacher salary, 26th in per-pupil expenditures, and 14th in class size. Minnesota, with the second-highest high-school graduation rate, ranks 12th in average teacher salary, 21st in per-pupil expenditures, and 26th in class size. Where there's a will, there's got to be a way.

When We Get Together on a Problem, We Solve It

Only about a decade ago, Americans were worrying about the doctor shortage. A 1974 *New York Times* story estimated the national shortage of physicians to be at least 30,000. At that time there were not even sufficient teaching facilities in America to handle such a severe shortage of doctors.[33]

Today we already have an oversupply of physicians in some specialties. The Bureau of Health Professionals estimates that by the end of this decade there will be a national oversupply of 51,000 M.D.'s. Some estimates run even higher.[34] our next problem may be: What do we do with extra doctors?

When Americans generate a kind of collective consciousness about a major problem with potential consequences for each of them, things suddenly begin to come together, get moving, and get solved. This also happened with the energy problem. It is already happening with the education problem. But each of us will have to *give* something to it, whether we have children in school or not.

Today's children are our children, too. Our future. And our responsibility and hope as Americans.

NOTES

1. *Education in the USSR* (Washington, D.C.: Division of International Education, International Educational Relations Branch, 1957).
2. Rudolf Flesch, *Why Johnny Can't Read and What You Can Do About It* (New York: Harper & Brothers, 1955). The new edition, issued in 1981, was *Why Johnny Still Can't Read* and was published by Harper & Row.
3. "Crisis in Education" series published in five parts in *Life* magazine (March 25, March 31, April 7, April 14, and April 21, 1985). Our quote is from the March 25 article, p. 25.
4. Landon Y. Jones, *Great Expectations: America and the Baby Boom Generation* (New York: Coward, McCann & Geoghegan, 1980), p. 51.
5. *A Nation at Risk: The Imperative for Educational Reform* (Washington, D.C.: National Commission on Excellence in Education, U.S. Department of Education, 1983).
6. Alvin P. Sanoff and Lucia Solorzano, "It's Our Language Is in Distress," *U.S. News & World Report* (February 18, 1985).
7. Basic data from National Opinion Research Center.
8. Sanoff and Solorzano, op. cit.

9. *Statistical Abstract of the United States 1985* (Washington, D.C.: U.S. Department of Commerce, Bureau of the Census, 1984), table 247.

10. Sanoff and Solorzano, op. cit.

11. "Rise in Scores on College Entry Test Is Lauded," Associated Press, (September 24, 1985).

12. Alec Gallup, *The Phi Delta Kappa Gallup Poll of Teachers' Attitudes Toward the Public Schools, 1985* (Bloomington, Ind.; Phi Delta Kappa, 1985).

13. Jeff Barnard, "Don't Touch That Dial; It's 'Homework Hotline,' " Associated Press (June 4, 1985).

14. "All About Teachers," *MacNeil/Lehrer News Hour*, Public Broadcasting System (June 14, 1985), Transcript 2535.

15. "California Faces Shortage of Math, Science Teachers," *The Wall Street Journal* (June 27, 1985).

16. Jackson Toby, "Pay Isn't Foremost of Teacher Tribulations," *The Wall Street Journal* (February 12, 1985).

17. Harry Chandler, *MacNeil/Lehrer News Hour*, op. cit.

18. Linda Darling-Hammond, *MacNeil/Lehrer News Hour*, op. cit.

19. Metropolitan Life Insurance Company survey of 1,846 public school teachers, and Harris survey of 1,253 American adults, reported by Linda M. Watkins, "Labor Letter," *The Wall Street Journal* (September 24, 1985).

20. Toby, op. cit.

21. Christopher Larson, "The Question Is Academic," *Northwest Orient Magazine* (August 1985).

22. *MacNeil/Lehrer News Hour*, op. cit.

23. 1985 report from the Committee for Economic Development quoted by James Kilpatrick, Universal Press news service (September 24, 1985).

24. National Education Association figure.

25. National Education Association survey data quoted from David Broder, "Today's Education," *Washington Post* (September 4, 1985).

26. Annual report on the economic status of the profession, 1985.

27. From material gathered by Jacquee G. Petchel, education writer for *Arizona Republic* (June 16, 1985).

28. Jacquee G. Petchel, "Magnet Plan," *Arizona Republic* (September 4, 1985).

29. Lucia Solorzano with Sarah Peterson, "A New Test Begins for America's Schools," *U.S. News & World Report* (September 9, 1985).

30. 1984 U.S. Department of Education survey, with representative demographic sample of population, except for education: 53% had attended college, compared to 33% in the nation as a whole.

31. National Center for Education Information report, quoted by Knight-Ridder news service (February 14, 1985).

32. National Center for Educational Statistics data.

33. *The New York Times* (January 13, 1974).

34. "Health & Medicine Employment Outlook," *The New York Times* (November 3, 1985).

Blessed Are the Boat-Rockers

Most of us Americans sail steadily through life on an even keel. We do what is expected of us: tend to our knitting; keep our noses clean; pull up our socks; steer a steady course; keep our powder dry; never get too far out; and certainly never rock the boat. And it's really just as well that most of us *are* like that.

But there are some, a very few Americans, maybe a million at a time, who are *boat-rockers*. They don't leave well enough alone, and they weren't born with an innate respect for the status quo. They go through life making a fuss when things aren't right, upsetting the comfortable decorum of the bureaucracy, and (this is the key point) fighting the fights for *us* that we don't fight for ourselves.

America has always had more than its share of boat-rockers. If it hadn't been for boat-rockers in the 1760s and 1770s, Queen Elizabeth would be using the White House as a western Buckingham Palace, and we'd all be driving on the wrong side of the road and talking through our noses like Margaret Thatcher.

America's boat-rockers have changed the course of history by jolting people and institutions out of ruts that were leading us in the wrong direction. I'll give you a few examples of some of my own favorite boat-rockers, just for starters:

Samuel Adams (1722–1803) not only rocked the boat of British government in the American Colonies; he also pitched part of its cargo overboard into Boston Harbor. He was unsuccessful as a businessman, so he got into politics, as failed businessmen often do. He first served a kind of apprenticeship in the lower house of the Massachusetts legislature, then became the "spokesman for the discontented" in resistance to British laws. He drafted a protest against the Stamp

Act; organized a nonimportation movement that forced repeal of the Townshend Acts; was constantly writing "crank letters" to the newspapers and stirring up trouble generally; and he signed the Declaration of Independence. He sent a circular letter to the colonies denouncing "taxation without representation," helped foment the Boston Massacre, and organized the Boston Tea Party and the radical Sons of Liberty. As a member of the Continental Congress the conservative members considered him an "irresponsible agitator." He wound up as governor of Massachusetts. Rocking the boat vigorously all the way, Sam Adams kept easygoing colonists who would have left "well enough alone" (and lost their chance for independence) stirred up and active for liberty.

Henry Thoreau (1817–62) was a small-town handyman who grew vegetables, did some surveying and odd jobs around the village, and served as assistant to Ralph Waldo Emerson. Thoreau was a stubborn individualist who broke the law by refusing to pay a poll tax that all the other good citizens of the community paid just as a matter of course. He said the tax revenues would be used to support the Mexican War, which he believed would extend slavery. Naturally, the town constable and tax gatherer had to make an example of Thoreau; he locked him up in the town jail. An anonymous friend bailed him out the next day, but Thoreau's view was that "Under a government which imprisons any unjustly, the true place for a just man is also a prison." His lectures on this theme and the book that grew out of his experience, *Civil Disobedience*, had a deep effect on people in the 19th century, and even more in our own. Thoreau advocated passive resistance against unjust governmental policies and had a profound influence on the development of the British labor movement in England, Mahatma Gandhi in India, and Martin Luther King and the whole civil-rights movement in our country. See what a single, passive boat-rocker can do?

The Man With a Dream for Us All

Martin Luther King (1929–68) was the son of a Protestant minister, and an ordained minister himself, with a Ph.D. from Boston University. A believer in the principle of passive resistance, he led the boycott by blacks in Montgomery, Alabama, against segregated buses there—a boycott that not only opened up the buses in Montgomery, but also opened up the way to civil rights in America. As head of the Southern Christian Leadership Conference, Dr. King spread the gospel of passive resistance and of civil rights throughout America. He was awarded the Nobel Peace Prize in 1964 for his efforts, and assassinated for them in 1968. This great "boat-rocker" for our society changed the direction of America toward equal rights more in a few years than it had moved in a century.

Vivien Kellems, who died in 1975 at age 78, came at society from a totally different direction, but she was also a boat-rocker for the general good. She ran a small manufacturing company. In 1948, when the government began requiring employers to withhold income tax, Vivien Kellems began her own kind of "civil disobedience." She announced publicly that the law was "illegal, immoral, and unconstitutional," refused to withhold taxes, and went to court to get the law changed. She was fighting for what she considered her employees' rights, but she lost.

Still, Vivien Kellems didn't stop boat-rocking. She went back to school and earned a doctorate in economics. Thus armed, she started suit to correct unequal taxation of single and married people. Kellems charged that the IRS had "stolen from me over the past 20 years because I have no husband." Again she lost, in Tax Court. She appealed again and again, until she was finally turned down by the U.S. Supreme Court. But even that didn't end the matter. In 1969 Congress changed the law, reducing the disparity between rates for unmarried and married taxpayers by as much as 22%. Vivien Kellem's legal boat-rocking had a lot to do with it.

Those four boat-rockers are now part of our history. But during their earthly years, all four were ridiculed, ignored, rejected, and/or actively hated by many "solid citizens." Establishments were irritated by these boat-rockers. All four were threatened with arrest, or actually put into jails. Boat-rockers are never liked by the people in charge of the boat. Many are thrown overboard and never heard from again. But their kind keep coming, thank heavens, and we have many boat-rockers among us today.

Yes, I said the *ACLU!*

The whole membership of the ACLU must be a bunch of dedicated boat-rockers. I'm sure everybody in the United

States must have been irritated with the American Civil Liberties Union at some time or other. I know I have been. Their own members have quit in droves because they disagreed with the ACLU. One attorney general of the United States even called the ACLU the "criminals' lobby."[1] But since 1920, when it was formed on the position that "all thought on matters of public concern should be freely expressed without interference," the ACLU has gone into court again and again in behalf of free speech in America and citizens' rights wherever the ACLU thought they were being threatened. And what violent waves they have made along the way!

The ACLU has been known to come to the aid of the Ku Klux Klan, American Nazis and Fascists just before World War II, civil-rights demonstrators during the 1960s, American Nazis' right to march in Skokie, Illinois, in 1977, Marine Corps Klan members, school newspaper editors threatened with censorship, university teachers similarly threatened, penitentiary prisoners—and most recently an ACLU project has reported that "at least 343 innocent people have been convicted in the United States since the turn of the century and 25 of them were executed."[2] The ACLU is out to change our death-sentencing laws. What has been labeled the "poisonous even-handedness" of the ACLU has been making waves nationally for over six decades now, but all for the purpose of defending *our* basic constitutional rights.

Ralph Nader is a major-league boat-rocker, too. His efforts over the past 20 years in behalf of greater car safety, clean food, clean air, and workplace safety have made him no friends in high places. But they have made changes for the better in the lives of all of us. We even owe him a vote of thanks for the fact that we can request smoke-free seating in airplanes. He's considered "old hat" today in some circles, but that has not stopped him from working continuously to change things for the better. As Nader has said, "The greatest patriots believe that loving their country means working hard to make it more livable."

Maggie Kuhn, the 80-year-old leader of the Gray Panthers, is another national boat-rocker. Her highly active multigenerational group works in many and often confrontational ways for peace and social justice, especially in eradicating age discrimination. The Gray Panthers helped to raise the national mandatory retirement age to 70. Now they're rocking the boat for a complete overhaul of our national health system.

Daniel Ellsberg gave the *Pentagon Papers* to the press in 1971, an act that not only rocked boats but also blew open a nationwide investigation and discussion of our Vietnam War involvement. Ellsberg still preaches civil disobedience and demonstrates against nucler proliferation, as he puts it wryly, "if I'm not in jail."[3]

W. H. Troxell was a boat-rocker in his community every day for 35 years. Back in the 1950s, Troxell got mad about how the government was wasting taxpayers' money, and what he considered the "erosion of America's rights and freedoms." He was convinced that "the liberal media" were "not presenting both sides and letting the public make up its own mind."

So Troxell spent his own money to buy air time ahead of the morning news on a local radio station, and started "rocking the boat" over the air six days a week, with his own ultraconservative commentary. "Trox Comments" became the longest uninterrupted radio commentary in history. After 35 years of speaking his mind for three minutes every day, for all to hear, Troxell's program was canceled by the station because of a change of station format. Troxell's parting words of advice to his listeners were in classic boat-rocker tradition: "Be not afraid to speak out in support of what you believe, no matter what the consequences."[4]

A Navajo Boat-Rocker

Mae Chee Castillo is a boat-rocker by tradition as well as by nature. She is a Navajo grandmother. Among Navajos, elderly people get much respect. They are expected to speak their minds, even in the highest tribal gatherings and places and even if it rocks the boat. So it was not out of character for Mrs. Castillo to make waves at the White House in Washington.

Mrs. Castillo was serving as a volunteer foster grandparent in a Head Start School when she rescued 10 children from a burning school bus. For this she was invited to Washington to be honored, along with 200 other senior volunteers. It was a fairly routine White House picture opportunity: Mrs. Castillo was allotted 20 seconds to say thank you to the president for inviting her, hand over some gifts, and shuffle briskly on in line.

Instead, Mae Chee Castillo took time to say what was most in her mind and heart about the needs of others: "We need to continue the current level of economic benefits, such as Social Security, since many, many Native American elderly depend on this support for their only source of income," she counseled the president. "We need funds for these services . . ." she went on as the president bent politely toward her and as minor White House functionaries fretted because Mrs. Castillo was overstaying her 20 seconds. "We need the funds because in Indian country there is little or no private sector. I ask for your support, Mr. President."

The President of all the United States promised to keep a safety net in place. Citizen Castillo was hustled off the scene— and appeared promptly on the front pages of newspapers all over the world. She had turned a routine government event into a media event simply by speaking her thoughts in the highest place of the land—rocking the boat for all of her people.[5]

Making Waves on the Farm

Wayne Cryts, a Puxico, Missouri, farmer, rocked the boat one rainy morning when he and 2,000 other farmers drove 78 trucks past FBI agents and federal marshals, broke into a sealed grain elevator, and carted away thousands of bushels of soybeans impounded there by a federal bankruptcy judge. Cryts went to jail, but in the process he set in motion long-needed legal efforts to test the constitutionality of the bankruptcy code as it applies to farmers.

Cryts had stored his soybean crop in a local grain elevator. The operator filed for bankruptcy, so the judge ordered all grain in the elevator sold to pay the operator's debts. Although the grain belonged to the farmers who had raised it and stored it there, the judge didn't consider their warehouse receipts sufficient proof of ownership.

Cryts and other farmers couldn't afford to lose their crops like that. They had big loan interest payments to make. If they couldn't sell their crops, they'd lose their farms. Cryts had $250,000 worth of soybeans locked up in the elevator. He was farming 2,000 acres with his father, brother, and brother-in-law. "This land has been in our family six generations," he said. "I just couldn't live with myself if I had to sell because someone had stolen my property and made me go broke."

So Cryts made up his mind to go get his grain, even if it did mean flouting the judge's orders. Word got around. The morning Cryts arrived at the elevator, there were 2,000 other angry farmers their waiting to help him. A wise federal marshal, who confronted Cryts and his supporters at the elevator, simply shook hands with Cryts and then stepped aside to let the trucks through so they could begin loading grain. "It didn't warrant killing people over basically a civil dispute," the marshal said.

The bankruptcy judge sent Cryts to jail and fined him on a civil contempt charge when Cryts refused to give him names of farmers who helped him reclaim his grain. But even in jail, the waves Cryts had stirred up in Puxico, Missouri, spread nationwide. They brought him thousands of letters, media interviews, and (more to the point) lawyers from the nonprofit American Constitutional Association, willing to work to get a bad law corrected and a good man out of jail.[6]

A federal district court jury took only 30 minutes of deliberation to acquit Cryts of contempt of court charges, though the federal judge disagreed with the jury's decision.[7] However, the next day the judge thought better of having scolded the jury for their decision. He had talked the case over with his mother. "She told me she was one hundred percent with the jury," the judge said, "and when you're in disagreement with the jury and with your mother, there's some reason to doubt that you are right." But he also added, of the jury, "I applaud it for its conscientious independence. But that doesn't mean that judges are not entitled to their own opinions, and they sometimes should be expressed."[8]

Let that be a lesson to all of us. If you have a conscientious, independent opinion, about a law or anything else, speak out—even if you're a judge. All of these boat-rockers did. They represent a wide spectrum of political shades, from ultraconservative to outright radical. But they all made waves and rocked the boat for what they were convinced was the general good, and to correct social wrongs. They all represent a great American tradition, and we should rock a few boats ourselves in their honor.

NOTES

1. Garry Wills, syndicated column for Universal Press service (October 23, 1985).
2. "343 People Convicted in Error, Study Says," *Los Angeles Times* service (November 14, 1985).

3. Karen De Witt, "Ellsberg in Pursuit of Peace," *USA Today* (August 3, 1985).

4. John Schroeder, "Patriot in Flagstaff Hangs Up His Mike After 35 Years," *Arizona Republic* (March 23, 1985). One other trenchant remark from Mr. Troxell deserves to be recorded. His original reason for going on the air: "I saw a gradual erosion of our freedoms . . . one little thing after another . . . I thought somebody ought to be talking about it rather than letting it happen." Right on!

5. "Navajo's Candor Upsets White House," *Arizona Republic* (April 27, 1985).

6. Lynda Schuster, "A Missouri Farmer Gets His Beans Back and Becomes a Hero," *The Wall Street Journal* (May 12, 1982).

7. *The New York Times* (June 3, 1983).

8. "Judge in Soybean Case Has Second Thoughts," *The New York Times* (June 5, 1983). As a footnote to a footnote, it should be recorded that Wayne Cryts became such a folk hero for reclaiming his own beans that a local poet memorialized his act in "Ode to Wayne Cryts," which ends:

> Though his song is not completed,
> He keeps singing of their rights,
> And the farmers of America
> Believe in Mr. Cryts.

III

The Way We Live

Freedom is an indivisible word. If we want to enjoy it, and fight for it, we must be prepared to extend it to everyone, whether they are rich or poor, whether they agree with us or not, no matter what their race or the color of their skin.

Wendell Willkie, *One World*

In all things that are purely social we can be as separate as the fingers, yet one as the hand in all things essential to mutual progress.

Booker T. Washington,
speech, September 18, 1895

We're Living Longer and Feeling Better Than Ever

★

Everybody knows health-care costs have gone up; we spend seven times as much for health care now as we did 20 years ago.[1] But look at it this way: We're also living longer than ever before in America, and feeling healthier, too. We have one of the lowest infant-mortality rates in the world—and it's just gone to a new all-time low. And according to the 1986 report on the nation's health from the U.S. Department of Health and Human Services, the average child born in America today can expect to live 74.6 years—an all-time high. So we're spending more—but we're also *getting* a lot more for most of us in terms of quality of life.

Up front, infant Americans have a better chance of surviving their first year than ever before in history. Estimated infant mortality dropped to 10.6 per 1,000 in 1984 compared to 10.9 the year before,[2] and 11.9 in 1981. When you think that as recently as 1970 we lost 20 infants per 1,000 in their first year of life, you see that we've almost doubled the chances for survival since then.[3]

Only a few years ago, rates of 10 or fewer infant deaths per 1,000 were thought biologically unattainable. Now, although our national rate is one of the best in the world, 10 other countries are even better: Canada (10); Taiwan (9); Denmark, Netherlands, Norway, and Switzerland (8); Iceland, Finland, Sweden, and Japan (7).[4] What a lot of lucky babies!

The main reason why infant deaths have been going down in countries like these are high living standards, improvements in their public and private health service, control of infectious diseases, better contraceptive techniques, legalization of abortion, and new and better ways of taking care of babies of low birth weight.[5] All of these factors also contribute to a lower fertility rate per woman. In 1900 an American woman who wanted to be sure that three of her children would become adults would have had to produce four, on average, and five if she really wanted to be sure of three reaching adulthood.

Not only are your survival chances better and better in the *early* years, they're also better and better toward the other end of life. Life expectancy at birth in the United States has been marching upward year to year for men (except in 1972 and 1980, when it remained same as the year before) since 1970. In that time, nearly three years of life expectancy had been added for men, from 67.1 years in 1970 to 71.0 years in 1983. For women, life expectancy has also marched steadily upward, except in 1980, when it fell back a fraction of a year. Female life expectancy grew from 74.7 years in 1970 to 78.3 years in 1983, a gain of 3.6 years.[6]

In recent years, the male life-span has been growing more rapidly than that of females. Doctors say this is because women smokers are dying earlier from lung cancer and chronic pulmonary disease, especially those who took up cigarettes during World War II. At the same time, men have been drinking and smoking less than they used to, eating and exercising better, and receiving better medical attention.[7]

Since the average life expectancy in 142 nations of the world is 62 years (73 years in developed nations; 59 years in developing ones), both Americans and Canadians (with a 74-year average life expectancy) have a substantial bonus of 12 added years of life expectancy above the world average. However, there are seven other nations where people can expect to live longer than we: Denmark, Netherlands, Norway, Sweden, and Switzerland (75 years); Iceland (76 years); and Japan (77 years). The average life expectancy in the Soviet Union is 70 years, and in the People's Republic of China, 67 years.[8]

In spite of this admirable health-improvement record during the past 15 years, people have been up in arms about the costs of the health-care services they've been getting. The nation's health bill has crept—no, *marched*—upward year after year, until by 1984 it was setting us all back over $1 billion a day, with expectations that it would reach $2 *billion* a day by 1990. "But we have hospital insurance," some people say. "It doesn't cost *us* much at all. We're covered!"

Not a bit of it. What you don't pay out at the hospital cashier's window or in the doctor's office, you pay in higher

insurance premiums, higher taxes, and increases in everything you buy. Since employers have to pay higher health-
care costs for their insured employees, they simply pass what
it costs them on to you, in higher prices for everything you
buy from them. Lee Iacocca, a constant campaigner to get
lower health-care costs for his Chrysler employees and for
you, has estimated that at least $600 of what you pay for your
American automobile goes to pay for the manufacturer's employees' health insurance![9]

Companies such as Chrysler, Motorola, Honeywell, and
others, consumer groups such as the American Association of
Retired Persons (AARP), the Gray Panthers, and Ralph Nader's
citizen-action groups, and insurance companies and official
medical organizations have been pushing for changes in the
health-care-system structure that would cut the cost of services. About six in 10 of the top 500 companies in America
have changed their health benefits and now encourage employees to shop around for the most cost-efficient medical
care.[10]

All this consumer action is getting results. For the first
time in 20 years, the number of hospital beds in the United
States went down, in 1984. Hospitals have been cutting the
charges for many of their services. Physicians are beginning
to freeze their fees. Americans are going to the hospital less
often and staying for fewer days. And, unfortunately, the
poor and the uninsured are being squeezed out of the health-
care market more than ever as the federal-state Medicaid
program is trimmed, and hospitals caught in a fiercely competitive market find it necessary to shuffle indigent patients
off to already overloaded public facilities.

These are days of radical change in the American medical
and health-care industry, and like any mass social change, it
is hurting many participants. But most of us Americans continue to enjoy one of the highest standards of health care in
the world. The United States spends substantially more in
public expenditures per person for care ($589) than the aver-
age among all NATO countries ($548) and more than three
times as much as the average among Warsaw Pact countries
($181), as well as more than Japan ($472) and China ($4).

We have a national average of 500 people per qualified
physician in America—that is, doctors in practice, teaching,
or research. The average among 142 world nations is 1,029
people per doctor.

We have one available hosptial bed per 166 people in America. The world average among 142 nations is 279 people per available hospital bed.[11]

All these figures show quantity of health care, and in those terms, America is well above the average among nations around the world. The figures don't show quality, of course. The indisputably authoritative *New England Journal of Medicine* has reported that because the medical profession has failed to police itself, and state governments have also been lax about acting against dangerous doctors, there are "at least 22,000 incompetent or impaired doctors . . . practicing medicine in this country," and there may actually be as many as 66,000 who are unsafe.[12] Even measured against the fact that there were 441,000 licensed physicians in the country in 1982, these are very unsettling figures for patients. Also for doctors, whose competence has never been brought into such open question before now.

But even this disclosure is beneficial and speaks well for our American system. Freedom of information has always helped to shake out and cleanse American institutions. It's time medical associations and state medical boards put an end to the conspiracy of protective silence that everyone has always known was there, shielding practitioners who should not be treating human patients. Now that the wrappings are off, the infection can and will be treated.

Meanwhile, the facts and figures show that Americans generally have never been healthier, nor had better prospects for a long and active life. And every year we're getting better. We must be doing a lot of things right!

NOTES

1. *Cut the Cost: Keep the Care* (Washington, D.C.: Healthy US, AARP, 1984), p. 4.
2. "1984 Infant-Death Rate in Nation Falls to Record Low; Births Rising," Associated Press, (October 12, 1985).
3. *Statistical Abstract of the United States 1985* (Washington, D.C.: U.S. Department of Commerce, Bureau of the Census, 1984), table 109.
4. Ruth Leger Sivard, *World Military and Social Expenditure 1985* (Washington, D.C.: World Priorities, 1985), pp. 38–43. It should be added to the other infant-mortality data that in China, the rate of infant deaths per thousand in the first year is 44. The author of this

remarkable and fascinating 56-page document, with many highly sophisticated and beautifully executed graphs and illustrations, now is the director of World Priorities, a non-profit research organization. Ruth Leger Sivard was formerly chief of the economics division of the U.S. Arms Control and Disarmament Agency. This 8½ × 11 four-color booklet should be in every library and on every coffee table for discussion by people interested in survival. It is called "The single most valuable compendium of armaments' social and economic costs," by *World Press Review* and is clearly the most up-to-date information on this subject. Single copies are $5 from World Priorities, Inc., Box 25140, Washington, DC 20007.

5. Victor R. Fuchs, *How We Live* (Cambridge, Mass.: Harvard University Press, 1983), p. 31.
6. National Center for Health Statistics data. (The 1982 and 1983 data are preliminary.)
7. Alan L. Otten, "Women Continue to Outlive Men but the Female Edge Is Narrowing," *The Wall Street Journal* (June 5, 1985).
8. Sivard, op. cit.
9. *Cut the Cost: Keep the Care*, op. cit.
10. Abigail Trafford, "Hospitals: A Sick Industry," *U.S. News & World Report* (March 18, 1985).
11. Sivard, op. cit.
12. Ronald Kotulak, "U.S. Has 22,000 Inadequate Doctors, Medical Journal Says," *Chicago Tribune* news service (March 24, 1985).

Want More Information About Health Care?

The federal government has been cutting back on its information sources and materials, but it has maintained the National Health Information Clearinghouse for citizens who need information on such topics as aging, arthritis, cancer, child abuse, consumer information, food and drugs, the handicapped, health planning, mental health, physical fitness, poison control—you name it, and ask about it! Contact the National Health Information Clearinghouse at P.O. Box 1133, Washington, DC 20013; or telephone, toll-free, 1-800-336-4797. In Virginia, call collect, 703-522-2590.

Elder Americans will find the free guidebook *Cut the Cost: Keep the Care*, from Healthy US, AARP, 1909 K Street, NW, Washington, DC 20049 full of valuable information about what they can do to help cut the cost of medical care.

There's No Better Place to Grow Old

★

"I never thought it would be so sad to get old," a 78-year-old retired craftsman said to me in 1972. At that time one in four older Americans was living below the government's poverty level. When the Leo J. Shapiro & Associates national poll asked people in 1972 if they thought "America is no place to get old," almost half of those over 45 years of age said, "Yes."

In 1985 the interviewers asked Americans across the country the same question again. Now just one in four of those over age 45 feels "America is no place to get old." Among Americans age 60 and older, eight in 10 *disagree* with the notion that this is "no place to get old"!

What happened in the past 14 years to make so many people feel more secure about growing old in America? A number of things. If you have to get old (and who doesn't?), there's never been a better place or a better time to do it than in our country, right now.

Elder Americans are much better off today than their predecessors were. Government figures show that between 1959 and 1963, poverty among American elders (65 years or older) dropped 55%—to about one in seven.[1] Thanks largely to the hearty growth of Social Security retirement benefits, real income of elderly Americans has gone up, both in absolute terms and in comparison to the income of people still in the labor force. When Congress tied Social Security increases to the cost of living annually (COLA) in 1972, the effect actually was to *over*compensate for inflation over a period of several years.

More Income; More Wealth

As of 1985, Americans aged 50 to 65 had an average household income of about $30,000 or 20% higher than the national average. Even the households of *older* Americans, aged 65 to 75, have a higher average income than do those of young Americans, under age 45.[2] How can this be, when so many of these older Americans are no longer in the labor force? During earning years, from ages 25 to 54, more than 90% of our income is earned by working. Even between ages 55 and 64, almost 80% of our income is earned. But at age 65, there's a kind of caterpillar-butterfly transformation: After that magic point, earnings make up only a fifth of our income, on average.[3] The rest comes from Social Security retirement benefits, income from interest and dividends, government employee pensions, private pensions, or public assistance.

Today's elder Americans not only have more average income; they also have more wealth (adjusted for inflation) than their predecessors. A 1985 study by the Conference Board found that eight in 10 Americans in the 50 to 65 age group are homeowners.[4] Since half of those homes are owned free and clear, the net home equity among elders aged 50 to 65 averages $70,000. Among those over age 65, more than 70% are homeowners, and eight in 10 have also paid off the mortgage. Add to this the fact that people over age 50 own 77% of all financial assets belonging to American households and that average savings of households of those aged 65 to 70 is a tidy $65,000 (more than twice the national average)—and you see that elders have come a long way in terms of security in the past decade or so!

We must pause here, however, to note that (as with any national-average figures) these *are* averages. The fact is, while income among elderly Americans is fairly evenly distributed, wealth is *not*. There's a big difference from top to bottom of the elder population when you look at ownership of controllable, transferrable wealth such as real estate, securities, liquid savings, insurance, and the like. One estimate, based on 1972 IRS data, found over 28% of all the wealth among elderly Americans is in the hands (or bank vaults) of just 1%. The top 10% of the elders owned 63% of the wealth in households of those aged 65 or over. And that top 10% of elder Americans averaged $241,000 in wealth per capita, while the remaining 90% averaged only $16,000.[5] So not everybody in what some young ad writer labeled "the Golden Years" is exactly rolling in resources.

Overall, older Americans in the 1980s are no more likely to be poor than are younger ones.[6] However, there are many bitterly poor elders among those living alone, particularly older women and blacks, and the chronically ill. Almost half of all widows during 1983 who were black and over age 65 were poor.[7] But even here, progress has been made: In 1959, a total of 62% of all persons living alone were living below the poverty level; by 1970, 47 percent; by 1982, 27 percent.[8]

More Buying Power

Older Americans today account for over 40% of consumer demand.[9] If you've been aware of more gray hair showing up in prime-time television commercials, and fewer "old-folks caricatures," it's because marketers have begun to discover the tremendous buying power among older Americans. On a per-capita basis, people in households headed by someone aged 55 or older have more discretionary income—money available to spend—than those in any other age group.[10] This is partly because the older household has fewer members than there are in younger family groups, so the income isn't spread across so many family members. But it still works out to more available spending money per person in the elder family. In 1980, people aged 30 to 39 had approximately $2,000 a year per capita in discretionary income. However, among those aged 55 to 59, there was $3,500 per capita; among those 60 to 64, $3,700; and people aged 65 or over had the highest per-capita discretionary income of all: $4,100. See why advertisers are very loath to poke fun at the old folks in commercials these days? Those are *customers* out their in Retirement City! Even if a substantial part of their income is from Social Security, the buying power of the average Social Security check has increased about 25% since 1970. The income of married couples over age 55 is likely to be very comparable to that of their young married offspring, and since the elders' family is smaller now, more of their income is available to spend.

In 19th-century America, "people looked so palpably old by the time they were sixty," a child of that time has written, that "it was an accepted truism that they had better act that way."[11] No more. Your 55-to-64-year-old today looks, thinks, and acts more like people did in their 40s, even 25 years ago. Elders are going in for exercise equipment, health clubs, diets, and cosmetic surgery. They are dressing younger, lead-

ing more active lives—and traveling even more freely than
young folks. (Guess who holds the biggest number of U.S.
passports? Until 1981, younger Americans—those under age
30—were America's biggest globe-trotters. Since 1981 there
are more passports held by Americans age 60 and over than
by any other age group—892,000 of them in 1983.[12]) A national survey during 1985 found that nearly one in four American elders was planning to take a trip by air during the
coming year; more than one in four planned to stay in a hotel
or motel during their trip.[13] We've changed a lot since the
old days when the "old folks" rocked away their last years on
the front porch at home.

The over-65 group today is also, by and large, much younger in looks, spirit, and activities than were their predecessors. They're "into" nutrition and healthful dieting;
health-insurance programs make it easier to maintain their
bodies in good shape; and they exercise as if their lives
depend on it, because now they know they do. A total of 16%
swim; 7% golf and bicycle; 2% run, jog, or take part in team
sports; and 1% play tennis, ski, or do horseback riding.

Not only do elders have more energy, they also have more
time, because tasks they used to have to do for themselves,
such as lawn care, snow removal, home improvement, house
cleaning, and even food preparation are done *for* them by
various services. The chores elders perform for themselves
today also have been made easier and quicker by power
equipment, convenience products, and new devices such as
the microwave oven, food processor, and large-capacity freezer.

Freed of many chores and financial burdens they carried
earlier, today's elder Americans have become a prime market
for all sorts of gear and gadgetry of the "good life." Automobile manufacturers have rediscovered them, especially in the
revival of large-size cars.

One in eight householders aged 60 or over was planning to
buy a new car during 1985 or 1986. Half of the Americans in
that age group were planning to make some kind of major
purchase during the year—everything from new cars and
housing to new television, appliances, or furniture.[14]

Homebuilders and real-estate developers were among the
first really to begin to grasp the enormous sales potential in
the "graying of America." Del Webb's Sun City, Arizona,
launched as a retirement community in 1960, now is a full-
fledged community with 57,000 citizens in America's fastest-

growing state. Builders who aim at the housing market for elders know in advance that they will be dealing with the most persnickety customers on site. Most elders have already owned three or four homes during their lifetime, and they know what to look for. "We find the average checkback before buying a new home is eight to 10 times," a home designer says. "They've got all the time in the world to check out every single thing." Builders also know the needs of elder customers and cater to them with no-upkeep surroundings, better-than-average lighting, nonskid tile floors, whirlpool tubs, hand grips in convenient locations, light sockets high on the walls, and absolute security.

More Options and More Fun

The "graying of America" has produced the "youngest" elders ever. Bernard Baruch, the self-made stock-market millionaire who became known as "adviser to U.S. presidents" from Woodrow Wilson on (and outlived them all, to the wise and witty age of 95), enunciated "Baruch's Rule for Determining Old Age: Old age is always 15 years older than I am." The current crop of American elders seem to be following this "elder statesman's" rule en masse.

Back in 1935, when the Social Security Act was passed by Congress, the average life-span in the United States was just 64. So it made sense to base Social Security on a premise of age 65 as a kind of "continental divide" in life, separating our productive years from old age and retirement. Now the life-span has stretched out by a full decade, to 74.9 years. And the people who *are* between 60 and 75 years of age today are likely to think of themselves as "middle aged." Not until ages 75 to 84 do you now move into "senior" status. Only when you cross the threshold of 85 do you step into truly "old age."

Elder Americans are taking advantage of the extra decades they've been given, to live a busier, far more enjoyable life than their predecessors had. In 19th-century America a writer describing life for those over age 50 wrote: "Vigorous-minded, formerly well-informed people grew silent and apathetic, uninterested, and eventually uninteresting because new ideas were cut off."[15]

Today elder Americans have more options than ever before. Three million (1.8 million men and 1.2 million women in 1983) have chosen to stay in the work force.[16] Millions are traveling. And although they're already the best-educated corp of elders the country has ever had, in the next decade or so their level of education will be even higher, with a projected median number of 12.1 years at school among Americans aged 65 or over. Better than one in 20 Americans aged 55 or over was enrolled in adult-education classes in 1981. Community colleges and four-year colleges and universities have grown accustomed to having a fair share of students in class who are considerably older than the teacher. (I know— I've been there for years.) A 68-year-old grandmother who recently earned her Ph.D. in psychology "with distinction," and her 68-year-old husband, who got his M.A. degree in humanities during the same month, said of their late-blooming college careers, "What do you expect us to do—sit home and watch game shows on TV?"

Millions of elders attend colleges and universities for short courses in this country and overseas, as part of the elder hostel movement; still others take part in similar programs offered through state universities. And for those who want to learn more about politics, there's the Close-Up Program for Older Americans, a national program in which men and women aged 50 or over descend on Washington, D.C., for a week-long educational program that involves them in person-to-person discussions, seminars, workshops, and study tours, where they sit face-to-face and exchange information and opinions with top national leaders and experts, members of Congress, administration officials, lobbyists, journalists, and political analysts. The foundation sponsoring Close-Up is nonpartisan and nonprofit. Since 1970 it's brought more than 150,000 elder Americans face-to-face with their government, at its very center. The fact that Close-Up exists and is so successful is a testimonial to the regard for elder citizens in America—as well as for their clout as voting members of their communities!

The percent of Americans aged 65 or older who are registered to vote has gone up in every election since 1974. It has never dropped below a ratio of one in seven elders. In the 1980 presidential election year over 24 million Americans of voting age were aged 65 or older; three out of four of them (74.6%) were registered; two out of three (65.1%) actually voted. The only age group with higher participation in the election was that of Americans 45 to 64 years old.[17]

You Don't Have to Retire

Whether elders "go out to pasture" at age 65 or not is up to them. In 19th-century America, by age 60, men and women were generally cut off from the work force, "amputated of a future," as one writer has put it. She describes how "most aging persons awoke in the morning to the knowledge that they had no plans to make. . . . Grandma tended and mended and knitted; Grandpa worked in the garden and did light chores; but the young folks made all the vital decisions. . . ."[18] It was customary in those days, especially in farming communities, for the "old folks" to turn their land and home over to their youngest married children and live on with them as wards. No more. Today's elder Americans aren't about to be pushed out of the work force or their homes until they are ready to leave. And Congress stands behind them.

In 1978, Congress made it illegal to force most employees to retire before age 70. Bills have been introduced in Congress that would end age-designated retirement, *period*. In the meantime, however, 20 states have gone ahead on their own to protect workers against mandatory retirements beyond the age of 70.

Self-employed workers have *always* been able to retire whenever they were ready to do so. Studies based on retirement-history survey data for the 1970s indicate that when all variables are equal, self-employed men are more likely to go on working beyond age 65 than are wage-and-salary workers. The self-employed worker has more flexibility in hours and can adjust the work schedule to fit the way he or she wants to work. And since many people retire of their own accord before reaching a mandatory age limit, one economist has estimated that in 1977 only about one in seven workers in the private sector was even subject to a threat of mandatory retirement.[19] Now even those elder Americans would be able to continue working, at least to age 70.

So you find redoubtable elders like the 76-year-old Palo Alto, California, machinist who continues in his 4-hour-a-week job running a lathe because "I would be lost if I didn't have something to do"; the 70-year-old Minnesota woman who describes herself as "the fat grandma type" modeling professionally for fashion photographers; the 87-year-old Maryland man who gets up at five and "works all day" every day as a sawmill operator; the 84-year-old South Carolina woman who still crisscrosses the country as an educator, giving workshops for teachers; the former advertising agency head, now in his 70s, beginning a new career as a full-time teacher at a prestigious Minnesota college; and the 64-year-old former schoolteacher in Cleveland, Ohio, who applied for a job as a police officer—and became the oldest person ever to pass Cleveland's tough certification test for city patrolmen. Five feet five and 118 pounds trim, she said she applied for a police-officer job because "older people have just as much right" to the job as anyone else willing to take the test.

You also find elder couples both working, like the pair past 65 and married "96 years—48 years for each of us"—with four children and three grandchildren. Their home is a huge 18-wheel truck in which they drive 150,000 miles a year as a team, making deliveries in 46 of the 48 states. In 1985, the wife outscored 3,000 men drivers to become regional driver of the year in an annual competition. She is the first woman to win the award—which her husband also won, in 1982. The two have each driven about 2.5 million miles without an accident. Trucking has become their "way of life," and they look to "keep on trucking" because they "wouldn't trade it for anything."

But while the way has been cleared for elders to work until their 80s, the fact is that in spite of lifting mandatory rules for retirement, the percent of men 65 or over still in the work force has dropped enormously since the end of World War II. In 1947 almost half the men that age in America were still working. By 1970 the proportion was down to a fourth. By 1983, only about one man in six among those 65 or over was still in the labor force. Women's participation at that age rose from 8% in 1946 to 10% in 1970 but has gone back down, to 7.5% during the 1980s.[20] A recent article in *Modern Maturity* magazine, a publication of the giant American Association of Retired Persons (AARP), commented on this trend: "The trend toward early retirement is accelerating, and older employees are continuing to leave the work force in droves."[21]

Why have so many elders been "opting out" of full-time jobs in spite of removal of mandatory retirement rules? Alan Pifer, president emeritus of the Carnegie Corporation of New York, suggested, "The main reason is a set of national attitudes that still regard older persons as obsolete or semiobsolete."[22] The 1981–82 recession bumped many elders out of their jobs during massive layoffs across the country, and they simply never went back to work. Other elders have been induced to leave their jobs by temptingly generous early-retirement packages developed by employers. A total of 60% of the companies surveyed in a national study by the Conference Board built special inducements for early departure into their retirement packages; only 3% encouraged employers to work beyond age 65.[23] Rapidly changing technology also is a factor. But probably the most important factor in the massive movement of elders out of full-time jobs is public pensions, especially Social Security retirement benefits. The dollar value of these benefits has been increasing faster than wages.

However, as the bulge of baby boomers moves inevitably into upper years, the working population is growing older. There are likely to be gaps in company work forces that need to be filled by experienced workers. Some employers are beginning to look for ways to raise the level of their available labor pools. Workers aged 50 or over have been finding themselves in a "buyer's market." The median length of time spent looking for a new job among *all* job-seekers was 2.8 months during the first quarter of 1985; but for experienced workers over age 50, the median time spent getting rehired was just 1.95 months. As one firm of outplacement specialists put it: "Employers these days are putting a premium on experience."

Such sophisticted major firms as Lockheed Missiles & Space Company; Honeywell, Inc.; Motorola, Inc.; Grumman Aircraft; and the Travelers Companies have been developing innovative ways to bring experienced elders back to work. These include "retiree pools" of ex-employees to fill part-time and temporary vacancies; increasing the number of hours retirees can work during the year without having pensions affected; job-sharing, in which two or more persons share one full-time job slot; retaining former employees as independent contractors rather than as employees; reclassifying retirees as "casual employees"; and retraining veteran employees aged 50 or over so they will be "up to speed" on the latest technological changes and can continue to be highly productive for another decade or more. Also, there now are firms that specialize in delivering highly qualified retirees (such as retired engineers, technicians, and professionals) on order to fill part-time jobs for employers.

All this gives today's American elders increased options,

and the opportunity to stay active in a job without working full-time, or endangering pension income. It's a far cry from the "amputated future" elders faced a few generations back.

Portable Empty Nests

Elderly Americans have never had so many options about where they'll live. Almost three out four Americans 65 or over own their homes. Over eight out of 10 (84%) of those are owned free and clear.[24] Since older householders are likely to have lived in the same house for many years and since housing values have increased meanwhile, this greatly increases living options for many elder Americans. Some take a reverse annuity mortgage on their home and are guaranteed lifetime tenancy, with the loan being repaid when they die and the home is sold. Meanwhile, they get a monthly payment as long as they live. Some use this extra income to help finance "snowbirding" trips in the winter, or a cool-off cruise or vacation in the summer. Others sell their homes, take advantage of the one-time tax-free IRS allowance on profit from selling their residence after age 65, and move into new quarters somewhere else.

Even with these options in hand, however, most elders opt to "stay put" in their homes. In fact, elders are much more likely to stay put than are Americans in general. Between 1981 and 1982, one in six (17%) of all Americans packed up and moved to a different house; but only one in 20 (5%) of those 65 or over did so. And while there's a sort of general impression that when the old folks move these days, they head for "sun country," down South or out West, it's just not so. Only 1.6%—one in 62 elder Americans aged 65 or over—moved to an area different from the one where they'd been living before 1981–82.[25] Over a five-year period between 1975 and 1980, 77% of elder Americans "stayed put"; 91% (including some who did change housing) stayed within the same country; and almost 96% stayed in the same state.

The Movers

Thus, over a five-year period only 4.4% of Americans aged 65 or over moved to "permanent" quarters in a different state—roughly 228,000 a year. Almost half of these headed for one of four Sun Belt states: Florida (25.9%); California

(8.8%); Arizona (5.7%); and Texas (4.5%). I'm not sure why, but the fifth most popular destination for elders migrating to another state was New Jersey, which has become the second oldest state in the nation in terms of median age.[26] In fact, among the 10 states in the country with the highest proportions of residents aged 65 or older, only one is in the Sun Belt. The 10 states, with their percentage of elder population, are: Florida (17.5%); Rhode Island (14.1%); Arkansas (14.1%); Iowa (13.9%); Pennsylvania (13.8%); Missouri (13.6%); South Dakota (13.6%); Nebraska (13.3%); Kansas (13.2%); and Massachusetts (13.2%). Just for contrast, Arizona has only 12% of its population aged 65 or over; California, 10.4%; and Texas, 9.4%.[27]

What kind of elderly people are these, who pack up their belongings and move to the Sun Belt from another state? Their average age is nearly 70; most are white, married, living independently, and with a total household income that's 200% above the poverty level. But as you can see in the following table, they vary, even in the averages, from state to state:[28]

Elderly Migrants to the Sun Belt, 1975–80

Characteristics	Ariz.	Calif.	Fla.	N. Car.	Tex.
Average age	68.1	69.7	68.3	69.1	69.6
Percentage over 75	15.9	24.3	16.3	20.5	25.8
Percentage of females	52.7	59.7	52.4	55.9	58.6
White	97.4	77.5	97.5	87.2	90.5
Married	73.4	53.3	74.2	60.0	56.2
Returning to state of birth	1.2	3.0	1.1	29.6	21.1
Living alone	13.7	18.2	13.9	18.9	18.0
Living independently	87.6	65.1	88.3	79.0	72.0
Average years of schooling	12.0	10.6	11.5	11.1	10.7
With over one year of college	34.6	27.8	27.4	32.0	27.5
In the labor force	12.7	18.5	11.4	14.6	19.3
Average total personal income in thousands	$ 9.4	7.3	9.5	8.3	8.3
Average total household income	18.1	19.1	17.7	17.0	18.0
200% over the poverty level	69.7	62.6	71.4	64.2	60.7
Below the poverty level	7.5	9.9	7.7	10.9	10.3

If you're looking around for a place to resettle that's *not* likely to be overpopulated by other inmigrants, you might want to consider New York State. In 1980, only 3.8% of its residents had moved in from another state during the past five years, compared to 19.6% in Florida and 23.9% in Arizona.[29] In Arizona, many people who have lived in the state for more than five years feel qualified to paste bumper stickers on their cars that identify them as "Arizona native." The state has had an increase of 215% in the number of elderly inmigrants between 1960 and 1980—the biggest increase in the nation.

And elderly Americans have never had so many options in housing. In spite of all this talk about picking up and moving, most elderly Americans do prefer to stay right where they've been all along. An increasing proportion are staying put in suburbia. The 1980 Census found 7.9 million Americans 65 or over living in suburbs, a one-third increase from 1970. Now, for the first time in history, there are more elder citizens living in suburbs than in central cities. Why should they move, after all? Most owned their homes, free and clear, and liked their neighborhood and neighbors. Besides, they couldn't see anything elsewhere that seemed to offer so much housing for so little money, even though they were finding it increasingly difficult to keep things up the way they used to, and they had more room to heat in winter and cool in summer than they really needed. One expert community planner has estimated that there are 12.2 million owner-occupied homes across the country sheltering just one or two people over 55 in five rooms or more.[30]

This "graying of the suburbs" is not without problems for the communities themselves. Suburbs have mostly developed since World War II. They were created to fill the needs of young families with growing children. They simply were never geared to serve a substantial population of elder citizens. Suddenly there have been organized property-tax revolts; elders thwarting bond issues for school improvements; and increased demands on the community for housing, transportation, recreation, and other services specifically to meet the needs of an aging population.

Meanwhile, as elders grow older, their homes, and the yards around them, are likely to deteriorate, causing neighborhood problems. John Logan, a sociologist at the State University of New York at Albany, said an aging population in the suburbs is bound to become "a state and national issue as communities find they don't have the resources to deal with the problems." Joann S. Lublin has written that "Some demographers fear that close-in suburbs could turn into unintended retirement communities" in which limited-income elders, living in deteriorating housing, would gradually wring the economic and social vitality out of the community.[31]

But America is a country that grew up solving people problems by community action. Some suburbs are changing zoning laws to permit adding separate rental units in single-family homes. This gives elders an additional source of income, provides more housing units in the suburb, and increases the property-tax base. Other suburbs arrange home-sharing, so older homeowners can provide living space for young tenants—who will do maintenance work on the home, and provide security at the same time, just by being there. In a number of large-city suburbs, unused school buildings are being converted into subsidized senior-citizen housing. There's more low-income public housing for elderly citizens today than ever before. In 1960 there were only 1,000 such low-income units occupied by elders in the whole country; by 1975 there were 288,000; and by 1983, 338,000. Even so, the waiting period to gain occupancy in one of them can run as long as five years in some suburbs. Meanwhile, town houses, retirement complexes, and "congregate living" apartment buildings and complexes—where residents have their own living quarters but share a common dining space and recreation facilities—are springing up, tailored to the needs of elderly people.

Those are all options for elderly couples and singles with enough income to pay fairly substantial rent. For elderly people on a more modest income, shared housing is a very attractive new alternative. This is particularly so for elderly people living alone. The housing coordinator for the American Association of Retired Persons (AARP) said that up to 40% of all people who go into nursing homes do not need the care but have no better place to go. In shared housing, they can find a comfortable private room, companionship, and help with living chores, at a cost far below that in an institutional setting.

Shared housing residences usually are single-family homes now occupied by five or more elderly people. Residents share meals and chores (studies have shown that elderly people prefer to help with household chores because this gives them a sense of being in control of their own lives) but usually have help with heavy housework, laundry, and house management. In Memphis, Tennessee, for example, a nonprofit community-development organization used church and government subsidies to open a shared house for seven low-income, elderly people. Residents paid $300 a month for a private room, all meals, and laundry services. On the basis of its experience with the first share house, the organization has opened two more houses with five residents in each and is planning for more shared housing.

A bed in a nursing home can cost from $15,000 to $30,000 a year. An apartment in a housing complex for the elderly averages $5,400 a year. A private room in a shared residence (depending on the level of service that comes with it) ranges from $2,400 a year with no services to $14,400 a year with all meals, laundry, and housekeeping services provided, according to the Shared Housing Resource Center in Philadelphia.[32] In one California shared house near Los Angeles, residents paid $350 a month for a private room and bath, all meals, housekeeping, and laundry services in an attractive house renovated to fit the needs of elderly tenants, even to the point of adding an elevator. The residents have help with heavy housework and yard care but are responsible for most household chores, cooking most meals, and shopping.

The idea of shared housing is one of those ideas whose time has come with the graying of America. It's still new, but in 10 years over 200 shared residences have been formed here and there around the country, mostly by churches and community groups but also by individuals with a lot of unused living space. The Census Bureau estimates that there are 253,000 elderly people taking part in some kind of shared living arrangement—and it sounds like there will be many more.

The Oldest in an Aging World

America's fastest-growing age group is its oldest age group. Nobody knows what the median average age of Americans was in our country's earliest centuries. We do know that in 1820 it stood at 16.7 years for all races. Since then, thanks largely to continually improving medical care, nutrition, and general living standards, the median age has mounted higher with every census-taking except those in 1960 and 1970, when "errors found in tabulations" confused things a bit and caused a temporary downward blip. In 1983 the median American age for all races was 30.9—getting very close to twice that in the early 19th century.[33]

Today the fastest-growing group is our oldest age group—that of men and women 85 and over. In 1940, there were only 365,000 Americans this old—one in 333 people. By 1982 there were 2.5 million of these oldest-old Americans—better than one per 100 younger Americans. By the end of this century the oldest-old will number 5.1 million—one in 50 Americans. And by 2050 every 20th American will be 85 or over.

Even at this great age, today's elderly are in better shape and more active than their predecessors were. But unless some enormous medical breakthrough occurs in our lifetime, the fact will remain that the older anyone gets the more vulnerable he or she becomes to disabling illnesses or other kinds of disability. As a friend remarked the other day, "After a certain point in life, it's just patch, patch, patch." Patching multiplies with the years: Government figures show that only one in 16 of the 75-to-84-year-olds is in a nursing home; among those 85 and older, it's more like one in five. This is a problem we're all going to have to cope with during the years ahead. An increasing number of elderly Americans are caring for oldest-old parents long after the time when elderly people used to be concerned with only their own ailments and expenditures. Younger Americans will increasingly be contributing to the care of the oldest with their tax dollars. A government economist estimated in 1984 that the government was providing $51 billion in payments and services just to people 80 and over and that by the year 2000 (just 14 years from now) it will be paying out six times that much (still in 1984 dollars) simply because the oldest-old population will have grown so much.

This is not uniquely an American phenomenon. The population is aging all over the world. The percentage of total population who are aged 80 and over is expected to rise between 1970 and 2000, not only in North America but also in Europe, the USSR, Latin America, East Asia, South Asia, and Oceania. Only in Africa, where human life has become so fearfully vulnerable, is the percent of 80-year-olds in the population expected to fall slightly by the year 2000.[34]

Yet, in this aging world, there seems to be no better place to grow old than America. And more of us are discovering that every year. There's no better place for growing old.

NOTES

1. Joe Davidson, "Differing Social Programs for Young, Old Result in Contrasting Poverty Levels for Two Groups," *The Wall Street Journal* (June 27, 1985).
2. Conference Board report, *Midlife and Beyond*, reported in *Business Week* (July 15, 1985).
3. Victor R. Fuchs, *How We Live* (Cambridge, Mass.: Harvard University Press, 1983), p. 203.
4. *Business Week*, op. cit.
5. Fuchs, op. cit., p. 205.
6. William Lazer, "Mature Market," *American Demographics* (March 1985).
7. Davidson, op. cit.
8. *Statistical Abstract of the United States 1985* (Washington, D.C.: U.S. Department of Commerce, Bureau of the Census, 1984), table 761.
9. *Business Week*, op. cit.
10. Lazer, op. cit.
11. Ethel Sabin Smith, *A Furrow Deep and True* (New York: W. W. Norton & Company, 1964), p. 171.
12. *Statistical Abstract, 1985*, table 397.
13. Leo J. Shapiro & Associates, national consumer poll (February 1985).
14. Leo J. Shapiro & Associates, 1985 second-quarter report.
15. Smith, op. cit.
16. *Statistical Abstract, 1985*, table 655.
17. *Statistical Abstract, 1985*, table 426.
18. Smith op. cit., p. 170
19. Dorothy Kittner quoted by Fuchs, op. cit., p. 193.
20. *Statistical Abstract, 1985*, table 655.
21. Elliot Carlson, "Longer Work Life?," *Modern Maturity* (June–July 1985).
22. Ibid.
23. "Trend Toward Early Retirement Continuing," United Press International, (February 3, 1985).
24. Lazer, op. cit.
25. *Statistical Abstract, 1985*, table 17.
26. Peter Francese, "People Patterns," *Register-Tribune* Syndicate (February 3, 1985).
27. *Statistical Abstract, 1985*, table 31.
28. Census Bureau data quoted in *Arizona Republic* (November 2, 1984).
29. *Statistical Abstract, 1985*, table 16.
30. Joann S. Lublin, "Growing Older," *The Wall Street Journal* (November 1, 1984).
31. Ibid.

32. Michael deCourcy Hinds, "Shared Housing," *The New York Times* news service (February 10, 1985).
33. *Statistical Abstract, 1985,* table 29.
34. Sheila M. Peace, *An International Perspective on the Status of Older Women* (Washington, D.C.: International Federation on Aging, 1981), p. 7.

We've Got All We Can Eat—
for Most of Us

★

Thanks to affluence, changing life-styles, and the most efficient food-production and distribution system on earth, most of us have been putting on weight. Seven out of 10 Americans come right out and admit it. One in five confesses to being overweight by more than 20 pounds—more than a "pinch."[1] Latest Metropolitan Life tables confirm statistically what most of us sense intuitively: One out of five American adults over age 19 is "obese."[2]

We're accustomed to think of encroaching fat as one of the many problems of aging. The fact is, obesity among teenage Americans has ballooned 40% in the past 20 years. Today better than one in five youngsters aged 12 to 17 is at least 20% overweight. Some experts blame the epidemic of anorexia, bulimia, and other eating disorders on this fact; youngsters see themselves getting fat, while their role models on television and in movies are all skinny as whippets. So they'll do anything to look like them.

We blame practically every problem these days on either a "down" computer or "too much television," and sure enough, nutritionists accuse television of putting pounds on us. We all spend so much of our lives watching juicy commercials for food and drinks on television that we've become like Pavlov's dog: A TV jingle spot can make us salivate all the way to the refrigerator. This hits teenagers hard. The average American teenager now spends 25 hours a week in front of television, and (you guessed it) a recent study by scientists from the New England Medical Center and Harvard School of Public Health finds that youngsters who watch a lot of television are more likely than average to be overweight.[3] Is this because they are less active than kids who are not watching the screen, or because they snack more while watching? The researchers admit they're not sure about this; it may be a combination of factors. But the end result (no pun intended) is fat.

Taken all together, government figures show that not only teenagers but also Americans at every age level have been growing heavier (and slightly taller) on average over the past quarter century.[4] We are—on average—the best-fed people on earth. I say "on average" because I am conscious that in the midst of all our plenty, and in a time of economic recovery, while most of us are putting on weight, more Americans than at any time since the 1930s are going hungry because they don't have enough to eat. The Physician Task Force on Hunger in America, with many of the most prominent names in American medicine, based their nationwide study that revealed the hunger around us on Census Bureau and Agriculture Department data. They said bluntly: "Up to 20 million citizens may be hungry at least some period of time each month."[5]

As for the lucky majority of Americans, no other national group in the world eats better—in quantity or in quality. The average American packs away 1,417 pounds of assorted food a year—49 pounds apiece more than in 1960. We average 3,450 calories a day. That's 270 calories a day more than the average in 1960[6]—the equivalent of one piece of pumpkin pie, or an egg salad sandwich-on-white-and-hold-the-lettuce. One piece of pie isn't bad. But 365 pieces of pie laid end to end across a year's time can send you out shopping for bigger slacks.

Not only are we eating more than we used to eat; we're also still snacking between meals about as much as we did in 1960. On average, Americans snack twice a day, and it's most likely to be a beverage or something sweet. The most discouraging part of this is that a recent nationwide survey of 2,000 homes found that people who say they're "on a diet" are more likely to eat between meals than are nondieters![7]

A Nation of "Grazers"

Of course, one reason why Americans snack is that snacks are so available to us, on all sides, all day. The sheer multiplicity of eating places where we make what sociologists call "food contacts" these days is overwhelming. In one 24-hour period across the nation, people reported they had eaten or snacked in fast-food outlets, friends' or relatives' homes, workplaces, hospitals, airplanes, drugstores, gas stations, supermarkets, country clubs, department stores, wine-tasting rooms, schools, fraternal lodges, hotels, shopping centers, convenience stores, and retirement homes. As more of us go off to work each day, and children go off to day-care centers or school, we've become what sociologist Leo Shapiro christened "The Grazing Society"—a nation of people who leave home during the day and "live off the land," picking up food and services as they move through the day, returning home to freezer and microwave at night.

But then, this has been a national inclination since long before Mother went out to work and left instructions for supper on the refrigerator door. Americans invented "eating on the run." John Montagu, England's fourth earl of Sandwich, did invent our national food staple back in 1762. After spending 24 hours at a gaming table without pausing to take any other food, he created a meal he could hold in one hand while he held cards in the other. But we've been improving on it by making food *faster* ever since. America produced the first cafeteria, first drugstore lunch counter, first Automat, first railroad dining car, first drive-in, and first fast-food franchise—not to mention electric toasters, Pop-Tarts, instant breakfast, TV dinners, and microwave ovens for grazers at home. We have also made a stomach acid secretion inhibitor, Tagamet, one of America's top-selling medications, and dieting a national preoccupation.

Take It Off, Take It Off!

We've been putting on pounds, but we're not just taking obesity lying down. America is fighting the Battle of the Bulge now on both front and rear. One out of three adult Americans has been dieting.[8] Calorie-controlled entrees are the hottest thing in the grocer's freezer bin. Also, we're being fussier about what's in our food: Six out of 10 food shoppers "read labels on all but the most trusted foods."[9] The government helps by requiring listing of ingredients in foods on labels, including the sodium content. The food industry also helps diet watchers in various ways: Meats may not be labeled, but most (55%) are USDA-graded for quality, compared to just 45% in 1975. Retailers now market meats leaner than what the USDA calls Prime and Choice. They offer these leaner (and often less expensive) cuts under their own generic and store-grade names rather than by USDA grade designation[10]—all because so many consumers are looking for leaner meats. In fact, since saturated fat was linked to heart disease as well as obesity, the meat industry has reduced fat by weight in its trimmed beef—from 15.4% fat in 1959 to just 11.6% in 1983. Pork now has less than half as much fat as it used to have. In fact, the percent of animal fats in our diet has fallen dramatically, and our share of fats and oils from vegetable sources (soybeans, corn, safflower, peanuts, and the like) has very nearly doubled since 1950.[11]

The effect of our growing concern about diet shows when you compare our per-capita consumption for various major food categories with consumption in major European countries. We eat less sugar than the Dutch, Poles, or Russians (but more than the French, Spanish, Swedes, English—and even the West Germans). We use less margarine and butter than West Germans, Italians, Dutch, Poles, Russians, Swedes, or English.[12] Europeans generally eat more fruit than we do, but the good news is that American consumption of fruit is going up—from 133.2 pounds per capita in 1970 to 143.2 pounds per capita in 1983.[13]

So with the help of our government, the food industry, and the world's most productive farmers, most of us are eating not only more but also better than ever. Now, if we can just keep from standing too long in front of an open refrigerator door . . .

NOTES

1. Epcot poll reported in *The Wall Street Journal* (June 18, 1985).
2. Claudia Wallis, "Gauging the Fat of the Land," *Time* (February 25, 1985).
3. Marj Charlier, "Teen-age Obesity Grows," *The Wall Street Journal* (July 1, 1985).
4. *Statistical Abstract of the United States 1985* (Washington, D.C.: U.S. Department of Commerce, Bureau of the Census, 1984), table 194.
5. "20 million in U.S. Hungry in Any Month, Study Says," Associated Press (February 27, 1985).
6. *Nutrition Week* (January 3, 1985).
7. MRCA Information Services report quoted in *U.S. News & World Report* (April 15, 1985).

8. Leo J. Shapiro & Associates poll (March–May 1984).
9. Betsy Morris, "Rise in Health Claims in Food Ads," *The Wall Street Journal* (April 2, 1985).
10. *National Food Review*, no. 27 (1984).
11. "Fat-Consumption Habits Are Changing," Associated Press report based on USDA Economic Research Service report (April 7, 1985).
12. *Statistical Abstract, 1985*, table 1484.
13. *National Food Review*, op. cit., pp. 30–32.

Freedom of Association

Americans are great associators. We like to seek out and get together with others who share our sometimes pretty arcane interests. Did you know that there are 17,644 different nonprofit associations scattered across the land? There are. In fact, without really thinking much about it, you are probably a card-carrying associate of one or more. There are the big ones everybody knows about, such as the American Association of Retired Persons (16 million members), the National Rifle Association (2.5 million), or the American Federation of Labor and Congress of Industrial Organizations (15 million), and the American Automobile Association (24 million), but these are just for starters.

What's really great is the heterogeneity of organizations in America. We have support groups for everybody. There's really no excuse for anybody feeling "out of it" in America. No matter how strange you may be, there are associations, federations, societies, councils, clubs, lodges, or a coven where you will be welcomed by like-minded strangers.

Hart's Law of Observation states; "In a country as big as the United States, you can find 50 examples of anything." Just to prove that Hart's Law still is being observed around here, I'll give you 50 examples of support groups across the country and bet that you can find one to your liking. I'll even add their mailing addresses in case you feel moved to associate with one before you leave these pages:

Aaron Burr Association, R.D. 1, Route 33, P.O. Box 429, Highstown-Freehold, Highstown, NJ 08520.

Automobile License Plate Collectors' Association, P.O. Box 712, Weston, WV 26452

Bald-Headed Men of America, 4006 Arendell Street, Morehead City, NC 28557

Baton Twirling Association of America and Abroad International, P.O. Box 234, Waldwick, NJ 07463

American Battleship Association, P.O. Box 11247, San Diego, CA 92111

Beer Can Collectors of America, 747 Merus Court, Fenton, MO 63026

January 12th, 1888 Blizzard Club, 4827 Hillside Avenue, Lincoln, NE 68506

National Button Society, 2733 Juno Place, Akron, OH 44313

The Byron Society, 259 New Jersey Avenue, Collingswood, NJ 08108

Guild of Carillonneurs in North America, 3718 Settle Road, Cincinnati, OH 45227

Cat Fanciers' Association, 1309 Allaire Avenue, Ocean, NJ 07712

Cryptogram Association of America, 1007 Montrose Avenue, Laurel, MD 20707

Descendants of the Signers of the Declaration of Independence, 1300 Locust Street, Philadelphia, PA 19107

American Dialect Society, MacMurray College, Jacksonville, IL 62650

National Ding-a-Ling Club, 3930-D Montclair Road, Birmingham, AL 35213

American Society of Dowsers, P.O. Box 24, Danville, VT, 05828

Dracula Society, 334 West 54th Street, Los Angeles, CA 90037

Southern Appalachian Dulcimer Association, 5313 Quincy Avenue, Birmingham, AL 35208

Electric Railroaders Association, Grand Central Terminal, 89 East 42nd Street, New York, NY 10017

Epigraphic Society, Inc., 6625 Bamburgh Drive, San Diego, CA 92117

Esperanto League for North America, P.O. Box 1129, El Cerrito, CA 94530

National Association to Aid Fat Americans, P.O. Box 43, Bellerose, NY 11426

Society for the Protection of Old Fishes, School of Fisheries, University of Washington, Seattle, WA 98195

George S. Patton, Jr., Historical Society, 11307 Vela Drive, San Diego, CA 92126

Goose Island Bird and Girl Watching Society, 301 Arthur Avenue, Park Ridge, IL 60068

Horatio Alger Society, 4907 Allison Drive, Lansing, MI 48910

Iceland Veterans, 2101 Walnut Street, Philadelphia, PA 19103

International Jugglers' Association, 203 Crosby Avenue, Kenmore, NY 12417

League of Lefthanders, P.O. Box 89, New Milford, NJ 07646

Lewis Carroll Society of North America, 617 Rockford Road, Silver Spring, MD 20902

Magicians' Guild of America, 20 West 40th Street, New York, NY 10018

Man Watchers, Inc., 8033 Sunset Boulevard, Los Angeles, CA 90046

Navajo Code Talkers Association, Red Rock State Park, P.O. Box 328, Church Rock, NM 87311

American Institute of Parliamentarians, 229 Army Post Road, Suite B, Des Moines, IA 50315

Committee for Pedestrian Tolls, P.O. Box 1578, New York, NY 10006

Pilgrims of the United States, 74 Trinity Place, New York, NY 10006

Procrastinators' Club of America, 1111 Broad-Locust Building, Philadelphia, PA 19102

Reed Organ Society, The Musical Museum, Deansboro, NY 13328

Richard III Society, P.O. Box 217, Sea Cliff, NY 11579

Samuel Butler Society, Chaplain Library, Williams College, P.O. Box 426, Williamstown, MA 01267

Sons of Sherman's March to the Sea, 1725 Farmers Avenue, Tempe, AZ 85281

Steamship Historical Society of America, 414 Pelton Avenue, Staten Island, NY 10310

National Association Taunting Safety and Fairness Everywhere, P.O. Box 5743, Montecito, CA 93108

Thoreau Society, 156 Belknap Street, Concord, MA 01742

Titanic Historical Society, P.O. Box 53, Indian Orchard, MA 01151

Ventriloquist's Society of America, 414 Oak Street, Baltimore, OH 43105

General Society of the War of 1812, 1307 New Hampshire Avenue, NW, Washington, DC 20036

Wilsonian Club, 1331 Parkside Drive, Riverside, CA 92506

Wizard of Oz Club International, P.O. Box 95, Kinderhook, IL 62345

Ziegfeld Club, 3 West 51st Street, New York, NY 10019

Put them all together, and these 50 marvelously varied American associative groups report a total of only 63,375 members. That's only about half as many as the free-swingers of the International Frisbee Association (110,000 human members and untold canines); less than a tenth the number of Odd Fellows (700,000). But what a wealth of enthusiastic sharing of highly specialized interests they represent, for everything under the sun!

Wouldn't it be great if they all decided to hold their national conventions *together* some year? It might change the world. And it certainly couldn't hurt!

Three Lines Could Change Your Life

★

Nobody knows how many million true life stories like this are written every day across America:

> We had this really lovely house. Suddenly the monthly payments were way over our head. So we absolutely had to sell right away or we'd lose everything we'd put into it. We put a little three-liner in the want ads. Would you believe it? The first couple bought our house! That really bailed us out so we could start again. . . .

In just one city—Atlanta, Georgia—the *Journal and Constitution* published some 3.5 million classified ads in 1985.[1] Imagine! Behind every one of those 3.4 million ads someone was waiting for the telephone or doorbell to ring, announcing an opportunity for change, whether small or large. Right now, all over the country, telephones are ringing. Strangers are saying to total strangers: "I saw your classified ad . . ."

Classified ads are a far cry from the macho-communication world of Madison Avenue and national advertising. There a prime-time national network television commercial can cost the advertiser $118,840 for 30 seconds. A 30-second commercial during *The Cosby Show* would set you back a cool $270,000 just for the time. You can say about 60 words in that much time, to people all over America. But if you don't need to talk to the whole country, then 60 words in a classified newspaper ad in a big-city daily paper will cost you about $30. And it could change your life!

An elderly retired business woman, living alone in her big-city apartment, was becoming more and more isolated. She had been in an accident, and while recovering she found walking very slow and difficult. It was hard to leave her apartment. Suddenly, after enjoying an active, people-filled life, she found herself spending long, empty days alone. It was demoralizing. She became more and more depressed.

A small classified ad in a suburban newspaper changed everything for her. The ad described her, her interests, and needs, and asked for someone who could provide part-time companionship and household help.

The ad brought so many interesting applicants, suddenly the woman found herself "scheduled up to here" just making time to interview people. Her married son (who had created and placed the ad for his mother) said, "That ad had more power to bring about change than I did, than a stable of doctors and the encouragement or even passivity of friends. Within one week, interest in activity quickened. My mother returned to a volunteer job with the Heart Association, and began to walk again with much more vigor."

That's what classified ads have to offer: immediate one-to-one human communication between utter strangers, addressed to specific human needs. This is why the want ads are America's most fundamental expression of free enterprise, and have been ever since the country began.

In Thomas Jefferson's earlier years, he kept in touch with the world by personally subscribing to almost $100 worth of newspapers a year. The papers in those days were violently partisan about politics and often opposed him. Jefferson said: "Advertisements contain the only truths to be relied on in a newspaper."[2] Later in his life, Jefferson wrote to an old friend, "I read but one newspaper and that . . . more for its advertisements than its news."

Reading the ads in a newspaper from Jefferson's time makes it easier to see why he savored them so. I have a treasured copy of the January 4, 1880 *Ulster County Gazette*, from Kingston, Massachusetts.[3] One of its four pages has a detailed account of George Washington's funeral. Another reports doings in Congress, and European battles during that Napoleonic era. These are interesting, but the liveliest, freshest part of that 186-year-old newspaper still is the want ads. A page and a half of them are printed right next to the account of Washington's funeral—business going on as usual in a growing community. A few samples will give you some of their flavor:

LOST, a watch, on Wednesday last. The person who has found or may find it will meet with a suitable reward by handing it to the Printers.

SECOND NOTICE of my wife HANNAH is hereby given, forbidding all persons whatever, from harboring or keeping her, and from trusting her on my account, as I am determined to pay no debts of her contracting. MATYS VAN STEENBERGH.

WANTED, as an Apprentice to the Clothier's Business, an active, diligent BOY, from 14 to 18 years of age. Enquire of William Peters, at Marbletown.

FOR SALE, a neat, elegant, well-finished Pleasure SLEIGH. Apply to James Hasbrouck, in Kingston.

FOR SALE. A number of choice LOTS, lying in the Military Tract, containing from 50 to 550 acres each. Indisputable title will be given. Also, one quarter Township of 4000 acres, in the Connecticut Purchase, at a moderate price. Persons desirous of becoming purchasers, may know the particulars applying to LODEWYCK HOORNBEEK, jun.

Want ads still are the liveliest, freshest part of any newspaper today; they have an intimate immediacy that neither news, display ads, nor editorial columns can approach. That's probably why want ads continue to be one of the busiest parts of the paper, day after day. In a single midweek issue of our morning newspaper, I found a total of 836 column inches of news, including all the sports news and scores from around the country. But in the same issue there were 2,720 column inches of classified advertising. That's over three times as much classified advertising in my morning paper as all the local, national, and international news put together![4]

Almost a fourth of all national advertising expenditures go into newspaper advertising. About one in every three dollars spent advertising in newspapers goes into the classified advertising pages.[5] No wonder my paper has such a hefty proportion of want ads—they not only work hard for the readers, they also work hard for the publisher!

You meet all sorts of people in the want ads. But put them all together, and want-ad users are a kind of composite average American. It's no coincidence that one carefully watched

indicator of how the economy is doing across the country is
the *Index of Help-Wanted Ads,* a monthly measurement of
how many jobs are being offered in the classified sections of
newspapers. The more help-wanted ads, the more jobs available around the country, and the more paychecks coming
home to families each month. There's nothing closer to daily
life in America than what you can read between the lines of
want ads. Want ads are people-advertising.

A special national survey of who advertises in want ads,
taken in mid-1985, found that almost two in five American
adults (37%) had placed an ad at some time or other.[6] Asked
if the ad "worked" for them, people were practically unani-
mous: It did. As the following table shows, the average want-ad
user turns out to be a fairly typical American:

People Who Have Placed a Want Ad Compared to All Americans

	All respondents	Have placed a want ad
Own their place of residence	69%	75%
Completed at least some college	47%	55%
Live in: 1MM + metro area	42%	39%
1MM − metro area	33%	36%
nonmetro area	25%	25%
Male	50%	52%
Female	50%	48%
Mean average age	44	42
Mean average income	$26,000	$27,000
Mean average persons in household	3	3
Better off financially than they were one year ago	43%	45%

SOURCE: Leo J. Shapiro & Associates national consumer poll special
questions, July, 1985

What's really remarkable about the humble little classified
ad is that its role has changed so little during the past 200 years
in America, while our society and way of life have changed so
much. Back in 1800, when my copy of the *Ulster County
Gazette* came off the press, Massachusetts averaged only 53
people per square mile[7] compared to 737 per square mile
today.[8] So in 1800 anyone who advertised in the paper might
know personally the person who responded to the ad. Today
most of us live among thousands of strangers in cities with
over 100,000 in population. And yet the little three-line want

ad you run in a metropolitan newspaper today does precisely the same job an *Ulster County Gazette* ad did 186 years ago: It reaches out into your community and singles out the *one* person or family that may be harboring your lost parakeet, or yearning for your 1983 Plymouth, your washer, water bed, or apartment and is willing to come all the way across town to talk it over with you.

What a vast parade of dreams, problems, opportunities, desires, and human stories are displayed every day in the want ads! Take these few, picked more or less at random from newspapers and magazines. Any one of them could be the start of a short story, a television drama—or a whole new life.[9]

ANYONE knowing the whereabouts of Jerry K. formerly owner of [company name; telephone].

I FIND MISSING PERSONS [telephone].

MOODY GROUCH, 52, seeks local female with late-model automobile. Automobile photo requested, returnable [box number].

LOST during windstorm white cockatiel with orange spots over ears, slight yellow under tail, around neck and head areas. We're lost without our baby [telephone].

I CAN TEACH YOU TO DANCE so that anyone would like to have you for a partner [name, telephone].

ENERGETIC young person wanted for lot attendant position in Airport. 18 years + with clean driving record, $3.50 per hour possibility of advancement [telephone].

DANCERS A great job, start immed. $1000 wk. [telephone].

PREGNANT WOMEN. Need extra money for baby & doctor bills. Telephone sales work guarn. salary. Will train. Apply [address].

1 WAY Phoenix to Anchorage coupon, must leave Sept. 20, $220, male or female [telephone].

THE NUDE YOU—Ever fantasized having a private portfolio of yourself in the nude? Museum-quality work by Parisian female photographer. Women only. A perfect gift for your loved one or just yourself [telephone].

BRILLIANT ROUND CUT DIAMOND, 13.99 Carats.
Grade: S-1-1. Color: Faint Blue. Best Offer [telephone].

Archaeologists sift through rubbish heaps and waste pits of
deserted cities, looking for clues to how people used to live
and what their values were. Today America's day-to-day record of our lives and values is in the want ads. As long as
want ads flourish, America still will be the land of opportunity, where anything is possible.

There's still a chance to change *your* life this very day.
Your future may be waiting just three lines and a phone call
away—in today's want ads.

NOTES

1. Van Wallach, "Aggressive Stance Transforms Classified Ad Sales,"
   Advertising Age (July 25, 1985).
2. Merrill D. Peterson, *Thomas Jefferson and the New Nation* (New
   York: Oxford University Press, 1970), p. 713.
3. *Ulster County Gazette*, Kingston, Massachusetts (January 4, 1800),
   for which I am grateful to that scholar and gentleman, Robert W.
   Stafford.
4. *Arizona Republic* (August 27, 1985).
5. *Editor & Publisher 1984 International Yearbook;* quoted in *Statistical Abstract of the United States 1985* (Washington, D.C.: U.S.
   Department of Commerce, Bureau of the Census, 1984), table 944
   (1983 preliminary data).
6. Leo J. Shapiro & Associates, national consumer poll (July, 1985);
   special questions on use of classified advertising, to national sample
   of 458 adults.
7. *Historical Statistics of the United States*, Part I (Washington, D.C.:
   U.S. Department of Commerce, Bureau of the Census, 1975), table
   A-196.
8. *Statistical Abstract, 1985*, table 11; 1983 population density figure.
9. Of these ads, culled from various sources and with names and
   telephone numbers deleted, only one is of continuing interest. It is
   "The Nude You," reprinted from an article about the photographer,
   Marie Claire, by Kevin McManus in *Advertising Age* (August 15,
   1985). The article, "Marie Claire: A Revealing Photographer," tells
   why and how Ms. Claire decided to advertise in the classified ads
   section of *New York* magazine. It is an interesting case history and
   background sketch. In the meantime, should you wish to respond to
   her want ad, the telephone number is 212-473-1566.

God Is Alive and Keeping Things
Stirred Up in America

Nine out of 10 Americans say they "believe in God," according to a 1985 national Gallup poll.[1] Just as many say prayer is part of their religious life.

We Americans agree about *believing*. But we never stop arguing about it and getting into trouble over it. The Pilgrims were hustled out of Europe in the 17th century and came to America because they were considered religious troublemakers. The Founding Fathers argued constantly during the 18th century about the role of religion in government, and of government in religion. In the 19th century we were arguing, demonstrating, and proselytizing in the names of various beliefs all over the country. All of Europe talked about the ferment of religious fervor here.

One of the most discerning and delightful tourists ever to arrive here, Mrs. Frances Trollope, came over from England in 1827. She was constantly fascinated by what she saw here during a three-year stay. But what seemed especially remarkable about us were what she called "strange anomalies" in our religious system:

> The whole people appear to be divided into an almost endless variety of religious factions. . . .

Flamboyant American religious practices made Mrs. Trollope long for something less argumentative:

> It is impossible, in witnessing all these unseemly vagaries, not to recognize the advantages of an established church as a sort of head-quarters for quiet unpresuming Christians, who are contented to serve faithfully, without insisting upon each having a little separate banner, embroidered with a device of their own imagining.[2]

The French political scientist Alexis de Tocqueville was here during the 1830s and came away bowled over by our religious involvement. He stated flatly that there was "no country in the world where the Christian religion retains a greater influence over the souls of men. . . ."[3]

Later in the same decade, Francis Grund, a German journalist who wrote a book about America and Americans for prospective immigrants, remarked:

> The religious habits of the Americans form not only the basis of their private and public morals, but have become so thoroughly interwoven with their whole course of legislation that it would be impossible to change them without affecting the very essence of their government.[4]

So you see, today's squabbling, jostling for leadership, and proselytizing is nothing new. It's been going on for a long time, and I think it's good for all of us. Today religion has tumbled out of its orderly Sabbath pews and plunged into our daily lives and thoughts.

That can challenge us not only to examine what we believe but also to put it to work in the world around us, where (Lord knows!) there's plenty to be done. Consider what's happening in American religious circles these days:

The Religious Right is up in arms about "secularizing trends" threatening "the American way of life." Conservatives have gone charging into politics, lobbying and advertising against abortion, for organized prayer in schools, and against pornography, even including *Huckleberry Finn*. They are being counterattacked by such groups as People for the American Way, and Americans United for Separation of Church and State.

The nation's Roman Catholic bishops are nailing their own series of controversial and provocative theses on the church door, attacking nuclear proliferation, and economic policies that ignore the desperate needs of America's poor.

The interfaith Sanctuary Movement, made up from over 200 religious congregations and many faiths, is harboring Central American political fugitives in homes and churches, setting up an "underground railroad" for them across the country, and fighting a full-scale legal battle with the United States government, which is now intent on sending them to jail.

Evangelical Protestants are shaken by heavy bickering between radical evangelicals, such as the Sojourners, and conservative evangelicals, such as the Moral Majority. Sojourners demand disarmament, an end to the death penalty in our legal system, and more public aid for the poor. They are prepared to punctuate their demands with nonviolent demonstrations and civil disobedience. The Moral Majority wants none of the above.

On the Air

Differences like these used to be aired from church pulpits, in revival tents, by pamphleteering, and in fringe-time radio in mid-America. Now the clergy suddenly appear in our living rooms and bedrooms via television, with all the gadgetry and pageantry of show business. According to the National Religious Broadcasters, a trade group, there were 996 different religious television programs on the air in 1982, and almost 100 more (1,081) a year later. There are 79 exclusively religious-oriented TV stations across the country and over 1,000 religious radio stations.[5] If all these stations suddenly spoke as one, with a single mission, what a mighty hymn of faith united they could sing!

Cable television has been heavily infiltrated by religious programming. Cable systems in many communities now carry not just one but three major religious networks. Religious programming on cable goes far beyond the pulpit-pounding of earlier years. There's still plenty of that to be seen, but religious cablecasters have become infinitely versatile and sophisticated in their programming, since they're now spending big money competing directly with one another for the hearts and minds of viewers. "Nowadays you have to compete with programs that cost a half-million dollars an hour to produce," the president of a major Christian cable network explained. "You can't just produce schlock."[6]

So religious cablecasting increasingly resembles the programming on secular commercial stations and networks. On their own cable system, Baptists present "Lifestyle" for women, "The Sunshine Factory" for children, "The Super Handyman" for Dad, and "The Plant Groom" for Mom. Catholics present dramas, magazine-format news, discussion shows, a marriage series. An Alabama Catholic nun has set up her own cable network and now reaches over 1.5 million homes with inspirational programs, talk shows, and reruns of such family-fare classics as *Lassie*. A 24-hour national Protestant network reaches 23 million homes with a blend of family-show reruns, news, documentaries, and straight-on religion. This is a far, far cry from the days a few decades back when many Protestants could go to a movie only at the risk of forfeiting their immortal souls. Today they sit at home and watch Christian talk shows, Christian soap operas, Christian quiz shows—you name it. Would you believe Christian rock?

What is the effect of all this religious show biz? It certainly draws a crowd—just as it used to fill tents in the small towns, and halls in cities back in the days of Billy Sunday, Luke Rader, and other great evangelists, long before television. The Ad Hoc Committee on Religious Television, a national coalition that includes groups ranging from fundamentalist Protestants to Roman Catholics, sponsored a major research study to find out about "religion and television." They found some 13.6 million Americans—6.2% of the national television audience—watching religious telecasts regularly.[7]

Most viewers told researchers they don't let religious programs take the place of attending worship services at church. Almost half (48%) attend services regularly. But does religious television make better people of them? Does it enrich their lives? Only God knows. According to the Ad Hoc Committee's report, really searching or profound religious issues seldom show up on the airwaves. More than half of the programs on religious television deal with political issues.

American Religions: Always Activist

That's not as surprising as it may sound. American religious movements have almost always had political ramifications. Evangelicals of the 19th century were in the forefront of the abolition, feminist, and prohibition movements. (Church historian Martin Marty of the University of Chicago said, "They tried to reform everything.")[8] Church groups also campaigned for tax reform, prison reform, the 10-hour workday in factories, against imprisonment for debt, against monopolies, for free education, and for world peace. Controversial religious activity and involvement in political gut issues is old stuff for American churches. It's just more universally visible today because of the electronic media.

To some people, this rough-and-tumble religion may be

upsetting. Like Mrs. Trollope, they would like a more "seemly" celebration of faith. There are, for instance, devout Catholics who are convinced that nuns and priests should "stay out of politics in Latin America and stick to spreading the Gospel." Also Protestants who complain abut ministers getting involved in the Sanctuary Movement. But a substantial majority of Americans continue to be active in their own churches and synagogues, as they have in years past. The 1985 *Yearbook* of the National Council of Churches reports that six out of 10 Americans—141 million of us—are members of religious denominatons. That's an increase of 1.2 million members in one year, or about the same rate of increase projected for the population itself. So in terms of membership, denominations are holding their own.

In terms of active participation, four out of 10 Americans said they had attended church or synagogue in the past 10 days. This ratio of Americans attending services during 1984 is about what it has been over the past 20 years.[9]

Cash contributions to churches have increased over the past 20 years. National Council of Churches figures showed a 7.5% increase in contributions from members during 1983 (the latest year for which data are available).[10] That increase more than doubled the rate of inflation that year. Actual dollar contributions increased from an annual $69 per capita in 1961 to $278 in 1983. After factoring out the effects of inflation during that time, there has been a real increase of 21.3% in per-capita dollar contributions.

More Young People into Religion

There's another, even more vital sign of increased religious involvement across the country today: More young Americans are studying religion—not with a view to making a career of it, but simply to gain religious knowledge. Rabbi James Rudin of the American Jewish Committee has said he finds signs of a "genuine hunger for religious knowledge" in America today as part of "the quest for personal identity in a big and impersonal society."[11]

Religious studies in colleges and universities used to be strictly for divinity students. Not today. Although few of the students plan religious careers, "Religion is becoming more accepted as one of the liberal arts," a Michigan State University educator said recently. At the University of Kansas, another educator complains that they "can't afford to expand religion courses to meet the record demand." The University of Arizona reports a 40% gain in enrollment for religion classes in the past four years. And in Minnesota, Bethel College, a private, liberal-arts college that describes itself as a school to attend for "integration of faith and learning," finds itself with students from 35 different religious denominations, 39 different states, eight foreign countries—and it's now one of the three fastest-growing colleges and universities, public or private, in a state where there are more than two dozen different four-year schools to choose from, several of them world-famous!

What's going on? Could it be that we're seeing the beginning of an increased personal involvement in religion in America? Some authorities believe we may. Dr. Gerson D. Cohen, chancellor of the Jewish Theological Seminary of America, has said that he believes ". . . religion in the United States will soon emerge from its present semistatic state and resume its position of strength and moral leadership in this nation." The Reverend C. J. Malloy, Jr., general secretary of the Progressive National Baptist Convention, said, "Religion appears to be gaining in popularity with all age groups." Ted Peters, associate professor of systematic theology at the Pacific Lutheran Seminary and Graduate Theological Union, said, "Religion is gaining strength in the United States both within the churches and outside. . . ."[12]

In a new national research study, Leo J. Shapiro & Associates asked Americans across the country if they agree with the idea that Americans are *losing* their religious faith rather than gaining it. A majority of older Americans agreed—52% believe we are actually losing faith. But in direct contrast to this, among America's youngest adults—the group under age 40—a majority *disagreed* with the idea that we could be losing our religious faith.[13]

But Can Faith Solve Problems?

At the same time, there's been a curious and worrisome decline of belief in the *power* of religion among Americans. That belief is weaker today than it's been in three decades. As we've seen, the vast majority of us believe in God. But since the late 1950s there has been a very substantial loss of belief that religion can solve today's problems. This is all the more sad because we are all aware of such immense social problems today, and we all share the burden of them.

In 1957, three out of four Americans believed that "religion can answer all or most of today's problems." Today only about two out of four of us believe that.[14] What a shame, at a time when we all need the reassurance that kind of belief would bring. "The uncertainty of world affairs, the era of rapid social change, the stress in business and employment, have brought many a deeper awareness of their spiritual needs . . . ," Dr. David Poling, a distinguished Presbyterian cleric, has noted.[15] But only half of us now think our religion can solve such needs.

The most hopeful fact is this: Of all the nations on earth today, none is more capable than ours, in terms of religion, to solve its social problems. Our denominations are fully free to act; there's no nation where religion is freer. We have three quarters of a million churches, synagogues, and temples in America—all open, all functioning freely.[16] We have 140 million committed members in our various denominations.[17] Not only is there a "mighty army" of believers in America, they can all be drawn together instantly by one great network today. The new "electronic church" has given religious leaders communication power that no other clergy in history have ever wielded. They now have the power literally to go into America's homes and talk to millions of people at the same time, on a "one-to-one" basis, through the combined television, radio, and cable-TV media of the country.

What a demonstration of the power of religion to solve problems it would be if America's religious leaders could get together and agree to address a *single* national problem shared by us all. What a way to win back that 50% of us who no longer believe religion can solve the nation's really big problems!

Actually, we've all seen what miracles a really dedicated little group of people can do when they work together to solve a specific problem. In a recent syndicated column, Erma Bombeck saluted women's groups in towns and cities all over America, whose social consciences turned them into "social do-gooders." She saluted them for having "silently built museums, sustained operas, fed the poor, funded shelters, erected hospitals, created parks, effected cures for diseases, raised money for research, provided schools and scholarships, perpetuated the arts, and brought dignity and opportunity to people they will never see, to lives they could never imagine."[18] Her column was an eloquent and well-deserved tribute. It also raises this question: If women's luncheon clubs can serve human needs this passionately and effectively, couldn't three quarters of a million churches, synagogues, and temples do the same thing for even bigger problems?

We've now seen global social problems of hunger, disease, and natural disaster taken on by rock music groups; national needs taken on by individual entertainment stars (Jerry Lewis is one example); the needs of American farmers attacked by country music stars. At a time when government is unwilling or unable to address some social needs, even individuals are summoning up the courage to take a try at it, using the power of the global media.

A new Jewish foundation, the Jewish Fund for Justice, is already making grants to help the poor: Navajos in Arizona, homeless blacks in Boston, low-income Mexican-Americans in Colorado. It plans also to give grants to poor communities in Tennessee and Mississippi, elderly in Montana, and indigent farmers in Minnesota. The fund's resources so far came from 150 donors, all but one of them Jewish individuals or Jewish-sponsored organizations. It hopes to give $1 million a year to help the poor of all races and sects to help them help themselves. Couldn't the example of the Good Samaritan move others to do likewise for children?

Wouldn't this be a shining moment in history if all the religious denominations of America agreed to get together— for example, to feed our children? One in five American children living among us today is living in poverty. They need food. They need clothing. These children are going to become a major part of the next generation of American adults. What memories will they have of their country? What will they believe in? Where will their loyalties lie?

Wouldn't it be a fantastic demonstration of the problem-solving, serving strength of religion if in 20 years those children could remember that when they were little and hungry *all* the churches of America got together for the first time and fed and clothed them? Many churches and synagogues are already doing it, alone. How much more exciting and memorable if they all did it together!

Only in America can we even think of such possibilities. Only in America can we dream such immense dreams. Only in America are religious gorups blessed with such power and such opportunities. Only in America could they magnify the power of belief in such human terms, for all of history to remember and celebrate.

NOTES

1. Steven Simpler, "Religion Retains Longtime Footing, Gallup Poll Find," *Arizona Republic* (August 17, 1985). Report of findings in *Religion in America: 1935–85* by the American Institute of Public Opinion.
2. Frances Trollope, *Domestic Manners of the Americans* (New York: Random House, 1949), p. 108.
3. Alexis de Tocqueville, quoted in *America Wants to Know*, Dr. George Gallup (New York: A & W Publishers, 1983), p. 174.
4. Francis Grund, *The Americans in Their Moral, Social, and Political Relations* (1837) quoted in *America in Perspective*, ed. Henry Steele Commager (New York: New American Library, 1948), p. 91.
5. Michael Doan, "The 'Electronic Church' Spreads the Word," *U.S. News & World Report* (April 23, 1984).
6. Ibid.
7. Ibid.
8. David Goddy, "Religion in the U.S.: Alive and Well—and Changing," *Scholastic Update* (March 1, 1985).
9. George W. Cornell, "Growth in Church Membership Barely Keeping Pace with Rise in Population," Associated Press (June 29, 1985).
10. Ibid.
11. Goddy, op. cit.
12. Quotes from Dr. Gerson D. Cohen, the Reverend C. J. Malloy, Jr., and Ted Peters in Gallup, op. cit., pp. 175–78.
13. Leo J. Shapiro & Associates special national survey conducted in June 1985 for this book.
14. Gallup Poll/Princeton Religion Research Center data quoted by David Goddy, op. cit.
15. Gallup, op. cit., p. 178.
16. *Statistical Abstract of the United States, 1985* (Washington, D.C.: U.S. Department of Commerce, Bureau of the Census, 1984), table 75.
17. Ibid., table 74.
18. Erma Bombeck, "Wealthy Do-Gooders Made Nation Strong," syndicated column (September 1, 1985).

Higher Education at the Grass Roots

★

The idea that practically any citizen able and willing to work at it can acquire even the *highest* levels of education in our country is one of the most shining demonstrations of the American promise. But a politican asked, "Why should we subsidize intellectual curiosity?" The answer is that we should encourage (yes, even subsidize) intellectual curiosity in our people because otherwise America will stagnate, feed off its past, and eventually dry up and die.

In earlier, simpler years, it's true that many people found their own ways to feed their intellectual curiosity. Abraham Lincoln said that in his days as a youngster in Indiana, "There was absolutely nothing to excite ambition for education." In the one-room schools, reading from the speller, a bit of writing, and "cipherin' to the rule of three" was all education could do for intellectual curiosity. Lincoln read Aesop's *Fables*, *Robinson Crusoe*, the Bible, and Parson Weem's *Life of Washington* out of his own sense of curiosity. Later Lincoln read Shakespeare, Voltaire, Paine, Robert Burns, Blackstone's *Commentaries*— everything he could get his big hands on.

Today the world is more complex; it moves in a far faster, more deadly dance. The Americans who will lead us in the next century must have their intellectual curiosity stimulated by information and questions that make them hungry to find out more. Intellectual curiosity needs to be fed, deserves to be fed. The history of America is one of feeding, and reaping rich harvest from the intellectual curiosity of our people.

In the earliest years of the country, colonial-era formal schooling was mostly for the sons of the rich, the elite. And yet America's first college, Harvard, was founded with a government grant in 1636 and subsidized by government grants until 1823. After the Revolution the country doubled in size within 50 years and became increasingly industrial and nationalistic. It became essential for us to have an educated people, not just an educated elite. The common school system was developed to fill the nation's need for the future. By the middle of the 19th century there were also some 17 state-supported colleges.

As the frontier moved westward and we became a great agricultural nation as well as an industrial one, new needs arose for higher education. The land-grant colleges came into being. Land-grant colleges were tailored to the nation's needs—practical, focused on agriculture, home management, and the business of living on the frontier. High schools in towns filled the gap between common school and college-level learning.

Community Colleges

The first community colleges were developed just after the turn of the century. They were aimed at expanding the high-school educational program so as to make the first two years of college courses available to students who might not otherwise be able to attend universities. The community-college system was America's answer to the needs of a people becoming increasingly urban, involved in problems of making a life and a living together in growing cities and suburbs, working in offices and factories of an increasingly complex industrial society.

Joliet Junior College opened its doors in 1901, the nation's first public, two-year college. By the end of the year there were eight such junior colleges in the country, with a grand total of fewer than 100 students among them!

Twenty years later there were 52 junior colleges in the country.[1] The junior-college movement was well on its way, with schools in Illinois, California, Iowa, Kansas, Michigan, Minnesota, Missouri, and Texas.[2] Their academic programs were designed around courses that could be transferred to four-year colleges or universities. Also, specialized vocational high schools were growing in states as far apart as New York, Oklahoma, Mississippi, and Minnesota. Their occupation-focused programs would eventually become part of the curricula of our present-day community colleges, with courses offered in automobile mechanics, computer science, public services, and business.

During the Great Depression years, junior colleges provided training and preparation for many thousands of people who may not have had regular work *then* but who were determined that when jobs opened up later, they'd be ready to make good in one. By 1940 there were 518 junior colleges in the country.[3] From then on junior colleges became a living part of the nation's educational framework and part of our view of American society.

In 1947, the Truman Commission on Higher Education endorsed the concept that a college education is not just for the elite and affluent citizens but for *all* citizens willing and able to work for it. The public community-college system was more or less appointed to carry out the concept. Ten years later, in 1957, another presidential commission, established by President Eisenhower, stated that community colleges were the best way available to meet the nation's critical higher-education needs.

By 1970 there were 892 junior colleges in the country, with nearly 2,250,000 degree students. Most recent available figures show 1,296 such colleges, with 4,772,000 students enrolled, in 1982.[4] In fact, there were very nearly as many Americans enrolled in two-year colleges in 1982 as were enrolled then full-time in four-year colleges and universities.[5] Better than half (55%) of the junior-college students are women; a decade ago, in 1975, only 45% were women. As more women work, especially in technical fields, the community college provides a source for advanced education and training close to home, at moderate cost, and with classes scheduled in early-morning and evening hours to fit work schedules of busy adults.

During this century the purpose and function of junior colleges flexed and changed to serve changing needs of American people. The colleges started out delivering freshman- and sophomore-level college education, mostly to people who probably would not go on to a higher level. Today two-year colleges serve a much more diverse public. It includes youngsters "trying out" college education before committing to upper-level college and university study; working adults attending before and after work, to raise their level of skills; elder citizens catching up on education missed earlier in life; and people taking courses in special-interest subject areas ranging from gold-panning and fly-tying to basket-weaving and pot-throwing. Every bit of it is enriching and intellectually stimulating.

The fact that community colleges are locally created and controlled, relatively inexpensive, offer a comprehensive and flexible curriculum with relatively flexible admissions policies, and have a student body as heterogeneous as the community itself makes them uniquely American in concept. So does the fact that community colleges are very largely paid for by local people who use them. Unlike state and private colleges and universities, community colleges get very little in gifts from foundations, individuals, business corporations, and the like. In 1983, private and public four-year institutions across the country received nearly $4.4 *billion* in such "voluntary financial support"; junior colleges received only $38 million. That's roughly $1 for every $115 donated to four-year schools.

Because their tuition fees are historically much lower than those at four-year institutions, community colleges get only 14% of their income from tuition and fees, compared to 30% among public four-year schools. Another third of the community colleges' income is from local taxes levied within the school district. Thus, locally raised dollars from tuition and local taxes provide almost half of the community college's operating funds.[6] Community colleges, like public four-year schools, receive substantial state financial support. But while public four-year colleges receive 10% of their income from federal funds, community colleges get only 5%. Thus, the community college is about as self-supporting and community-supported as a public school can get. Community-college authority Glen Gabert has stated flatly: "No other segment of public higher education receives such a significant proportion of its revenue locally.[7] That's what you might describe as "holding up your own socks."

Fitting the Community's Needs

Northland Pioneer College, a 10-year-old community college in Navajo County, Arizona, is a good example of how community colleges "flex" to fit the needs of the people they serve. Northland Pioneer serves an 11,000-square-mile area, which includes three Indian reservations (Hopi, Navajo, and Apache) and some of the most spectactulary beautiful scenery in America, including the Painted Desert, Monument

Valley, and the Sitgreaves National Forest. Combining arid, desert-like high plateau country with vast, empty mesas to the north and heavily wooded rugged mountain area to the south, Navajo County has a population density of about seven people per square mile—less than that in either North or South Dakota. The very idea of creating a "community college" to draw all that immense area of largely unpopulated territory together seems an incredible educational challenge—but when Northland Pioneer College was planned a decade ago, the school's charter governing board made the challenge even tougher. They stipulated that *no future student* of Northland Pioneer College *should have to drive more than a half hour to get to class!*

With that sort of commitment, it was obvious that the college must go at least partway to meet its students. The result was a community college with an average 5,100 students but no major campus at all. The school's administrative offices are in the county seat of Holbrook, roughly midcountry, geographically. "Minicenters" and smaller "satellite" units of the college are in small communities with historic western names such as Winslow, Snowflake, Show Low, Kykotsmovi, Kayenta, and Whiteriver. Initially, the college rented classroom space in local schools or empty buildings; now its 42 full-time faculty members and 300 associate faculty members hold class in a remodeled hospital; a remodeled grocery store; and 43 modified, double-wide mobile-home units strategically located across its huge service area.

Two years after Northland Pioneer College opened, it had full-time equivalent student costs that ran $600 higher than those of any other community college in the state. It was in a bit of "disarray," the present college president, Dr. Marvin L. Vasher, recalls. But by 1985 the school had awarded some 600 associate degrees and an additional 100 educational certificates and had the second-lowest full-time student cost in the state! Northland Pioneer celebrated its 10th anniversary with a kind of "homecoming" for the whole community, including 1,000 graduates and friends. The celebration was entirely fitting for the school itself: Spread out over 10 days, it included decentralized "birthday parties" in four different towns where its major classroom centers are located. "We are now accepted as a legitimate model of the delivery of educational services in a rural area," said Dr. Vasher proudly.[8]

America's Best Buy in Education

A student simply can't get a better buy in college-level education anywhere than at his or her local community college. Tuition and fees have risen steadily in recent years, and every year students demonstrate against this. But, after all, teachers must be paid at the going rates, modest as they are. Even so, the annual cost of attending classes for credit at the average community college ($510 in 1984) is less than half that at a four-year public university ($1,270) and only one twelfth that at a private four-year university ($6,140). And the credits you earn in the community college classroom carry just as much academic weight as do credits for the same courses at a fancier, larger, far more costly university. Truly, as Glen Gabert has called it, the public community college is "the people's university."

Beyond the first two years of college, even a heavily work-scheduled or completely homebound person can continue to learn, grow, and acquire academic credentials. It's not easy, but you can move steadily forward from undergraduate to graduate-level study, all the way to fully accredited master's and doctorate degrees—and do it without ever having to set foot on a campus. Over 70 American colleges and universities offer fully accredited external degrees in practically very subject short of brain surgery. It's much easier to sit in a classroom, taking notes, while a teacher feeds you elegantly organized information than to dig for your learning alone at home, guided only by a correspondence course syllabus and your instructor's notes on papers you send in. But there is no richer, better way to learn. And you do it in your own time, on your own schedule. America's highly innovative network of external-degree colleges and universities is so unique and effective, it draws hundreds of thousands of students from all over the world—by mail.

Now you can even take college courses from 1,700 fully accredited colleges and universities throughout the United States through your personal computer, at home, linked directly to the school and your instructors by telephone. The three-year-old Electronic University expects to have 100,000 students enrolled in courses for college credits by the end of 1986. If you have a compatible personal computer and $35 to $100 per course, you can earn associate degrees, a B.A. or B.S., or a master's degree in your choice of three kinds of business administration—while just sitting in front of the monitor at home, communicating back and forth with your instructor "across the keyboard." "What hath God wrought," indeed!

Part of the whole picture of egalitarian education in America is this: Among the young college students who are living at home and still dependent, 51% of parents had no savings stored up toward education.[9] We hear about "families with big incomes and cars" borrowing from the government for their children's college educations, but those are exceptions that make the news. In 1983, the median family income among all dependent colleges enrollees in America was $33,149, just $4,000 over the median average income for *all* American families with four members.[10] However, among the families of white dependent college enrollees, the median average income was a bit higher, $35,000; while for black college enrollees, it was just $14,875—about half the national median average income for a four-person family.[11]

For these youngsters from lower-income families, ambitious to get the education they need to climb in America, financial aid is *essential*. It has been available—through Pell grants, supplementary educational opportunity grants, national direct student loans, college work study programs, and guaranteed student loans. The average grant is not large, ranging from $545 a year to an upper limit of $2,308—but for many Americans it makes all the difference between a college education and no college education.

In addition to loans, there are literally hundreds of major grant, endowment, and fellowship programs with thousands of potential recipients, actively looking for individuals and schools who need and deserve financial support to pursue learning. There are almost 22,000 nongovernment, nonprofit foundations across America with funds available to support "social, educational, religious, or other activities deemed to serve the common good," including thousands of grants and scholarships.[12] As the federal government increasingly turned away from social welfare during the 1980s, these private foundations gave a larger share of their grants (24.5% in 1980 and 28.4% in 1983) to direct social welfare and correspondingly reduced grants for education (22.4% in 1980 and 16% in 1983).[13] But any talented and determined learner in America who needs financial help in pursuing a program of study probably can find it.

"The strength and spring of every free government," Moses Mather said in 1775, "is the virtue of the people; virtue grows on knowledge, and knowledge on education."[14] George Washington wrote "with indescribable regret" of "the youth of the United States migrating to foreign countries" for education; he worried that we might be "sending abroad among other political systems those who have not well learned the value of their own." He feared that they might be "imbibing maxims not congenial with republicanism" in the European schools and believed that "education generally is one of the surest means of enlightening and giving just ways of thinking to our citizens."[15] A few months later, in Washington's eighth annual address to Congress, he proposed the establishment of "a national university and also a military academy."[16] Washington's idea was later championed by Thomas Jefferson, who also called on Congress, in his second inaugural address, to press for a constitutional amendment authorizing money for "the great objects of public education, roads, rivers, canals, and such other objects of public improvement as may be thought proper." Unfortunately, the grand design got lost in a political shuffle in Congress, where public education was not considered a vote-getting issue, even then.

But as a means of improving the individual and the nation, education became part of the American theme and the American dream. In 1830, a French magistrate, visiting the United States for a nine-month tour, marveled: "The effort made in this country to spread instruction is truly prodigious. The universal and sincere faith that they profess here in the effaciousness of education seems to me one of the most remarkable features of America. . . ."[17]

Education was a means to equality. It *still* is in America. We've got education here for everybody who wants it—right down to our grass roots!

NOTES

1. *Historical Statistics of the United States* (Washington, D.C.: U.S. Department of Commerce, Bureau of the Census, 1975), series H-690.
2. Glen Gabert, *The Public Community College: The People's University* (Bloomington, Ind.: Phi Delta Kappa Educational Foundation, 1981), p. 10.

3. *Historical Statistics*, op. cit.
4. *Statistical Abstract of the Unied States 1985* (Washington, D.C.: U.S. Department of Commerce, Bureau of the Census, 1984), table 253.
5. Ibid., table 247.
6. Walter Garms, *Financing Community Colleges* (New York: Teachers College Press, 1977).
7. Gabert, op. cit., p. 16.
8. John Schroeder, "Decentralized College Comes into Focus," *Arizona Republic*, (March 31, 1985).
9. *Statistical Abstract, 1985*, table 260.
10. Ibid., table 736.
11. Ibid., table 254.
12. Ibid., table 651.
13. Ibid., table 652.
14. Gordon S. Wood, *The Creation of the American Republic 1776–1787* (Chapel Hill: University of North Carolina Press, 1969), p. 120.
15. Letter to Alexander Hamilton (September 1, 1796), quoted in Saul K. Padover, ed., *The Washington Papers* (New York: Grosset & Dunlap, 1967), p. 390.
16. Ibid., p. 300.
17. Alexis de Tocqueville, quoted in G. W. Pierson, *Tocqueville in America* (Garden City, N.Y.: Doubleday & Company, 1959), p. 294.

Almost Any American Girl
Can Grow Up and Become President

★

Many people will remember 1984 as "the year a woman ran for vice president." That one of the two major American political parties finally got around to full recognition of women was a victory for all of us. But there have been well over a dozen woman candidates for vice president of the United States, nominated by smaller parties, since 1892. An exceptionally qualified woman, Congresswoman Shirley Chisholm, was picked from the floor at the 1972 Democratic National Convention to run for president. She wasn't nominated by the party, but that did prove that you could be both black and female and run for the highest office in the land without being struck down by the jealous Spirit of Jehovah or one of the other Founding Fathers.

I believe an even more momentous event passed relatively unnoticed in the presidential year of 1984. That was the first year in American history when the voting turnout rate of women was higher than that of men. A total of 61% of voting-age women reported having voted, compared to 59% of voting-age men.[1] That's one statistic to be remembered; the other is that this was the second presidential election in which women cast a fairly substantial majority of all the votes across the country: 52.9% in 1980; 53.5% in 1984.[2] Since 1980, women have been more likely to vote than men.[3]

All I can say is, Mabel Millard and all the other antisuffragists of past years must be whirling, wherever they may be today. Ms. Millard was secretary of the Iowa Association Opposed to Woman Suffrage in 1920. At that time the 100% male legislators in some states still were trying to decide whether or not the little women could be trusted to vote. Ms. Millard fired off a semihistoric telegram to the legislators, begging them to "Please consider the wishes of the people of the states which have voted against woman suffrage by overwhelming majorities and remember the serious menace which votes of women would be."[4]

The fact that such a wimpy message could actually be sent, presumably in all seriousness, to a state legislature, which filed it in all seriousness, as recently as 1920, and in America, just goes to show how close to the dark ages we still may be. On the other hand, it also shows how far we have come into the light.

It's good for us to remind ourselves today that American women didn't find their right to vote under a cabbage leaf—it came as the result of persistent day-to-day volunteer work by many thousands of heroic women (and some men, too, don't forget!) over two generations of time. Historian Aileen S. Kraditor reminds us, "The early pioneers for women's rights were subjected to humiliation and occasional violence."[5]

Women were considered qualified to express their opinions in school board elections long before the men would trust them with wider issues. As early as 1838 Kentucky became the first state to let women vote in school elections, followed by Kansas in 1861, Michigan and Minnesota in 1875, and 13 other states in 1890. This established not only a precedent of sorts but also a pattern. One state "tried women out" to see if they could bear the burden of voting on local issues, while other states watched to see what might happen. After a quarter century or so, others began to take the plunge.

Granting full suffrage followed somewhat the same pattern. Wyoming has the honor of being the first state in the Union to make women full citizens, in 1890, followed by Colorado (1893), Utah and Idaho (1896), Washington (1910), California (1911), and Oregon, Kansas, and Arizona (1912). The first state east of the Mississippi River to grant full suffrage to women was Abraham Lincoln's old home state, Illinois, in 1913.

The process of gaining the vote was nowhere near as smooth as this steady march of dates may suggest. In the face of obdurate resistance, not only from men but also from many of their "sisters," women fought all the way through 56 separate popular-vote campaigns over a spread of 50 years, "traveling over immense western distances in bad weather and with dreadful transportation, speaking again and again before voters and legislators. Defeat after defeat rewarded their efforts."[6]

The National American Woman Suffrage Association records the fact that this struggle involved 480 campaigns to get state legislatures to submit amendments to their voters; 277 campaigns to get women suffrage planks into state party platforms; 19 campaigns with 19 successive Congresses; plus the final ratification campaign of 1919–20.[7] It was women who fought the good fight through all of these campaigns, but again we should remember that the state legislatures and U.S. Congresses involved were 100% male bodies at that time, and there must have been a lot of enlightened males among them who also helped, or the amendments would never have gotten out of committees.

Why Women Should Not Vote!

People keep repeating that "history repeats itself," and so it does, but always with changes. It is interesting that some of the most persistent arguments made against woman suffrage in the 19th and early 20th centuries have been taken out of mothballs, dusted off, altered to fit today's fashions, and paraded against the Equal Rights Amendment (ERA) in the 1980s. Some of the major arguments against woman suffrage were:

God made men and women for different roles. Genesis made it clear that men were intended to earn bread by the sweat of their brow and be concerned with things of the world (such as government); women were supposed to mind things at home, and have children, which would occupy them full-time.

Men's and women's minds are wired to work differently. Men have judgment. They are practical. They think things out sensibly. Women are weak, nervous, and emotional. They jump at conclusions intuitively. This may make them ideal as wives and mothers, because it makes them sensitive to others and their needs—but it is all wrong for deciding affairs of state.

If women began getting involved in men's areas of responsibility, society would fall apart. They would have to become involved and politically informed and would be expected to devote their time and thoughts to activities (accosting strange men on street corners to solicit their vote!) unsuitable for them. In the meantime, they would be neglecting their children, juvenile delinquency would rise, and so would divorce. Moreover, women taking upon themselves men's prerogatives would lose their traditional protected status and lose the respect of men.

A pamphlet addressed to *"Housewives!"* reasoned:

> You do not need a ballot to clean out your sink spout. A handful of potash and some boiling water is quicker and cheaper. . . . Control of the temper makes a happier home than control of elections. . . . Good cooking lessens alcoholic craving quicker than a vote on local option."[8]

Fortunately, right prevailed; women won the right to vote *and* keep the sink spouts clean in 1920. The world didn't fall into ruins. Instead, as often happens with technological progress, when women found they didn't have so much time left as before to be Cinderella at home while waiting for Prince Charming to get home from work and the voting booth, manufacturers developed a whole houseful of products, gadgets, and equipment to give women time; and even Prince Charming found a politically literate helpmate more challenging and interesting, and he began to help around the house, too.

Is there *still* danger, now that women are beginning not only to outnumber men at the polls but also be more active politically than they are? Will the weight of all those women standing in the booths on the same day unbalance the elective process so we'll suddenly have an all-*woman* government instead of the all-*man* government we used to have? Nonsense. Of course not. Women don't think as a bloc, any more than men do. More men than women did vote for the incumbent president in 1984, but a majority of *both* sexes voted for him. The women in Congress are a mixed group politically, and even when some wanted to form the Congresswomen's Caucus in 1977 to help bring attention to legislation dealing with women's rights and economic equity, its effectiveness was blunted because it was such a small group—some congresswomen had refused to join!

The history-making woman who ran for vice president in 1984 has said that when her running mate asked her to campaign with him,

> . . . he opened a door which will never be closed again. That is a victory of which every American can be proud. Campaigns, even if you lose them, do serve a purpose.

My candidacy has said the days of discrimination are numbered. American women will never again be second-class citizens.[9]

When I was growing up, they used to say, "America is the land where any little boy can hope to grow up and become president." It wasn't true then, of course, and it's still not true. But we're on our way and making progress toward making it true for any little boy *or* girl. We open more doors every election.

NOTES

1. Adam Clymer, "Women and Blacks Were Keys in Voting Rise," *The New York Times* (January 28, 1985).
2. Ibid.
3. *Statistical Abstract of the United States 1985* (Washington, D.C.: U.S. Department of Commerce, Bureau of the Census, 1984), table 426.
4. Michelle Williams, "Women Vote; World Survives!," *Arizona Republic* (August 25, 1985).
5. Aileen S. Kraditor, *The Ideas of the Woman Suffrage Movement 1899–1920* (Garden City, N.Y.: Doubleday & Company, 1971), p. ix.
6. Ibid., p. 3.
7. *Victory: How Women Won It: A Centennial Symposium, 1840–1940* (New York: H. W. Wilson, 1940).
8. Pamphlet published by the Women's Anti-Suffrage Association of Massachusetts.
9. Geraldine A. Ferraro's statement the night of the 1984 election, quoted in *The New York Times* (November 7, 1985).

America's Amateur Ambassadors

Every year we send a quarter million or so young ambassadors to foreign countries. Most are of high-school age, but some are as young as 11 years old. Some 50,000 to 60,000 are foreign-bound American students, part of the President's International Youth Exchange Initiative of the U.S. Information Agency. This joint project of government and private not-for-profit organizations encourages young Americans to visit other nations. It also encourages youngsters from other countries to come here and get to know us.

Some foreign-bound youngsters travel simply to enjoy exploring another country and culture. Many spend a semester or a year attending school. Most live with host families during at least part of their stay abroad. They all gain by the experience—and so do we, as a nation. As Mark Twain put it after having been just such an "innocent abroad" himself: "Travel is fatal to prejudice, bigotry and narrow-mindedness—all foes to real understanding. Likewise tolerance or broad, wholesome, charitable views of men and things cannot be acquired by vegetating in our little corner of the earth all one's lifetime."

The idea of spending a year of study abroad is not new. Many Americans spent years in Europe during the 19th century to study with the world's best teachers of medicine, engineering, the sciences and art. Today this cultural exchange process is flowing our way: A total of 339,000 foreign students were enrolled in almost 2,500 American colleges in 1984. In fact, some American schools have been finding it necessary to limit foreign enrollment in certain graduate fields. In 1983, for example, a majority of all U.S. doctorates in engineering (54%) went to foreign students, as did more than a third of those awarded in mathematics and agriculture. A fourth of the graduate-school enrollment at the Massachusetts Institute of Technology, now one of the world's most prestigious learning institutions, comes from foreign countries.[1]

One of the present student exchange organizations, Experiment in International Living, introduced the idea of living as part of a host family overseas ("homestay") over 50 years ago. Another, AFS International/Intercultural Programs, was formally founded in 1947. But it grew out of an idea originated earlier by American Field Service volunteer ambulance drivers in World Wars I and II. They set up an international exchange program for students as their peacetime contribution to world understanding. The first year just 52 students took part. Since then over 130,000 have lived with host families in over 80 countries worldwide as part of AFS programs.[2]

During this past decade overseas study programs for teenagers have been booming. A handbook of summer programs abroad during 1985 listed 939 different choices. That's 40% more than were offered just a decade ago. In part, growth has been stimulated by our strong dollar; it made going to college overseas almost as affordable during the 1980s as living at a public university here at home. But much of the growth of overseas study has come from the traditional desire of parents to give their kids a "better head start than we had" into a career. As *Business Week* writer Bradley Hitchings put it: "More parents, school advisers, and students themselves are thinking that America's oft-bemoaned ignorance of foreign languages and cultures may one day give a career edge to Americans with international experience."[3]

Actually, a summer in a foreign country, with a few weeks of daily dunking in a new language, isn't likely to open doors to jobs. American corporations have been cutting back on staffs of Americans abroad and reducing incentives for foreign work. It costs them less to staff with personnel from the country where they have their office or plant, since most educated people in foreign countries are multilingual and are likely to speak our language as well as their own.

What study and even a brief exposure to living abroad *is* likely to open is the mind of the student. It can make him or her a more mature and knowledgeable citizen of the world, with new perspectives on other cultures and our own. The breadth of experiences available to high-schoolers or high-school graduates through the various international programs is really immense. To take just a handful from hundreds of examples:

Overseas Study Opportunities

People to People International, launched in 1956 by President Eisenhower, sends about 1,500 carefully selected high-schoolers overseas each summer to make contacts in 30 countries. Each student receives orientation at home and two days of briefings in Washington, D.C., before leaving, travels in troupes of 30 to 35 with three or more teacher leaders, and lives for 12 to 15 days with families in several countries of the world. The program provides a very extensive and intensive educational travel experience. Students get briefings on economics and government from officials in the countries they visit; take field trips to factories and farms; visit universities and historical sites; and attend cultural affairs. They are called "student ambassadors," and that's the sort of VIP exposure they get in the countries they visit.

Amigos de las Americas gives youngsters an opportunity to combine homestays in 13 Latin American countries with learning job skills; studying the history, culture, and language of the area; and hands-on volunteer experience actually helping the people. This seems ideal for youngsters with an interest in entering a helping profession. After preparatory training here, they spend a summer in a Latin American country in such humanly useful activities as giving inoculations, teaching community sanitation, teaching dental hygiene, conducting vision screening clinics, giving animals rabies vaccinations, and in reforestation and national park services. Doctors recommend Amigos as an excellent training ground because of the growing need in our own country for knowledge of the Spanish language and Latin American culture for anyone wanting to go into private medical practice.

Council on International Educational Exchange provides a wide range of educational and travel opportunities throughout the world for both high-school and college-age youngsters. It also offers summer work experience abroad and in our own country.

For high-schoolers, there are summer language programs that plunge them into a second language 24 hours a day during a summer in France, Germany, Spain, or Italy. Also, there are voluntary service projects lasting two to four weeks that combine manual and social work in a foreign land. During 1985 CIEE even had a voluntary service project where participants aged 16 to 30 could spend three weeks living and working with Americans and foreign volunteers on grounds-keeping projects as part of the historic Ellis Island-Statue of Liberty restoration project. Lee Iacocca, chairman of the foundation responsible for promoting this enormous project, has said that every American should be able to "personally participate in this project" because "they deserve that opportunity. The Statue belongs to the people."[4] CIEE gave young people a chance to participate right on the site and in person, becoming part of the historic project themselves.

American Institute for Foreign Study offers young people a really mind-boggling (and mouth-watering) selection of what seems like hundreds of semester and full-year degree and summer courses at major universities all over the world. They can learn Russian in London, Moscow, Leningrad, and in Krasnodar, in the Northern Caucasus; Chinese at the Beijing Language Institute of the People's Republic of China; French at the University of Paris (Sorbonne) in France; Spanish at the University of Salamanca in Spain; or spend a year in Homerton College at Cambridge University in England. The Institute has already had over 300,000 students and teachers enrolled in its courses overseas since 1964, including 1,200 in 1985 alone.

Future Farmers of America enrolls over 350 young Americans a year in their Work Experience Abroad program. FFA members get to live and work for a summer with farm families and others involved in agriculture throughout the world. The FFA believes in "learning by doing," and that's exactly what youngsters get from this program. Intensive language study and practice, and three to six months of hands-on work experience on foreign farms combined with group meetings and travel make this a lifetime learning experience for America's future farmers and gives them a world perspective necessary to survive in today's world of international agribusiness. A unique feature of the FFA programs is that after spending two weeks as guest on a family farm in Canada, Europe, Africa, or Asia, a son or daughter from the foreign host farm pays a similar exchange visit to the American participant's home for two weeks—a true people-to-people program!

America's Best Ambassadors

Operation Crossroads Africa, Inc., sends American college students to work in African development projects for five-week stints among villages in Botswana, The Gambia, Ivory Coast, Kenya, Lesotho, Liberia, Sierra Leone, Sudan, Tanzania, Zimbabwe, and other nations. At the same time, it arranges for professionals from Africa and the Caribbean to visit the United States, living among volunteer host families here. The professionals, selected by their governments, represent such fields as engineering, education, and business.

One of the most exciting aspects of Operation Crossroads Africa is that it encourages participation by working and middle-class families, and families from other groups that normally don't get involved in exchange programs. The American youngsters who take part are also special in that although OCA is the least expensive program of its kind in Africa, participants are expected to dig up their own funds for participating; they are "self-starters," but the organization does give them fund-raising counsel and even makes small grants. Once in Africa, Crossroaders serve in community work-camp groups, participating with professionals and local craftspeople in community construction, agricultural/farming, archaeology/anthropology, and medical projects. This is not a summer holiday fiesta by any means. It involves a lot of very mature commitment and hard, often grubby work. One young OCA volunteer, heading out toward a summer of manual labor in an African village, gave his reasons for going: "I'd like to get to know the African people and give them an impression of the American people that I can be proud of, an impression of Americans as loving, caring people."

How fortunate America is to have tens of thousands of these young amateur ambassadors representing us overseas every year! They come unarmed and with open minds. They live among the people of the countries they visit, eating their food, sharing their homes, at least trying to speak their language. They show their respect for the cultures of other countries by studying them as eager learners. They don't leave just dollars behind them when they come home—they leave good works contributed and good friends made. And they bring back with them a first hand people-to-people awareness and appreciation of the world that officials and executives need but almost never get. Neither can most journalists, who can't speak the local language and who don't live among the local people; these journalists bring back what is given to them by government functionaries.

We couldn't have a brighter, better corps of representatives for America among the peoples of the world than this yearly batch of young ambassadors. They do us all proud. One of them said of the experience: "I came home, not with a lot of pictures of beautiful places, but with something much more meaningful to me: a memory of many terrific people who will always be my true friends." America can't get too many true friends. This is one of the best, brightest, and most attractive ways to get them.

NOTES

1. Lucia Solorzano, "Colleges Turn Abroad to Find More Students," *U.S. News & World Report* (March 11, 1985).
2. John Hildebrand, "More U.S. Students Are Going Overseas to Study Business," *Newsday* (September 1, 1985).
3. Bradley Hitchings, "Student Summers: A World of Choices," *Business Week* (March 4, 1985).
4. Lee Iacocca, speech at West Point, N.Y. (October 18, 1985).

Want to Know More About International Exchange Programs?

U.S. Information Agency, 400 C Street, NW, Washington, DC 20547, is a good place to write first. Ask for a free copy of *One Friendship at a Time: Your Guide to International Youth Exchange*, a booklet produced for the President's Council for International Youth Exchange and the Consortium for International Citizen Exchange as a volunteer effort by the Advertising Council. It tells you what's involved in becoming an exchange student or a host family; describes a number of youth exchange organizations; and gives you guidelines to help in selecting a program.

Addresses of the specific organizations mentioned in this chapter are:

People to People International, 2420 Pershing Road, Suite 300, Kansas City, MO 64101; telephone 816-421-6343.

Amigos de las Americas, 5618 Star Lane, Houston, TX 77057; telephone 713-782-5290.

Council on International Educational Exchange, 205 East 42nd Street, New York, NY 10017; telephone 212-661-1450.

American Institute for Foreign Study, 102 Greenwich Avenue, Greenwich, CT 06830; telephone 203-869-9090.

Future Farmers of America, WEA; National FFA Center, International Department, P.O. Box 15160, Alexandria, VA 22309.

Operation Crossroads Africa, Inc., 150 Fifth Avenue, New York, NY 10011; telephone 212-242-8550.

Helping All of Us—The American Foundation

★

Chances are you've never heard of Charles Kenneth Blandin. But I'd bet 10 to one that when you do, it will make you feel even prouder of being an American.

Blandin's life story sounds like something straight out of a Horatio Alger story. Born to a dirt-poor farm family near a Wisconsin town so small you have to track it down on the map, he left school at age 12 to become an apprentice on the local weekly newspaper. Two years later, with "a mother's tears, a father's blessing," and almost nothing else, young Charley left home to become an itinerant worker in southern Minnesota.

He managed to become a rural schoolteacher despite the fact that he didn't have a high-school diploma. Later Blandin admitted he "just barely managed to keep ahead of the better students by studying every evening." At age 20 he married a pretty farm girl—also a schoolteacher.

The young couple moved to the tiny farming village of Walnut Grove, Minnesota, a year later. This was the town made famous by Laura Ingalls Wilder's *Little House on the Prairie*. There Charles and Jennie Blandin managed to scrape up and borrow enough cash to finance the town's first newspaper, a weekly. When their first child was born, Charles carried out the many duties of a small-town publisher while Jennie "rocked the cradle with one hand and set type with the other."

Ten years and three papers later, the Blandins were in the big Twin Cities of Minneapolis-St. Paul, Charles as a daily paper subscription salesman, selling door-to-door. At age 32 he was circulation manager for the *St. Paul Pioneer Press*, and seven years later he was business manager of both St. Paul papers, the morning *Pioneer Press* and the evening

198

Dispatch. In the first four years under Blandin's guidance, the company's net profit quadrupled (not bad for a self-educated 35-year-old in the state's capital city!).

Another 10 years later, after having "borrowed a dollar from everyone," Blandin was able to buy half the stock in the publishing company. At age 45 he became co-owner and publisher as well as president of the two big daily papers, plus a northern Minnesota paper mill that made their newsprint. For the first time, Charles and Jennie Blandin were able to move into a larger house, in a more affluent neighborhood. They rented it.

Then Charley Blandin fell in love—with a town! Grand Rapids, Minnesota, where his paper's mill was located, is a Mississippi river town almost 200 miles north of Minneapolis-St. Paul, near the Canadian border. Always a small-town boy at heart, Blandin was "strongly attracted to Grand Rapids from his first association with the town." He became its most enthusiastic and influential booster as well as the town's biggest employer. When he sold the two St. Paul newspapers, for just under $5 million at age 55, many people expected Blandin to retire. Not Charley. He headed for Grand Rapids and the papermaking business. Thirty years later, at age 85, he had to be carried to his car, but he attended the annual employees' picnic. Charles Blandin died a few months later, in 1958. At his request, he was buried in a little plot of land across the river from the paper mill. But (and this is the real point of this little biography) he still "has a hand in" making life better for all of the people in Grand Rapids and in the state of Minnesota, through a foundation set up in his name after his wife's death in the 1940s.

An Ancient Idea, Perfected Here

If you're like me you have only a very rudimentary picture of what a foundation is and harbor a vague suspicion that its main purpose is to dodge taxes. Blandin was very clear about that: He left specific instructions that his foundation should *not* replace tax revenues. He believed normal governmental functions should be supported by taxes. But he specified that his foundation should spend its assets on "advancing the quality of life" for the people in *other* ways—assuming social responsibility where government could not or would not. *That's* what a foundation should do.

Americans didn't invent the philanthropic foundation, but Americans have brought it up to date and perfected it as a legal and social instrument to apply private wealth to public services. Philanthropy generally, and charitable endowments, have existed since very ancient times. The words "philanthropy" and "charity" both come to us from the Greeks (*charitas*, or love); the word "foundation" is from the Middle French *fondation*. In the fifth century B.C. there are records of well-to-do Greeks making generous philanthropic bequests— to care for strangers, sick, poor, and old. Later, in the third century B.C., they built public works using their own money and endowed temples or universities. In Renaissance Italy, every Florentine who made a will left money in it to be distributed to the poor in his church parish. Much of this money was administered by various civic organizations, and Florence alone had 73 such organizations in A.D. 1500 devoted to works of charity, with funds left to them by endowment. So the idea of foundations has been around for a long time, probably as long as the idea that "You can't take it with you."

But the modern foundation is essentially an American innovation of our own century, probably a reflection of our Judeo-Christian tradition that "He who gives to the poor will not want" (Proverbs 28:27) and "It is more blessed to give than to receive" (Acts 20:35). The general foundation, with its breadth of purposes and flexibility of action, has really blessed us all through such founts of philanthropy as the Smithsonian Institution, created "for the increase and diffusion of knowledge"; the Peabody Fund, which promotes education in the South; the Carnegie Foundation; the Rockefeller Foundation; the Ford Foundation; the Russell Sage Foundation; the Simon Guggenheim Memorial Foundation; the W. K. Kellogg Foundation; and nearly 30,000 more American foundations that distribute some $3.5 billion worth of grants a year for welfare (28%), education (16%), health (22%), culture (15%), science (9%), social science (7%), and religion (2%).[1]

But figures as huge as these, followed by percentages that somehow make them even more impersonal-sounding, are hard to "get one's mind around." Let's see how the single, relatively modest Blandin Foundation, administered by a very professional and socially perceptive staff in Grand Rapids, Minnesota, is "promoting the well-being of mankind" throughout Minnesota—but especially in the economically hard-hit northern region, which includes Grand Rapids. The Blandin Foundation spends approximately $6 million a year through grants and program-related investments (loans) and in sponsoring conferences and initiating programs that address specific needs and opportunities in the community.

Blandin considered himself a progressive, and he thought of his company as "more of a community ownership than a personal one."[2] He believed that money amassed by industry should somehow be used to promote social well-being and wrote, "There is no question but what business has failed in many respects concerning the social and economic needs of the state and the nation."[3] Personally, Blandin lived comfortably, and he enjoyed having money in his last years. But he was also frugal (at age 84, when told his six-year-old Cadillac needed new tires, he had them recapped). He wanted his foundation to support the efforts of others in enriching human life and helping human beings grow.

Let's look at just a sampling of how many ways slightly more than *half* of the 1984 grants made by the Blandin Foundation have done this for thousands of people of all ages and at all levels of Minnesota society. Here is where $3,549,630 in grants were distributed:

In and around Grand Rapids:

$40,000   General operating support for community orchestra that serves children and adults through group instruction and concerts.

26,500   Feasibility study concerning development of northern Minnesota-based arts program for young artists and avocational artists; purpose: interaction and creation of new artistic productions.

303,000   Educational awards to 379 students in county high schools, plus merit awards to 13 students.

35,000   Study feasibility of constructing two-way, interactive television system for school districts and community college in three-county areas where rural area schools have trouble financing low-enrollment courses in upper division science, math, and language. System would allow them to offer these courses.

110,000   Funding for developing home-based mushroom
           industry to create jobs in northern Minnesota.

1,025,000 Develop Small Business Investment Corpora-
           tion to foster expansion of small businesses and
           increase job opportunities in northern Minnesota.

450,000   Foster development of winter recreation, tourist
           promotion, and seasonal employment in county
           area.

337,200   For 58 projects to help range communities expe-
           riencing high unemployment and its resulting
           problems.

15,000   Investigate need and feasibility for comprehen-
           sive chemical dependency aftercare services in
           the area.

75,000   Three-year planning grant to support staff posi-
           tions and initiate major efforts to modernize ser-
           vices in town public library.

20,000   Provide emergency trail rescue equipment on
           350 miles of county outdoor winter recreation
           trails.

29,250   Initial operating support for self-help organiza-
           tion operated by and for unemployed, to help
           families deal with stress resulting from unem-
           ployment, operate self-directed job search train-
           ing and preparedness programs.

7,590   Expand three-county program that assists in in-
           struction of handicapped and special-education
           students.

1,500   Assistance in providing for amplification devices
           for all-volunteer senior-citizen musical group.

In St. Paul and Minneapolis:

150,000   Start-up support for newly built music theater.

86,000   Planning and start-up support for professional
           summer repertory theater to produce regional
           history plays in Grand Rapids.

5,000   Minneapolis Society of Fine Arts.

5,000	Minnesota Museum of Art.
11,000	Guthrie Theater.
5,000	St. Paul Chamber Orchestral Association.
11,000	Minnesota Orchestral Association.
5,000	Public Television membership challenge.
15,000	Public radio for regionally based Minnesota *In Concert* series.
25,000	To pilot test leadership training institute for elected and appointed officials from communities under 25,000, conducted in a Twin Cities college.
45,000	Two-year grant to assist excavation of mid-18th-century French fort near Little Falls, Minnesota.
20,000	Establish comprehensive peace education program created to invite young people to express thoughts and feelings about nuclear war.
124,500	University of Minnesota Department of Forest Resources for increasing state's forest productivity through mycorrhizal symbiosis.
50,000	Two-year program-related investment to provide operating capital for start-up of firewood business on Indian reservation.
60,000	Start-up funding for the Governor's Council on Youth.
25,000	Expand number of receivers for loan to blind persons so they can receive Radio Talking Book broadcasts.
80,000	Funds to establish Grand Rapids as site for national demonstration project five-year program with youth and parents to help them impart a value system to restrain or decrease teenage sexual activity.
7,000	Support for Minnesota Special Olympics Winter Games serving 350 mentally handicapped persons.
2,500	For intercultural adoption counseling at Children's Home Society of Minnesota.

1,000   Campership for low-income children.

In smaller communities around the state:

5,000   Public Television membership challenge in northern Minnesota.

8,000   Establish maple syrup operation that will help environmental education program become financially self-sufficient.

7,390   Establish leadership effectiveness seminar conducted by community college faculty members from fields of business, industry, community, and economic development to provide educational leaders with new management skills.

90,000   For three-year program creating summer institute for retraining 40 experienced teachers to become certified to teach science or mathematics.

19,700   Funding to partially overcome isolation of far-northern community in state by equipping a new library building with telephone and satellite communications systems to receive cultural and educational programs, and tape programs of educational significance for county schools.

20,000   To University of Minnesota at Duluth for feasibility investigation of furniture blank manufacturing process using presently wasted wood.

15,000   Help purchase rescue equipment for fire department serving three isolated rural townships.

25,000   Help train Native Americans as mental-health specialists.

9,500   Complete renovation of senior-citizen center.

30,000   Two-year grant to develop culturally adapted mental-health service program for Native Americans, combining traditional Indian techniques with mental-health therapy.

15,000   Help fund domestic abuse intervention clinic.

7,000   Rebuild volunteer fire department fire protection equipment.

7,000   Start-up funding assistance for athletic program at new Indian school.

83,000   Development of emergency medical services association serving northeastern Minnesota.

Think for a minute of all the ways in which all the different kinds of people are truly enriched, helped to grow with this money. It's "small potatoes" compared to Washington-type outlays for various kinds of government hardware. But how big it is in terms of belief in the human will to grow!

James P. Shannon, chairman of the National Council on Foundations, has remarked that it's patently impossible for private philanthropy to make up for cuts in the federal budget. But he added, "It is possible for a creative, well-managed foundation to use its limited resources, arm in arm with government and other creative people, to develop ways and means of helping all of us use our God-given talents more creatively and more productively than would have been possible without the facilities of the foundation."[4]

Now that you know a little about Charles Kenneth Blandin, don't you think he would have agreed?

NOTES

1. *Statistical Abstract of the United States 1985* (Washington, D.C.: U.S. Department of Commerce, Bureau of the Census, 1984), tables 652, 651.
2. Donald L. Boese, *Papermakers: Biography of Charles K. Blandin* (Grand Rapids, Minn.: Charles K. Blandin Foundation, 1984), p. 231.
3. Ibid.
4. James P. Shannon, "The Altruistic Gene," *Blandin Foundation 1984 Annual Report* (Grand Rapids, Minn., 1985), p. 9.

Together Maybe We Can Turn Off Terrorists

Americans differ among themselves on all sorts of issues, from A (abortion, of course) to Z (Zaire's government, probably). But whenever we feel threatened as a nation, suddenly we all seem to recall some collective pioneer impulse to "circle the wagons" and pitch in together in defense of America and Americans. That national ability to pitch in together when we're threatened suggests to me that there's something we might do together now to turn off terrorism, or at least turn it down.

There have been many instances of Americans' spontaneous unity, but none more dramatic than what happened on December 8, 1941. As historian Samuel Eliot Morison recalled, during the 1930s:

> Had any pollster been looking for one idea on which the vast majority of the American people agreed, when under the New Deal experiment they agreed on nothing else, it would have been that if Europe were so wicked or stupid as to start another war, America would resolutely stay out.[1]

As the Nazis bullied their way across Europe and finally began systematically destroying Britain from the air, America sent aid to Britain "short of war." But Americans were split right down the middle about going to war ourselves:

> The issue was fought out in the halls of Congress, in the press, over the radio, on public platforms, in bars, offices, and homes. Party lines were shattered, labor organizations split, business relations strained, old friendships broken.[2]

Then, on December 7, 1941, everything turned upside down. Japanese aircraft devastated Pearl Harbor, their troops landed on the Malay Peninsula, and Guam came under bombardment. At first Americans were incredulous; then, as we got more details by radio, and the full realization sank in that American territory had been attacked and was vulnerable, incredulity became cold anger, and anger became determination to strike back. The next morning Congress declared war with only one dissenting vote, and there were long lines of men waiting to be sworn in to the armed services when recruiting offices opened. Americans had settled their differences overnight, spontaneously. We had been attacked. We were united.

Next, the Arabs

Again in 1973 we suddenly felt attacked, in a different way. The oil-producing Arab countries declared an embargo against us and began steps to double the price of oil, essential to our national security. As soon as the impact of this hit them, Americans began to draw together again, to cut our oil consumption and develop alternate energy sources.

We insulated windows, wrapped water heaters in blankets, recruited car pools, turned thermostats back, bought bicycles, even adopted year-round Daylight Saving Time for a while, to save fuel. We also began to buy smaller cars, install solar heaters, and alter our energy habits simultaneously at all levels, all across the country.

Americans' per-capita consumption of energy dropped almost 7% in the next two years. By 1983 it was down 14%.[3] We had all cut back and changed our life-styles spontaneously in a single decade once we felt threatened and angry together as Americans.

What threatens us today is terrorism, especially in Europe and the Mediterranean area. From 1970 to the beginning of 1985 there were over 22,000 terrorist attacks in the world—assassinations, bombings, hijackings, kidnappings, maimings, attacks on various facilities. The average was 10 terrorist incidents a week in 1975; by 1985 it had risen to 10 a day.

Citizens of all nations were victims in these terrorist incidents, but with growing frequency Americans, or American property, have become specific terrorist targets. Over 3,000 of the 22,000 terrorist incidents since 1970 were aimed against

Americans.[4] Between 1982 and October 1985, 263 Americans were murdered by terrorists in Europe and the Mediterranean area.

What the United States Did Right . . .

What can be done to protect Americans and citizens of other nations who travel to those areas? Our own government began tighter screening of air travelers and put armed sky marshals on vulnerable flights in this country over a decade ago. Passenger screening alone caught nearly 3,000 unreported firearms in the boarding areas for flights during 1984. Since the TWA hijacking and the Air India mystery crash at sea in 1985, the FAA has tightened security even more, especially on international flights from America.

But the fact is that governments and government agencies in Europe and the Mediterranean area, living side by side with terrorists, often have been lax about security and slow to capture and prosecute terrorist killers. They have political pressures, religious and ethnic pressures, and logistical pressures in being in one of the world's most heavily traveled areas; all of these factors hamper efforts to control terrorism in their area. As a result, Americans who travel in those countries are jeopardized.

In our own country, when the federal government applied pressure to keep hijackers off flights, the drop-off in air piracy was dramatic and massive: Between 1969 and 1972 there were 125 hijacking incidents on U.S. aircraft before our government clamped down; in the next four years there were just 25. In fact, once our government tightened security on flights, there were only 122 hijacking attempts here in 12 years—fewer than in the four years just before security was tightened.[5] A government determined to keep hijackers off airplanes can do it.

. . . Other Governments Can Do

What might induce other governments in Europe and the Mediterranean area to tighten security against terrorists as effectively, for instance, as Israel has done on its El Al flights? El Al hasn't had a hijacking since 1968, before Israel tightened the screws on its security. El Al is probably the safest airline in the world to fly today, because of Israeli security.

Here is a modest proposal that might encourage governments in the terrorist-plagued areas to turn off hijackers as firmly as America and Israel have done:

Over 5 million travelers from the United States flew to Europe and the Mediterranean area in 1983. Their average length of time there was about three weeks, and even with our superdollar, in 1983 American travelers spent an average of $878 per person while touring in Europe and the Mediterranean area, in addition to what they spent for transportation over there and back. That adds up to big money: $4.4 billion spent in Europe and the Mediterranean area alone in one year.

Now let's add what we spent for transportation over and back. We spent over $5.5 billion for overseas tickets on foreign-flag airlines alone. A little more than half of our overseas flights were to Europe and the Mediterranean area. Based on these facts, we can estimate that Americans brought some $7.8 billion in tourist money into that area in a single year.[6] As Everett Dirksen once said, "Now you're talking big money!"

We've seen in the past that when Americans feel threatened *as* Americans, we spontaneously get together in a unified effort. Maybe terrorism is that big a threat to us—big enough to mobilize us to encourage overseas governments to really clamp down on terrorism. If so, *what if Americans decided to turn off terrorism by turning off tourism in Europe and the Mediterranean area during 1987?*

Obviously we can't all stay home from there, even if we want to. Business travelers go where business is, terrorism or not. But let's imagine what would happen if three out of four American travelers stayed home from Europe or the Mediterranean area all during 1987. We'd be turning off the flow to that area of about $5.4 billion in good, hard American dollars. Hotels, restaurants, airlines, retailers, cab drivers, cruise lines—they'd all set up a roar of dismay you could hear in Turtle Lake, Wisconsin, with earmuffs on!

Don't you think that uproar from their tourist industries, plus the decline in trade, would get the attention of governments in most European and Mediterranean countries? Wouldn't they take some steps to make life safer for innocent people in their airports and on their transportation and streets?

A Great Place to Start

Now let's take a brief look at the other side of the $5.4 billion coin: We know Americans aren't going to stay home altogether if they don't cross the Atlantic in 1987. We're the travelingest people on earth. We don't spend vacations shingling the chicken coop. We *go*, man. But now, think how much farther and fancier we'd be able to go touring with $5.4 billion to spend in our own neighborhood! Think how beneficial it would be to America's balance of trade for that $5.4 billion to be spent in travel around home. And think how welcome an extra 3.8 million paying guests would be during 1987 to tourist industries in America, Mexico, Canada, and the Far East!

We say we're concerned about terrorism. We say somebody should *do* something to stop it. We feel threatened ourselves. But do we feel it strongly enough actually to do something about it ourselves? Something as drastic as trying to turn off terrorism by turning off tourism to Europe and the Mediterranean area in 1987?

I'll start. I'm going to suggest to my wife that in 1987 we fly American—and really see America. We've been to Europe and the Mediterranean area before, and do you know something? As many times as we've crossed the Atlantic, we've never seen the Statue of Liberty.

What a great place to start seeing America!

NOTES

1. Samuel Eliot Morison, *The Oxford History of the American People* (New York: Oxford University Press, 1965), p. 987.
2. Ibid., p. 997.
3. *Statistical Abstract of the United States 1985* (Washington, D.C.: U.S. Department of Commerce, Bureau of the Census, 1984), table 952.
4. Basic data from Risks International, Inc., quoted in "The Rise of World Terrorism," *U.S. News & World Report* (July 8, 1985).
5. Basic data from U.S. Department of Transportation.
6. Basic data from U.S. Bureau of Economic Analysis, *Survey of Current Business*, quoted in *Statistical Abstract 1985*, table 399.

IV

The Way We Make
Our Living

★

On the whole, with scandalous exceptions, Democracy has given the ordinary worker more dignity than he ever had.
> Sinclair Lewis, *It Can't Happen Here*, 1935

I never did anything worth doing by accident, nor
did any of my inventions come by accident; they
came by work.
> Thomas A. Edison (attributed)

There's No Better Place to Work

We've seen so many pictures of smiling Japanese workers singing their company's corporate anthem before trooping happily to their machines and assembly lines; smiling Japanese workers exercising happily together in harmonious unison during what *we* would call the coffee break; smiling Japanese workers reluctantly leaving their factories on bicycles at the end of the shift, that it came as a bit of a shock to many of us to hear that American workers are a whole lot *happier* about their jobs than are their Nipponese counterparts. That's right. An international study of workers' satisfaction with their jobs, conducted by the University of Indiana, reported during 1985 that 53% of Japanese workers are happy while they work . . . but 81% of Americans are happy about their work![1]

That's great to know. We have more Americans working and bringing home paychecks today than ever before in our history. It's good to know that most of them are happy about what they're doing. Of course, "happiness" is compounded of different ingredients for different people. They're not all happy, or unhappy, about the same things. Another research study reported "what workers want from their jobs" in America during 1985. A big sample of almost 1,000 employed adults named "ingredients of happiness at work" in this order:[2]

1. A good salary
2. Job security
3. Appreciation for a job well done
4. A chance to use your mind and abilities
5. Medical and other benefits
6. Being able to retire early with a good pension

Actually, I think this is an excellent list of the ingredients Americans have more of today than ever before, and the reasons why there's no better place on earth to work in today's busy, changing world.

A good salary. In 1985 an average American worker's annual take-home earnings after taxes "went farther" in buying basic goods and services needed to live comfortably than did the earnings of workers in 12 other highly developed countries: Netherlands, West Germany, Hong Kong, England, Italy, France, Brazil, Sweden, Australia, Israel, Japan, and Canada. Only Swiss workers' earnings went farther in providing food, housing, clothing, appliances, automobiles, and the other basics for modern living.[3]

Job security. As I write this in December 1985, eight out of 10 American households report that no one in their family has been laid off; lost a job; or had hours, commission, or overtime cut during the past year. And, mind you, eight out of 10 American families have been reporting this same good news every month, month after month, since February 1984! *That's* job security that expands out into the great majority of our American homes. And when people were asked if they expect any layoffs or income cuts during the year ahead— month after month for 22 months, an average of seven in 10 American households said they expected *no* layoffs or income cuts in the year ahead. That's job security, too, that can be multiplied 59 million times!

That same Leo J. Shapiro & Associates national survey, conducted in November 1985 as part of a massive continuing study of American society, found most families (54%) had increased their income during the past year; and almost as many (53%) were expecting their incomes to increase again during 1986. *That's* job security combined with the assurance of growing income.

Appreciation for a job well done. There are a lot of ways in which an employer can show appreciation, and they vary a good deal because differences in company size make a difference in how personal the relationship can be between employer and employee. Just getting to keep your job is certainly a very basic form of appreciation. Another is when the employer strives to protect you on the job. As more people (and especially more new people) go to work each day, the incidence of job-related injuries and illnesses is likely to go up. But occupational injuries and illnesses in 1984 (the most recent year reported) were just 8 per 100 full-time workers during the year, compared to 10.4 in 1974.[4] That's a major improvement in job safety for 79 million American workers in private industry, with employers showing they value workers by protecting them.

A chance to use your mind and abilities. Again, this is a job quality that is often inherent in the task itself. Some jobs are stultifying because they treat the work as a *thing*. But it should be noted that our American companies today are in the forefront of the new world workplace revolution of automation, robotization, and computerization, which is replacing much of the kind of work that used to treat workers as "things" and parts of the machines they worked on, with machines to do that sort of unthinking, repetitive gruntwork.

American industrial ingenuity created the first mass-production computers; an American company's subsidiary developed the first installed industrial robot in 1961; and American companies spent more on R&D in 1983 than all the nations in Europe, plus Japan.[5] Much of that money went into computer development, including the kind of fifth-generation hardware needed to enhance greatly the capability of robotics in future factories. American machines are going to get a lot smarter, and the smarter they get, the more opportunity there will be for workers who use their minds and abilities.

Already, one in four of all adult workers in our American work force has a college degree, and another sixth of all workers have at least some college schooling. By 1995, if current trends continue, half of all American workers will have had college-level training.[6] The number of college graduates in the work force has already increased by 144% since 1970—and more come to work every day. Such a smart work force will be *expected* to use "mind and abilities" in jobs of the future. Why else would nearly 8 million workers be already enrolled in vocational courses run by companies for their workers at all job levels? American companies have been spending over $40 billion a year on education and training of workers,[7] *polishing* their minds and abilities.

"Fringes" Worth $7,500 a Year

Medical and other benefits. American workers have never had as many valuable and varied job "perks" as they do today. Would you believe that worker benefits account for more than a third of all corporate payroll costs these days?

The average American hourly worker picks up over $7,500 a year worth of benefits.[8] We can thank America's unions for much of this, in the beginning. They fought for, struck for, and went to court for many rights that workers take for granted today. We've come a long long way from the days when a railroad superintendent refused to roof a loading platform where men had contracted rheumatism and asthma from work exposed to the wintry cold, because "Men are cheaper than shingles. . . . There's a dozen waiting when one drops out."[9]

Today the faster-growing (and most costly) packet of benefits includes pensions, insurance, short-term disability, and other items agreed upon by workers and employers, which cost employers an average of $54.10 per employee a week. Those "other items agreed upon" as fringe benefits for employees these days are very likely to include child-care assistance. One authoritative study during 1985 found a third of companies had some sort of employer-supported child-care assistance program, and three fourths expect to support child-care services in years ahead.[10] Another national study found 1,800 companies providing child-care services for employees, compared to just 600 three years before![11]

Being able to retire early with a good pension. In the 19th century, "Aged workers were given jobs as sweepers or submenials, preferring to labor 12 hours for 75 cents rather than face a pensionless retirement."[12] Now when most American workers retire, they are covered by some sort of pension plan or plans. In 1982, a total of 43.8% of all civilian workers had pension-plan coverage,[13] and so did 6.2 million government employees at federal, state, and local levels.[14] Retirement plans in America today are so generous that an increasing percent of elder workers are taking early retirement.

When you put all these ingredients of employment together with the fact that there's no nation in the world where workers are more free to move around wherever and whenever they want to find better employment opportunity, you see why there's no better place to work than right here in the U.S.A.

NOTES

1. University of Indiana study reported by Associated Press (May 28, 1985).
2. Louis Harris & Associates, Inc., survey conducted for *Business Week* (July 8, 1985).
3. Union Bank of Switzerland study reported in "Paycheck Power—from Houston to Hong Kong," *U.S. News & World Report* (October 28, 1985).
4. "Occupational Injuries and Illnesses in 1984," U. S. Department of Labor *News*, (November 13, 1985).
5. Kenneth Fleet, "A Robot Era?," *The Times* of London (August 24, 1985).
6. Peter Francese, "Better-Educated Work Force Turns to Government for Statistics Supply," Cowles Syndicate (May 12, 1985).
7. "At Work," *Changing Times* (July 1985).
8. John Conniff, "Worker Benefits Rising in U.S.," Associated Press (May 12, 1985).
9. Otto L. Bettmann, *The Good Old Days—They Were Terrible!* (New York: Random House, 1974), p. 71.
10. American Society for Personnel Administration, *Resource*, quoted in "At Work," *Changing Times* (July 1985).
11. Glenn Collins, "More U.S. Employers Now Help Workers Find, Pay for Day Care," *The New York Times* service (June 26, 1985).
12. Bettmann, op. cit., p. 69.
13. *Statistical Abstract of the United States 1985* (Washington, D.C.: U.S. Department of Commerce, Bureau of the Census, 1984), table 615.
14. Ibid., table 617.

American Workmanship May Actually Be Better Than Ever

I drive the oldest car on our block. It may even be the oldest car in the neighborhood. It's a 1963 Ford Fairlane 500, and I've never met an automobile mechanic who wasn't ready to buy it from me. "Old Blue" was my father's car. He gave it to me when he got too old to drive. We used to drive it into his barn up in Wisconsin late in fall, take out the battery, and leave the car there all winter, while snow piled higher and overnight temperatures went lower and lower. In the spring we'd run an extension cord out from the house across the snow, hook up the electric engine-block heater to warm the half-frozen oil overnight, put the battery back in, and in the morning "Old Blue" would start up "just like a charm." Today mechanics shake their heads admiringly over the engine that's hauled it 150,000 miles: "Look at that. That's beautiful. Look at all that extra space under the hood!"

Cars today are infinitely more complex and packed with intricate components than they were a few years ago because they do a lot more things for you than cars used to do. The 1917 car had about 2,500 parts; the 1976 model, 14,000; the 1986 models, even more. And yet, these complex, mass-produced mechanisms our American plants turn out are miracles of dependability. My wife's 1976 Buick has nearly 100,000 miles on it, and it runs like it's just getting really limbered up. The clothes dryer that came with our house 17 years ago complains a bit but still turns out nice, dry, fluffy clothes. And our Hoover vacuum cleaner has been beating and cleaning carpeting for decades.

Sure, I know that even our oldest All-American brand-name products are now full of components from other countries. More and more, "Made in America" means put together here. But that's not because of workmanship. It's a matter of a strong dollar, which has appreciated about 50% since 1980[1] compared to a combination of foreign currencies; this makes it cheaper for manufacturers to buy overseas. Even the IBM PC has a monitor from Korea; floppy disk drives from Singapore; and semiconductors, power supply, graphics printer, and keyboard from Japan.[2] And now, more and more American companies are opening plants overseas to use cheaper labor producing things to sell not only overseas but also in America.

Better than Japanese

But again I say, *not* because of American workmanship. An average American worker's hourly output still exceeds that of his or her Japanese counterpart, although Japanese manufacturing workers' production has been growing at a faster rate than ours. Since 1974, Japanese manufacturing workers' productivity has increased 104% compared with 17% in our country.[3] But in terms of *fine* workmanship, Nissan has said that our U.S. workers in its Tennessee plant turn out cars "as good as or better than those made at plants in Japan."[4] And Shoichiro Irimajiri, of Honda of America Manufacturing, said of the cars his company turned out in Marysville, Ohio, during 1984, "The quality, I think, is better than in Japan."[5]

Even with our expensive American dollars that made U.S.A. products extra expensive overseas, we sold $54.3 billion worth of machinery; $5.9 billion worth of sophisticated professional, scientific, and controlling instruments; and $28.3 billion worth of transport equipment, including $12.2 billion worth of aircraft and parts, to foreign buyers in 1983.[6] And in 1984, we sold $31.8 billion in electronic products alone to Canada, Great Britain, Japan, West Germany, and Mexico.[7] These people buy from us because the products we have to sell them, and the workmanship, exceed what they can get anywhere else. If that weren't true, they wouldn't buy.

That's why most of the world's major airlines buy and fly aircraft made by Americans, for one example. The design and the workmanship are unequaled for the money anywhere else.

American workers created and built the most sophisticated flying machine ever built: the Space Shuttle. Until the tragic *Challenger* accident our shuttles lifted satellites, scientific gear and experiments, and human explorers into space and brought them safely back again and again, 24 separate times in five years. That's an incredible performance record for flights in and out of an alien physical environment. At the same time, our unmanned space-probe vehicles have been exploring Earth's remote sister planets, farther out in space than human-made devices have ever ventured before. In 1983, after 11 years in space, *Pioneer 10* became our first space-probe to fly beyond the planets.

Voyager 1 and *Voyager 2* explored Jupiter in 1979 on their way to Saturn. Both sent back spectacular pictures and an incredible amount of scientific data. When the rugged little 1,819-pound *Voyager 2* whisked past Uranus at 45,000 mph on January 24, 1986, it had been traveling for nine years in a curving trajectory that carried it over 3 billion miles. Approaching Uranus, it was 1.8 billion miles from Earth—so far away that its radio signals took 2 hours and 45 minutes to reach home, even traveling at the speed of light. Yet, every American-made component of the infinitely intricate craft performed perfectly. In fact, when *Voyager* approached Uranus, it was only about a minute off the flight schedule calculated for it five years and nearly a billion miles before!

In early February 1986, a nationwide Shapiro poll asked hundreds of Americans: "By-and-large, are you pleased or disappointed with the job that industry has done for the space program?" Nine out of ten of those answering (87.6%) said they are "pleased" with the job American workers and industry have done for space exploration. And we should be.

It's about time we began really appreciating and encouraging American workmanship. Our standards of quality in production are as high, dollar for dollar, as any in the world. One of the most visible (and manufacturers might even say ubiquitous) examples of this determination for excellence is the motor-vehicle-defect recall program of our National Highway Traffic Administration. In 1983 alone, some 3,021,000 cars were recalled by our four leading American manufacturers, to correct defects. Slightly more foreign models (3,024,000) were recalled in the same year.[8] This represents an enormous effort and investment by our government and our manufacturers to guarantee superb product quality. It deserves appreciation.

There are signs that we Americans are finally beginning to recognize the quality built into our own products. Thirteen years ago, in 1972, Leo J. Shapiro & Associates conducted a national consumer survey in which they asked people across the country if they would agree or disagree with this statement: "Americans have become a nation of lousy workmen." Believe it or not, in 1972 almost two out of three American adults *agreed* with that lousy statement. Actually, in 1972 over 61% of Americans said, "Yes, we are a nation of lousy workers."

Now, in 1985, the Shapiro organization conducted a new national survey for this book. They asked men and women the same question asked in 1972. In 1985, six out of 10 Americans flatly *disagree* with the statement that we are a nation of lousy workmen. And although a majority of Americans in all age groups disagreed, the most heartening thing of all is that the Americans who feel *proudest* of American work quality are the baby-boom generation of Americans—the ones making up most of our work force!

In fact, with so many Americans feeling so proud of the quality of our workmanship these days, I may even turn in my 1963 Ford—or better still, offer it to the Smithsonian, or the St. Vincent de Paul Society. The car still has another 100,000 miles in it. But it's time to shop for one of those 1986 vans—*made in America!*

NOTES

1. United Press International, "U.S. Firms Importing Machinery" (May 23, 1985).
2. Data from *Future Computing,* Businessland, Inc., quoted in "America's High-Tech Crisis," *Business Week* (March 11, 1985).
3. Basic data from U.S. Department of Labor, Japan Statistics Bureau, and Japan Productivity Center, quoted in "Face to Face in the Factories," *U.S. News & World Report* (September 2, 1985).
4. Richard Alm with Maureen Walsh, "America vs. Japan: Can U.S. Workers Compete?," *U.S. News & World Report* (September 2, 1985).
5. Barry Stavro, "Made in the U.S.A.," *Forbes* (April 22, 1985).
6. *Statistical Abstract of the United States 1985* (Washington, D.C.: U.S. Department of Commerce, Bureau of the Census, 1984), table 1445.
7. Data from Electronic Industries Association quoted in *The Wall Street Journal* (May 6, 1985).
8. Leo J. Shapiro & Associates national consumer survey (June 1985) conducted especially for this book.

"The Hand That Rocked the Cradle"
Now Steadies Our Economy

★

When I was a kid there wasn't a house in our neighborhood with more than one "breadwinner." Dad went out to work and brought home the bacon. Mother stayed home and cooked it. That was the way it had been; that was the way it was *supposed* to be in our working-class area.

What a long time ago, and how far we have come! By 1981 nearly two in three married couples (62%) in America were both working. The increase in women working outside the home has been called "the most important social change of the 20th century."[1] It's more than that. It's also a revolutionary force in our consumer economy.

Women have moved into two out of three of the new jobs created in America during the past decade.[2] By 1982 they held more than half of all "working class" jobs in America: clerical, service, and manufacturing jobs.

Not only are women stepping into more jobs, they are also stepping up in the pay scale. For decades it seemed women's earnings would never go above 60% of men's average earnings. In 1939, a woman's wages averaged 59% of a man's. A whole generation later, in 1970, that ratio was still exactly the same. But lately the scale has finally tipped in favor of women: As of 1985, U.S. Department of Labor figures showed median earnings for women had climbed to 66% of men's.

Women's earning power is still well below that of men. But as women gain experience in jobs and as they come into the job market with more education in high-paying disciplines, their earning power and clout in the job market is rising. And make no mistake about it: Young women coming out of our colleges and universities today are "ready for bear" in business or the professions. Let's take a look at the 1982 graduating class at American colleges and universities.

221

Women now earn almost two out of five undergraduate degrees (39%) that are granted with majors in business and management. They also earn 28% of the master's degrees in business and management. In the physical sciences, such as chemistry, physics, and geology, women earned nearly one in four of the undergraduate degrees granted (22%).[4]

In the professions, back in 1960 only one in 20 M.D. graduates was a woman. Today the ratio is one in four. In 1960, one in 120 degrees in dentistry went to a woman; today it is one in six. In 1960, one in 40 law degrees was earned by a woman. Today it's one in three.[5] "Things they are a-changin' —fast!" Women college graduates are already increasing their earning rate faster than men with the same qualifications, as the following table shows. And women are really just getting started!

10-Year Increase in Median Incomes Among Those Completing Four Years of College[6]

	1972	1982	Increase
Men	$14,879	$28,030	88%
Women	8,736	17,405	99%

Now, what happens to a family's income when there is more than one paycheck coming in? That extra check each payday makes an enormous difference in the buying power of the family and in its life-style. Let's look at the difference a second paycheck makes in dollars and cents:

During the fourth quarter of 1984, two out of three American households—41.4 million of them[7]—had wage or salary earnings. Of those, over half (56%) had two or more people working. In married-couple families where only one person was bringing in a check, median earnings were at the rate of $29,536 a year. But among families where both husband and wife were getting paychecks, median earnings were at the rate of $34,632.

That extra $5,096 a year makes a big difference in how a family can live. It also makes a big difference in spending. A national survey of over 3,000 households during 1984 compared households with one employed worker and those with two or more working.[8] The survey found that households with two or more people out working were more affluent, and confident that they would continue to be affluent in the year ahead; more likely to be spending freely day to day for items such as food, clothing, transportation, and medical services; and also more likely to make major purchases in the year ahead, such as for housing, cars, furnishing, appliances, and travel.

Not only does the added income of a second earner make families feel more secure about spending in good times, the second paycheck also makes them more secure against unemployment in bad times. Nearly two thirds of American families where there was unemployment during 1984 still had at least one other wage and salary worker bringing in a check. In married-couple families where the husband was unemployed and the wife was the only earner, median earnings for the household were $206 a week. That's not much, but it could provide a temporary "safety net" combined with the husband's unemployment insurance payments.

Put all those millions of wives going out to work every day and bringing home paychecks together, and we have a very important potential "cushion" for the economy that never used to be there, if unemployment sets in, as it did in the four recessions hit us between 1969 and 1981. But there's one other interesting factor that seems to make that cushion even more important: Women are more likely to be working in "recession-resistant" jobs than men are.

As we've already mentioned, a very high proportion of women who go out to work are employed in service jobs, including clerical work. Service industry employment has proven surprisingly recession-resistant in recent years. A comparison of the payroll changes between jobs in the production of goods and jobs in services during four recent national recessions demonstrates this recession-resistance factor:[9]

Changes in Employment During Recessions

(Payroll changes—thousands of workers)

Period	Jobs in Production	Jobs in Services
July–Dec 1981	− 788,000	+ 114,000
Jan.–July 1980	− 1,243,000	+ 507,000
Nov. 1973–Mar. 1975	− 2,736,000	+ 1,298,000
Dec. 1969–Nov. 1970	− 1,651,000	+ 796,000

Economists have been almost constantly surprised during the past few years at how resilient the American economy had become. They kept putting their figures together and comparing them to past experience and predicting that the economy was about to come down like Chicken Little's sky. But each time, the enormous consumer buying power in America has swept in and buoyed the economy again. I believe that the added energy of women's income, as it continues to grow, is helping to fuel and stabilize our whole economy.

So here's to woman power! The hand that used to rock the cradle now steadies our economy, too!

NOTES

1. Eli Ginzberg, human-resources authority and adviser to every president of the United States since Franklin Roosevelt, quoted by Theodore Caplow, Howard M. Bahr, Bruce A. Chadwick, Reuben Hill, and Margaret Holmes Williamson, *Middletown Families: Fifty Years of Change and Continuity* (Minneapolis: University of Minnesota Press, 1982), p. 97.
2. Karen Pennar and Edward Mervosh, "Women at Work," *Business Week* (January 28, 1985).
3. Karen Sacks in *The Women's Annual 1982–1983*, ed. Barbara Haber (Boston: G.K. Hall & Company, (1983), p. 264.
4. *Statistical Abstract of the United States 1985* (Washington, D.C.: U.S. Department of Commerce, Bureau of the Census, (1984), table 266.
5. Ibid., table 267.
6. U.S. Departments of Commerce and Labor, basic data.
7. U.S. Department of Labor, Bureau of Labor Statistics, *News* (January 30, 1985).
8. Leo J. Shapiro & Associates, January–September 1984 summary of data from monthly national surveys covering a representative sample of over 3,000 households in the nine-month period.
9. Bureau of Labor Statistics data reported in *The Wall Street Journal* (January 15, 1982).

Even Our Worst Inflation Was Temperate

When people across America were asked, "What are the nation's major problems?" shortly before Thanksgiving in 1985, one in seven said, "inflation."[1] This was at a time when the national inflation rate was running below 3% and when one in six consumers was considering borrowing to buy a new car!

Of course, people worry because they've been through the double-digit inflation in the 1970s, and that was very painful. But look at it this way: Even at its worst, the inflation rate in America during the 1970s was one of the lowest in the whole world.

Compared to 104 other countries of the world, including the most developed and least developed, the United States had the *seventh lowest* average inflation rate in the world during those high-inflation years. The 1970s were marked by a slow but steady rise in prices among both healthy and unhealthy economies throughout the world. Some, such as Chile (185.6%) and Argentine (130.8%), had triple-digit inflation. Ours averaged out to just 7.1%. The British had 14.4% inflation, more than doubling ours. And the only highly developed nations with *lower* inflation than ours between 1970 and 1980 were Austria (6.3%), Singapore (5.1%), West Germany (5.1%), and Switzerland (5.0%).[2]

Sure, we all keep watching the prices every time we go to one of our many favorite supermarkets or super drugstores. And we all worry about prices going up again. But in the meantime, let's count our blessings while we count the change. We have one of the most inflation-resistant economies on this planet. And you can count on that.

NOTES

1. Leo J. Shapiro & Associates, national consumer survey (November 1985).
2. *World Development Report* quoted in G. T. Kurian, *The New Book of World Rankings* (New York: Facts on File Publications, 1984), table 71.

The Lion and the Lamb Sit Down Together and Work Things Out

★

A quiet but important victory for America took place in 1984. Most of us were not even aware of it. In 1984 there were fewer major strikes or work stoppages across the country than at any other time in the 38 years the U.S. Department of Labor has been keeping count! The year 1983 had also been a record one, with just 81 major stoppages nationally, but 1984 was the most peaceful year ever, with only 62 stoppages.[1]

Not only that, but there were fewer workers out in labor stoppages during 1984 than ever before in U.S.D.L records: 376,000. Working days lost in stoppages during 1984 (four days per 10,000 worked) also hit an all-time low level, equaling the previous low in 1982.[2]

Just for comparison, and to give perspective to these cool statistics, let's go back one decade and see how the Great Peace of 1984 compares with what happened just 10 years before. In 1974 there were 424 major work stoppages across the country, compared to 1984's 62—almost seven times as many strikes that involved 1,000 or more workers. In 1974, 1.8 million workers were involved in major strikes, compared to the 376,000 in 1984—nearly five times as many people off the job. And in 1974, a total of 16 work days were lost per 10,000 across the country, compared to just four days in 1984—four times as many days off the job.[3]

What's going on here? Are the unions getting too weak to strike? Or are the employers making so much money they don't want to fight? Neither of the above. It's true that unions represent a far smaller share of American workers today than they used to. In 1950, about three in 10 American workers belonged to a union; by 1980, fewer than two in 10 (17.9%) did. But unions, like American business, are in the midst of a

227

monumental changeover in the kinds of products we turn out
and the work we do. For three decades, the old smokestack
heavy industries have been losing their steam in this country,
and losing jobs and union members. Copper and coal mining
have also changed enormously. Four out of five construction
workers are now nonunion. But this doesn't mean unions are
going away; they are growing where the new growth is in
jobs. In terms of numbers, there were more Americans holding cards in AFL-CIO–affiliated unions in 1983 (13.8 million)
than there were in 1971 (13.2 million).[4]

What's happened, and happening, I believe, is that lions
and lambs have learned to sit down together and reason out
their differences, so strikes have become less necessary in
America. There was a time when there was no other way out.
In 1932, when nearly 3,000 unemployed men marched to the
gates of Ford Motor Company's plant in Dearborn, Michigan,
the marchers

> planned to ask Ford company officials, through a com-
> mittee, to give them work . . . but before it was over
> Dearborn pavements were stained with blood, streets
> were littered with broken glass and the wreckage of
> bullet-ridden automobiles and nearly every window in the
> Ford plant's employment building had been broken. . . .[5]

In a confrontation among marchers, Detroit police, and Ford
Motor Company fire department workers with hoses, four
men were killed and at least 50 more injured.

Again, in 1937, when UAW members, headed by their
union leader, Walter Reuther, gathered at the gates of Ford
Motor's Rouge plant, with written permission from the city of
Dearborn to hold a peaceful demonstration, they were met
by a "cadre of guards identified as bruisers, ex-baseball, and
-football players and jailbirds,"[6] and when the men and women
in the UAW group retreated they were met by still another
group of Ford thugs:

> One grabbed Reuther from behind, knocked him to the
> ground and, after kicking his head and body, flung him
> down the steel steps. Another unionist had his jacket
> pulled over his head to immobilize his arms and was then
> beaten. A woman was kicked in the stomach. Another
> union man had his back broken.

> Newspaper photographers . . . were the next targets. They were beaten, and their cameras confiscated. But enough escaped to provide front-page coverage of the vicious asssault for the next day's newspapers and for national magazines.[7]

We've certainly come a long way from that kind of "negotiation." Today, company management realizes that they must serve a consumer economy to survive and that workers and their unions are consumers, as well as big stockholders, through pension funds. Management must also keep production humming to stay ahead of foreign competition as well as competition here at home. For their part, union leadership realizes that if the companies can't compete in the world market their members' jobs will be lost when plants close and the work moves elsewhere. So they and their members are more willing to yield on some issues than in the past, in exchange for job security.

This new level of pragmatic understanding between labor and management, confronted by worldwide competition, has led to less confrontational, more productive negotiations. When Chrysler Corporation's contract with the UAW ran out in 1979, the production lines kept running and the workers kept at their jobs. Chrysler was in terrible economic trouble, and negotiating not only with the union for a new labor agreement, but also with the federal government for $1.5 billion in loan assistance, in order to stay in business.

The union, led by Douglas Fraser, did its part by offering Chrysler a contract with concessions worth about $400 million, part of this in deferred payments to the Chrysler workers' pension fund. The company and Chrysler workers approved it. Congress and the federal government gave Chrysler its needed loan guarantee. By each of those involved sacrificing something for the common good, one of America's top ten companies was saved from going down the tubes, and hundreds of thousands of American jobs were saved. That's what cooperation instead of confrontation can do.

Of course, the government helped. But as Chrysler's chairman, Lee Iacocca, put it, "The real reason Chrysler is alive today is people—people who faced up to the company's problems and accepted sacrifices to see the company through."[8]

Once Chrysler had its loan guarantee locked in, the spirit of cooperation didn't stop. Four months after Congress approved the loan, Iacocca nominated the head of his company's employees' union to Chrysler's board of directors. Fraser became the first union leader in history to serve as a member of top management in a major American corporation.

Douglas Fraser is a tough, hardheaded Scottish immigrant union man. He also knows how business works, and like Iacocca he recognized that the time has come for American industry to work hand-in-hand with labor and government to iron out problems that could affect us all. Chrysler gained an outstanding board member, and the country gained a new kind of labor-management level of cooperation.

That's the spirit. That's the kind of cooperation America needs when we're competing together against the whole world. Our most persistent competitors, the Japanese, have their own share of labor disagreements and strikes. They had 893 strikes and lockouts in 1983, which cost 507,000 days of production. That's over 14 times as many strikes as we had in America in 1984. But the Japanese settle their differences more quickly than we do; they stay off the job for an average of 2.3 days in their strikes, compared to an average of 22.6 days in our country. We need to learn how to settle our differences together *before* they shut the plants down. We have to reason together, or we'll all collect unemployment together.

That's why the day industrialist Lee Iacocca stood up to welcome unionist Douglas Fraser to the board of directors of one of America's most powerful companies was a great day for all of us. We're on our way. Government figures on collective-bargaining agreements reached during 1985, and the figures on a new low in work stoppages across America in 1984, are proofs: The lions and the lambs are working together to keep America working and growing.

NOTES

1. "Major Work Stoppages: 1984," U.S. Department of Labor, Bureau of Labor Statistics, *News* (February 27, 1985).
2. Ibid.
3. *Statistical Abstract of the United States 1985* (Washington, D.C.: U.S. Department of Commerce, Bureau of the Census, (1984), table 710.
4. Ibid., table 708.

5. Richard Hofstadter and Michael Wallace, eds. *American Violence: A Documentary History* (New York: Vintage Books, 1974), p. 357. Quotes from *The New York Times* (March 8, 1932).
6. David Abodaher, *Iacocca* (New York: Kensington Publishing Corp., 1985), p. 91.
7. Ibid., p. 92.
8. Lee Iacocca, "Straight Talk," *Los Angeles Times* Syndicate, October 13, 1985.

We Never Stop Looking for
Better Mousetraps

Does this line sound familiar to you?

If a man has good corn, or wood, or boards, or pigs, to sell, or can make better chairs or knives, crucibles or church organs, than anybody else, you will find a broad hard-beaten road to his house, though it be in the woods.

It's a line written by American philosopher and poet Ralph Waldo Emerson in 1851. He also used it in a speech, and about 40 years later, a lady named Sarah S. B. Yule remembered it, and wrote it down like this:

If a man can write a book, preach a better sermon, or make a better mouse-trap than his neighbor, though he builds his house in the woods the world will make a beaten path to his door.[1]

Sarah Yule put the mousetrap in, took out a lot of other merchandise, and made Emerson's line a lot better. Later, we Americans shortened it to just

Build a better mousetrap; the world will beat a path to your door.

That's the way it is with Americans. We're always improving things, making better mousetraps. This persistent national urge has made us the most innovative, technically advanced society on earth. We abhor the status quo.

Americans in the 19th century didn't invent the steam engine, the dynamo that made electric generation possible, the gasoline engine, horseless carriage, mechanized agriculture, steam locomotives or steamboats, or the telegraph—but we took the basic technology and made them all practical and mass-marketable.

Americans in the 20th century didn't invent the radio, jet engine, plastics, artificial rubber, airplane, television, or space rocketry, either—but again, we took basic technology from Europe and turned it into a technological revolution that swept us all into the space age. The basic principle of the computer was developed in Europe, but it took American engineers to turn theory into the Mark I digital computer at Harvard University in 1944, and the first transistors at Bell Telephone Laboratories in 1948 to make today's computers possible.

Today we're busier than ever exploring the universe, creating and developing new technology and products. We spend at the rate of $185,000 a second on research and development in America today—$266 million a day discovering "new mousetraps" and developing better ones.[2] In fact, we budget more spending nationally for research and development than ever before. Figured in constant (1972) dollars (to take out the effects of inflation), we're investing more than twice as much in R&D in America today as we did in 1960. Almost two thirds of that is invested in *non*military R&D, to produce better products and better living for all of us.

Over 750,000 scientists and engineers go to work in America every day, working strictly in research and development— half again as many as we had in R&D in 1965. About two thirds of them work for industry.[3] With all this money and all this scientific brainpower dedicated to the exploration of new and better ways to do things, and developing new methods and materials to use, we have an endless flow of technology for American entrepreneurs to put to work for us creatively.

Unbundled Opportunity

At the same time, "unbundling" industries tied up with regulations until recent years has thrown open millions of new doors and windows in our economy for new companies and new products to grow through. Since 1980 legislation made it easier to get into the trucking business, for example, the number of interstate carriers in America has grown by 70% to almost 31,000. And since deregulation in the telephone business, more than 100 new companies have moved

into phone manufacturing alone.[4] Not only has taking down
the bars in giant industries opened the field to thousands of
new businesses, it's also created new opportunities for consumers. We have more choices, and more companies competing for our business than ever. With more companies
competing, the average price to ship a truckload of freight is
25 to 30% lower today than it was four years ago. As for
telephones, have you shopped for a new push-button headset
this week? Or compared prices for long-distance calls? It's
like shopping in a discount market!

The competition is fierce out there, but there's never been
a better environment for growing new products and companies in America. Some 600,000 new corporations opened—
their doors for the first time in 1984—almost double the
number starting business 10 years ago.[5] Most are small. Many
will fail. But in our free-enterprise environment, practically
all look for ways to "build a better mousetrap" that will catch
sales in a consumer marketplace receptive to new ideas and
new products. "New" and "improved" are the most powerful
attention-getters in the American consumers' lexicon. We
love to be the first in our block to try something new.

Today the air is full of new ideas; the marketplace is full of
new, improved products; and our cities are full of new
companies that didn't exist even a few years ago. Most have
been built simply by improving a "mousetrap" that was already there. Others have created a brand-new innovation.
Together they're changing the face and the life-styles of America. Consider just a few giants serving us today that didn't
exist 10 or 15 years ago:

"Absolutely, Positively"

Federal Express. Fifteen years ago, the only way you could
get a letter or a package across country overnight was to send
it by courier, or take it to the airport yourself and get it on an
individual airline flight. Today you simply pick up your phone
and call any one of a whole gaggle of overnight small-package
air-express companies, including Emery, Airborne, Purolator,
and the giant UPS. They'll pick up your letter or package and
deliver it overnight practically anywhere in the country for
less than it would cost you to take a cab to the airport. Even
the U.S. Postal Service has gotten into the act and will

deliver overnight—if you bring your package to them. We already take all this fast-flying superservice for granted.

This $3.5 billion-a-year industry started with a college term paper by a young fellow named Fred Smith. Fred's term paper laid out his notion that by melding jet planes, computers, jet-age communications, and automation, a nationwide system could be constructed that would carry messages, packages, and inventory from any city in America to any other city overnight, running as efficiently and dependably as a giant quartz watch. Fred got only a C on his paper. But what seemed like a crazy idea then became Federal Express in 1973. The little company delivered just 18 packages in its first night's trip to 13 airports. But it turned its first profit just three years later, in 1976.[6] Now Federal Express delivers about 250,000 packages a night and does 42% of the $3.5 billion overnight delivery business.[7] And Fred Smith is CEO of the whole shebang!

MCI. William McGowan bought half of the stock in a little company called Microwave Communications of America for $50,000. McGowan "didn't come from the telephone industry, so I didn't have any preconceived notions."[8] He demonstrated that by going to court against one of the biggest, most secure monopoly companies in the nation, AT&T. He was determined to force the world's biggest phone company to deliver calls made long-distance over *his* company's microwave equipment, to their final destination over local wires. McGowan also persuaded the Justice Department to begin antitrust proceedings against AT&T.

It took six years of battling in the courts, but McGowan won in 1980. A historic judgment gave him $1.8 billion in damages; and the government's action ended in a consent decree that split AT&T seven ways and opened the lines for a whole new long-distance telephone industry. Then a federal appeals court threw out some of the charges on which MCI's historic award was based and sent the case back to the lower court to decide how much MCI should be awarded for the other counts that it had upheld. Five more years, and 21 volumes of evidence, later, in 1985 a new jury awarded MCI $37.8 million. Under the Sherman Act, the verdict was automatically tripled—to $113.3 million. Today McGowan's Microwave Communications of America (now MCI) is the largest of many new long-distance phone companies. And as for

AT&T, it and all its seven regional corporate split-offs are growing and scrambling for business, too!

Therapeutics, Plant Foods and Beer

Biotechnology. The enormously complex and potentially tricky business of splicing and altering genes of bacteria and other organisms to create new genetic engineering products has captured the imagination and dollars of investors. It also intrigues companies making a wide range of things, from human therapeutics to plant foods and even beer. However, the most significant products of genetic engineering now in development are pharmaceutical preparations. A recent estimate showed about 90 genetically engineered products being developed. The biotechnology industry in America already includes some 200 high-tech companies.[9] And biotechnology itself still is only about 10 years old! Companies in the industry are just beginning to bring their first products to market; in 1985 there was only one recombinant human therapeutic product on the American market. But the worldwide potential for biotechnological products is enormous. Genetech, one of the industry's two leaders at this point, along with Cetus Corp., had seven products under consideration for FDA approval during 1985. These included such medically innovative products as an antiviral and anticancer agent, a human-growth hormone, gamma interferon, a tissue plasminogen activator, a blood-clot dissolver, a vaccine for hepatitis B, and a tumor necrosis factor. The company's president has said that the tissue plasminogen activator (TPA) alone is potentially "a $500-million to $800-million-a-year-product." Its CEO has said flatly, "Our goal is to be a *Fortune* 500 company." This from a company only nine years old![10]

But you don't have to be a giant, or even a potential giant, or be part of a newly created nationwide industry to flourish on the strength of an idea in America today. Thousands of successful new products and services, in every corner of the economy, didn't exist a decade or less ago. Some have attracted big-league investment capital. Some are still being financed out of the owner's hip pocket. All illustrate the fact that a better mousetrap still can draw buyers and profits to your door.

Communications. Everybody seems to agree that we're in the midst of a "communications revolution." But sometimes we overlook how varied and wide a revolution it is. Here are just two examples of widely different entrepreneurial successes in totally different fields; both are part of America's multifaceted communications field today:

• Larry Beyer and his friend Jay Schultz saw opportunity shaping up in 1979 in the growing number of VCRs in homes. They figured that owners of VCRs would like to put them to work showing "movies on demand" at home. Beyer and Schultz began distributing uncut feature-length films to video specialty shops in the Cleveland area. In the first year, they sold $1 million worth. By 1982, it was $10 million worth. By 1985, Beyer estimated that they would make $80 million in sales in a field where the pretax profit on sales probably is 25% of sales.[11] And they don't even have a factory!

• Kathy Kolbe was born a dyslexiac (for whom it is hard to tell left from right), but she says her disability is "one of the greatest advantages I have." She was concerned that her own gifted children, ages six and eight, were being held back and bored in school, because the school was not geared to serve above-ordinary children. Kathy first started a summer school to teach children how to think creatively and critically by using both sides of their brains. The school grew to 200 students, at $60 a week each. But then Kathy was frustrated because she couldn't find special learning materials for gifted children. She used $500 of her savings to start a company called Resources for the Gifted. She wrote a series of "Thinkercises" to stimulate and teach gifted children. Using a spare bedroom at home as the company's headquarters, Kathy wrote a catalog and mailing for her line of products, which were warehoused in the closet! Orders came hard at first. But six years later she was grossing $3.5 million a year—without a single government or corporate grant.[12] "I enjoy a challenge," said Kathy Kolbe. She found a need to be filled; she's helping children; and thus she's building a flourishing business. That's *accepting* a challenge and putting it to work earning a profit.

Re-Inventing the Airplane

Transportation. Deregulation created many new opportunies for entrepreneurs, on the road and in the air. But that's not the *only* route to success in transportation these days.

• By starting where the Wright Brothers did, almost a century ago, with a hang glider, immigrant aeronautical engineer Julian Wolkovitch is revolutionizing the airplane. Back in the mid-1970s, Wolkovitch began tinkering with an idea for a new, safer hang glider shaped a bit like a flying picture frame. Called a "joined-wing aircraft," the glider had wings both fore and aft, joined together at their tips. Joining the wings added structural strength. Since the pilot sat amidship, the forward wings also created an added crash barrier for protection. It seemed a promising design, but in practice Wolkovitch found that his new, safer hang glider was too awkward to handle as a manually launched "space vehicle." Fortunately, he didn't stop there.

When he used his computer to analyze the hang glider's aerodynamics, Wolkovitch realized that his diamond-shaped joined-wing design created a lighter, stiffer aircraft than the conventional monoplane design. Thus, joined-wing aircraft could theoretically carry more passengers or cargo weight, and do it farther on the same amount of fuel than a conventional single-wing plane of similar size. In fact, a NASA executive who has said "all the studies so far indicate there are no stoppers" to developing a practical full-size joined-wing demonstrator aircraft, estimated that the joined-wing assembly alone could be up to 30% lighter than the wing-plus-tail assembly on a conventional monoplane. Wolkovitch estimated that replacing the weight saved by his design with fuel could extend the flying range of a twin-engine transport by 40%—to over 2,000 miles.

NASA expected to issue a contract for developing a full-size demonstrator of Wolkovitch's new aircraft to be flight-tested by 1987–88.[13] A privately built, one-person, ultralight prototype already has been built and flown successfully. If the big one flies as well as it sounds, "Wolkovitch's mousetrap" could revolutionize business aircraft, medium-size commercial airliners, and military transports in the future.

• As a youngster in Kentucky in the early 1960s, Danny Lawson had no choice: He sat in the back of the bus. As a teenager, Danny was a high-school all-American in football, basketball, baseball, and track. This won him a football scholarship to Oklahoma State University, and after graduation there, a chance in pro football with the Washington Redskins. A serious knee injury ended that career and sent Lawson back to college for his master's degree in marketing.

After graduation, Lawson entered a manager-trainee program with Federated Department Stores, and then an accelerated management program for Gulf Oil Company's marketing department. This gave him an opportunity to run management projects in a major corporation as if they were his own business. That was just what young Lawson needed: opportunity to grow.

In 1975, Gulf lent Lawson to the city of Houston to become public transit administrator. When OPEC raised oil prices out of sight in the late 1970s, Lawson looked for an answer to Houston's problem of how to operate public-transit buses on the least possible amount of fuel. He discovered that midsize buses were more versatile and more cost-effective than the 40-foot monsters cities were using. He also found a great need for midsize buses nationwide.

In 1978, Lawson borrowed $10,000 from his mother, a retired schoolteacher. He used that to set up his own company, marketing midsize passenger buses. Seven years later, Danny Lawson and his company had sold more than $110 million in municipal contracts for buses; 1985 sales were pegged at $37 million. Today Lawson heads the fastest-growing transit company in America, a six-year-old company to market, service, and assemble buses for major cities, including Chicago, New Orleans, San Francisco, Los Angeles, and Minneapolis-St. Paul. Minorities make up about three out of four transit riders in the nation's major cities.[14] "Blacks have long been the backbone of public transportation in this country," Lawson said. "Now we need to become makers and sellers of those buses." He's come a long way from the back of the bus. Asked about his early days, Lawson says, "The experience helped give me the courage and inspiration to forge ahead."

• Six years ago, David R. Leggett quit school and went into business. He had worked as a garage mechanic and junkyard attendant while earning his way through college, and the experience gave him a big idea. Legett realized that an old but well-made car, on its way to the scrap heap, could be totally rebuilt "good as new." With prices climbing ever higher on new cars, many owners of high-quality cars really wanted to hang onto the old buggy—but didn't know how to refurbish it themselves. So David Leggett started his own company to remanufacture aging and derelict Volvos and BMWs.

Five years later, Leggett grossed $1.2 million turning battered, worn old cars into showroom-quality beauties. Each car carried a one-year, 12,000-mile warranty and sold for about $9,000—less than half the price of a new model. "We're saving a tremendous amount of material and energy," Leggett said proudly. One authority in the remanufacturing field estimated that remanufacturing technology takes only one fifth the energy and one tenth the raw materials necessary to build the same product from scratch.[15] By 1985 there were 600 companies remanufacturing various vehicles and machines across America, twice the number four years earlier. They found a need to fill and an opportunity for service and profit in remaking "better mousetraps."

Putting Your Medical History in Your Pocket

Low-budget, high-tech. High-technology manufacturing is also high-budget manufacturing. But that doesn't mean there isn't room in it for shirt-sleeves inventor-entrepreneurs who have know-how and a new idea. Take the 19-year-old computer "hacker" who figured out how to put your life history onto a credit card.

• Douglas Becker was a teenage high-school graduate "into computers" and laser-optics technology. What he and four of his computer hacker friends developed as a "brainstorming idea" may very well get them into your *pocket* in the next year or so. They devised a way to store up to 800 pages of information on a plastic wallet card.

Becker and his friends knew that laser-optics technology used to make audio and video disks could also be adapted to create encoded cards with special accessing codes that would "unlock" information stored on them only for someone with the code—an authorized health-care provider, for example.

The youngsters put this knowledge together with their interest in computer technology and "brainstormed the idea until we knew it could work." What they came up with was a design for a billfold card that can carry your complete medical data, including X-ray and electrocardiogram records, drug prescriptions, lab-test results, allergy alerts, and surgical history, plus your photo, signature, and details of your insurance plan benefits—all in the space taken by your current plastic Blue Cross or Blue Shield card.

Over 1.5 million Blue Cross and Blue Shield subscribers in Maryland will be trying out the new identity card during 1986–87.[16] After that? The young investors may find time (and plenty of money) to go back to school for their college education!

• In 1982, Wilton H. Jones "didn't even think I'd have a company." Then, at age 38 and after 17 jobs in 20 years, he won a $250,000 contract to develop a personal computer word-processing program for the Connecticut Mutual Life Insurance Company.

As a teenager, Jones dropped out of high school to go into the Air Force. Later he dropped out of the University of Houston to take a computer programming course. Many jobs in data processing followed, with a number of insurance companies. Finally Jones became a consultant to Connecticut Mutual. That's when he suggested the new software program. It turned out to be Multimate, one of the most popular of all word-processing programs. Jones kept title and marketing for the software and became head of Multimate International Corporation, the company set up to publish his program.

In 1985, Jones's company was acquired by a much larger software corporation for some $19 million in cash and stock.[17] A pretty fair return in three years, and Wilton Jones gets to keep his job, besides!

Feeding Grazers

Serving people in a grazing society. In an increasingly urban society, where 47 million working couples leave home each day, consumers need all the help they can get.[18] That's spurred the proliferation of convenience foods, all-night supermarkets, microwave ovens, and various services created to fill the needs of people who are too busy to cook from scratch and can afford to pay for help. Here are a few instances of how entrepreneurs with a new food-service idea can quickly turn it into a going business:

• In your grandparents' day the grocer who wouldn't make up your order for you when you phoned it in, and deliver it the same day, didn't stay in business. Home delivery was an accepted part of the grocery business. *No more*. Nowadays you're lucky if some warehouse supers will give you a bag to put your own groceries into before you carry them out to the car yourself!

So the new grocery shopping services developed by entrepreneurial and energetic women in Washington, D.C., and Columbia, Maryland (areas with high employment and incomes to match) are so welcome.[19] The services are like old times, brought up to date! You simply phone your grocery order to them in the morning. They do your shopping for you during the day, deliver to your kitchen in the afternoon—and will even put everything away for you. In Washington the rate for all this starts at $6 for the first $50 worth of groceries and runs up to 10% of orders over $200. For an additional fee, you get fresh seafood bought for you at the city's waterfront market. In Columbia the fee is $10 for five bags of groceries, and $1 for each additional bag.

This is a good example of finding a consumer need and then filling it. As our population grows older and cities become more crowded, home delivery and personal-shopping services are going to become increasingly attractive to more people besides working couples.

Just 22 and a year out of school at Yale, financial analyst Myra Evans fell in love in San Francisco. She fell in love with *gelato*, a frozen Italian dessert. To learn the secrets of how to make the delicacy, Evans traveled to Italy to study the methods of the masters. When she came home to America she was ready to get down to business.

First Evans got a childhood friend to become her partner. Then, in six weeks' time, she induced 30 investors to put $200,000 into the *gelato* business. The company, Gelato Modo, Inc., was capitalized at over $1 million, with Evans, her partner, and relatives holding just over half the stock. By the time the company opened its first four Gelato Modo shops in Manhattan, sales were projected at $1 million for 1985, and Evans had requests for information about franchising from 2,500 people.[20] Talk about *la dolce vita!* This is *vita* with a double dash of good old American marketing savvy.

• There are a flock of chickens in the fast-food field, but Dick Lipson aimed to make El Pollo Asado the biggest, most successful bird of all. Lipson and his two associates broiled a flavorful difference into their product. *Pollo asado*, a Spanish specialty, is charbroiled after being marinated in herbs and fruit juices. Then it's served with salsa, tortillas, beans, and side orders. "It's a great product," Lipson said. "Acceptance is wonderful. People love it." And indeed they must: The first El Pollo Asado restaurant opened in Phoenix in 1983; two years later it had hatched a clutch of six company outlets and three franchise shops in the same metropolitan area. Thirty-nine more were in planning, or had received franchise commitments, in Texas, New Mexico, Arizona, and California. And Lipson was aiming at having 400 restaurants nationally by 1988, with one in four of them company-owned.[21]

• Americans munch $5.1 billion worth of pizza a year. That's only about a fourth of what we invest in hamburgers, but the pizza business has been growing faster, at a 21.5% annual rate.[22] In a country spending an average $61 per family a year for pizza, you know there's a great big hungry market out there, just waiting for your product to come out of the oven. But it's also a great big *competitive* market. The food giants are into it. You can buy pizza ready to eat in fast-food places at practically every major city intersection, and the grocer's freezer section is loaded. Is there any more room for a new pizza to roll up sales in such a crowded market?

Neal Andrews found it. His company sells supermarkets with a deli section the makings for fresh, unbaked pizzas; shows them how to make and sell fresh pizza; then keeps them well supplied with his ingredients. Shoppers buy ready-to-bake fresh pizza at the store and pop it into the oven to finish at home. It's the quickest, easiest way in the world to make your own home-baked pizza, and you can add your own touches.

Do people like unbaked pizza? They eat it up. Andrews' company has been selling the ingredients for pizza to nearly 5,000 supermarkets, which adds up to a lot of dough. In the past five years his company's sales zoomed from $11 million to an estimated $65 million[23]—all on the strength of a *fresh* approach to a market that's already well stocked with competitors.

This "dissertation on a mousetrap" has covered a wide gamut of products and services, all successful in their segment of the market. At first glance, they all seem to have taken different routes to reach success:

Federal Express proved that it could do a better job in providing a necessary service than the government was doing. They *positively* delivered the mail overnight.

MCI proved that it could deliver a necessary service more economically than a giant monopoly could do it.

The new biotechnology firms are creating products that never existed before, to serve existing human needs.

Larry Beyer and Jay Schultz found a need the consumer was *going* to have even before most of us had it.

Kathy Kolbe found a very special need in our society and created the materials to fill it.

Julian Wolkovitch created a totally new design concept in a field where "everything had been discovered."

Danny Lawson found a way to save resources and money for society itself, in a field that serves society.

David R. Leggett re-created and preserved quality products that people wanted to save in an era of disposables.

Douglas Becker and his friends related two unrelated sophisticated technologies to a mass-market opportunity.

Wilton H. Jones created an exclusive new product in a market where many people were already looking for it.

Home delivery of food re-creates a lost service that's needed now more than ever.

Myra Evans, Dick Lipson, and Neal Andrews found fresh ways to serve our grazing society.

All of these various products and services, with their many different approaches to a market, share one ingredient of success: Each basically represents an innovator who has either "made a better mousetrap" or made one where no mousetrap existed before. What was true for marketers over 100 years ago in America is even more true today. American consumers are as open to new products and new services today as ever. There are more consumers than ever, with more money to spend.

If you have a new idea for a "better mousetrap" in any field, there never was a better time to develop it. And never a better place than here in America.

NOTES

1. Sarah S. B. Yule and Mary S. Keen, *Borrowings* (1889).
2. *Statistical Abstract of the United States 1985* (Washington, D.C.: U.S. Department of Commerce, Bureau of the Census, 1984), table 988.
3. Ibid., table 1000.
4. "Living Without Shackles," *Time* (December 12, 1983).
5. *Statistical Abstract, 1985*, table 876.
6. Cindy Skrazycki, "An Industry That Keeps Promises—Overnight," *U.S. News & World Report* (October 22, 1984).

7. Susan Spillman, "Overnight-Mail to Deliver Us Some Messages," *USA Today*.

8. Otto Friedrich, "Seven Who Succeeded," *Time* (January 7, 1985).

9. David Stipp, "Biotechnology Becomes Business in Transition," *The Wall Street Journal* (October 15, 1985).

10. Marilyn Chase, "Genetech Gears Up to Enter the Marketplace," *The Wall Street Journal* (October 15, 1985).

11. Alex Ben Block, "Hard Dollars in Video Software," *Forbes* (June 17, 1985).

12. Friedrich, op. cit.

13. Jerry E. Bishop, "Technology," *The Wall Street Journal* (October 11, 1985).

14. Lloyd Gite, "Lawson National Travels the Road to Riches," *Black Enterprise* (June 1985).

15. Roger Schulman and Margaret Sabin, "A Growing Love Affair with the Scrap Heap," *Business Week* (April 29, 1985).

16. "The Story of Your Life, Wallet-Size," *U.S. News & World Report* (May 20, 1985).

17. "Success of Multimate Gets Ashton-Tate to Bid," *The New York Times* (July 31, 1985).

18. U.S. Bureau of Labor Statistics data (June 17, 1985).

19. "Tired of Carting Groceries?", *Changing Times* (July 1985).

20. "People," *Business Week* (June 10, 1985).

21. Sam Stanton, "Bird in Hand: 3 Crow over Chicken Chain," *Arizona Republic* (May 12, 1985).

22. National Restaurant Association data quoted by Peter Francese, "Americans' Increasing Incomes Keep Restaurants Cooking," Cowles Syndicate (March 24, 1985).

23. Toni Mack, "Pizza Power," *Forbes* (September 23, 1985).

The Invisible People Who Keep the Country Going

★

Who runs America? Nobody runs America. America is too big, too complex for one person or party to run it. Just making and interpreting our *laws* is a continuous mass-production process. There are 7,419 state legislators, 100 U.S. senators, 435 congressmembers—7,954 lawmakers, all grinding out legislation as fast as they can go. Fifty state supreme courts and the U.S. Supreme Court all try to help us sort out and understand the legislation, with the nine U.S. Supreme Court justices alone docketing over 5,000 cases a year. At the same time, you have 542,000 lawyers across the country trying to find ingenious ways to get around the laws.

Obviously, no one person or even a White House full of movers and shakers can actually run America. But I'll tell you who *keeps* America running: It's the invisible people who come out to take charge every night.

The invisible people work and live on a shift different from the rest of us. You'll never see them on *Meet the Press*, *Time's* cover, or even in *People* magazine. But without them, the president would go hungry, Congress would adjourn, Wall Street would close down, all monthly bills would go unpaid, and the Social Security checks would not arrive. America would come to a grinding stop. Who are these invisible and uncelebrated powers?

Cleaning people who take over offices after hours and clean up the mess we made there during the day, without interrupting the unfinished work on our desks and in our machines.

Rubbish collectors who spirit away our daily debris—the 100 million tires, 20 million tons of paper, 28 billion bottles, and 48 billion cans we throw away during a year[1]—while we try to sleep through the grunting, clanging, and whirring of their compactor trucks.

Street cleaners who work under the arc lights, hauling away the husks of abandoned cars, scrubbing, sweeping, flushing streets in the vacant hours before we come out to begin littering them again.

Truck drivers hurtling through the night across countryside and trundling through sleeping cities so our cereal, produce, milk, and beefsteak will be in the store, and the catalog stuff we ordered will arrive tomorrow.

Postal workers wrestling packages and sorting letters, pumping past them in endless flow all night under the post-office lights so we'll find them in the mailbox in the morning.

Air express pilots crisscrossing the country in the dark, seven miles up, on instruments all the way while cities glisten like powdered diamonds far below and lightning flickers on the horizon—tomorrow's business riding in the holds of their jets.

Newspaper printers and circulation crews working all night every night of the year so there'll be a familiar newspaper waiting for us when we open our door in the morning.

Airport workers loading and unloading, fueling, dumping wastes, cleaning, checking, maintaining, and guiding flights through the night so people and packages will be somewhere else in the world tomorrow.

Communications workers in windowless rooms somewhere who are always there whenever you call, controlling the endless flood of sound and pictures from around a world that never stops talking, night and day.

Hospital workers in emergency rooms, in the wards, in kitchens, laundries, boiler rooms—caring for the sick, recovering, and dying, for us.

Transportation workers—cab drivers cruising vacant streets downtown, hunting out the house where a lady wants a ride to the hospital before her baby arrives; bus drivers talking baseball with a lone passenger while waiting for a stop light to change; commuter train crews getting equipment ready for the morning's rush hour; subway attendants swaying warily through the rocketing cars underground.

Street construction crews working in water and mud under an intersection, trying to piece together pipes and wire in time to get the intersection open to morning traffic.

Hotel and restaurant workers polishing, mopping, cleaning equipment, emptying wastebaskets and ashtrays, restocking supplies, shining shoes, vacuuming carpets, taking calls, monitoring halls, baking breakfast rolls, bringing produce in, doing the chores for tonight's guests and tomorrow's diners.

Police and fire department people, always there at any hour; cruising the secret city streets and alleys while the rest of us sleep, snug behind locked doors, security systems glowing, phone and panic button right next to the bed.

Night security guards hustling through shadowy warehouses and parking lots, scanning television monitors in smoky little booths, trotting down hotel corridors, rattling doors, sniffing for smoke, lighting corners, and listening for sounds in the night for all of us.

Military personnel on guard duty in sentry posts under the night sky, buried under the prairie in missile silos, flying night maneuvers, taking a turn as C.Q., or on watch as the ship wallows through the sea.

Morgue and mortuary attendants turning down *The Late, Late Show* or putting aside their schoolwork to answer the telephone, pulling the hearse out onto the dark street, hurrying to gather up the dead before the living rise for their own new day.

Nursing home R.N.s and assistants, gliding down long nighttime corridors in nursing homes to look in on 1.4 million sleepers every night, like mothers watching over their aged children: the parents of America.

Radio and television people on the studio floor or on the air all night, doling out entertainment, cheer, information, companionship; reassuring listeners awake here and there across the sleeping country that they're not alone and that the night will end.

These are just a few of the invisible people who do the jobs we can't or don't want to do for ourselves every night of the year. They keep America running for us while we sleep. Let's pause for a moment and give thanks for them. Imagine what would become of America if all these invisible people suddenly decided to take two weeks off at the same time.

NOTE

1. *Solid Wastes* (New York: Educational Services Department, National Audubon Society.)

Even Our Millionaires Are Egalitarian

America must surely be the only country in the world where even working stiffs like yours truly have a copy of *Forbes'* annual catalog of America's richest people on the living-room cocktail table. We are truly a nation of card-carrying capitalists, whether or not we carry much capital.

So the day the latest millionaire scores came out in mid-1985, it was almost enough to overshadow baseball talk. (In fact, of course, a lot of baseball players had contributed to fattening the census of millionaires, since athletes no longer perform for peanuts and all the chewing tobacco they can stuff in.)

The news that the number of adjusted gross annual incomes of $1 million a year or more in America had doubled between 1980 and 1982 didn't come as an overwhelming surprise.[1] We had already seen Washington's latest official report on American incomes, which showed that those in the top 20% were getting richer and those in the bottom 80% were getting poorer. (The administration was already planning to cut the funds for preparing such reports by the Bureau of the Census in the future.)[2] It was just a little startling, though, to see that the number of million-dollar incomes had increased by over 800% since 1970, when there were a paltry 1,000 in the country.

But when you get into these stratospheric income levels, it's necessary to step back and take a wider perspective before turning green with envy. First: Here at home, our gross national product increased over 300% in those same years; so did our national personal income, which increased 318%.[3] So I guess once your salary gets up over the first half million a year, it can be expected that you'd out perform us average types, plodding along with a 318% increase. Right?

Stepping still farther back to gain further perspective on

the increase of rich and super-rich in America in the most recent decade, let's see how we stood internationally. As economist G. T. Kurian has pointed out,

> The percentage of national income received by the richest 10% presents a reliable index of the concentration of wealth in a country. Even in countries traditionally regarded as bastions of capitalism, this percentage is being whittled down by a combination of political and economic forces.[4]

In a list of 69 nations of the world, including the more developed and less developed, the richest 10% of the population received *most* of all the national income in 1980 in five nations: Zimbabwe, Ecuador, Kenya, Gabon, and Brazil.

In 58 of the 69 countries, the richest 10% of the population received a *fourth* or more of the national income during 1980. America is among those 58 nations. In fact, among the 69 nations, the percentage of our national income garnered by the richest 10% of Americans in 1980 ranked fifty-fifth. The richest received just 26.6% of national income in the United States.[5]

So you see? We have more rich than ever before in America, and most of them have arrived in the past decade. But in terms of world-class rich, we remain egalitarian. The fact that there's this much room at the top suggests that there may be more hope for those of us who are still on our way, even pretty far down. On the other hand, the facts show that even our richest aren't raking in too much of the national income compared to world standards. We are comparatively egalitarian, even among the millionaries, here in America!

There. Doesn't that make you feel better?

NOTES

1. *The Wall Street Journal* (July 24, 1984), p. 1.
2. "Rich Getting Richer," *U.S. News & World Report* (July 22, 1985).
3. *Statistical Abstract of the United States 1985* (Washington, D.C.: U.S. Department of Commerce, Bureau of the Census, 1984), table 717.
4. G. T. Kurian, *The New Book of World Rankings* (New York: Facts On File Publications, 1984), comments on table 67.

5. Data from *World Handbook of Political and Social Indicators* quoted in G. T. Kurian, *The New Book of World Rankings*. It may be of interest to note that the 10 nations with the lowest percentage of national income received by the richest 10% are, in order, Australia (23.7% of national revenue), United Kingdom, Yugoslavia, Norway, Sweden, Poland, Hungary, Bulgaria, Czechoslovakia, and East Germany (16.9%).

V
The Way We Govern Ourselves

★

As the happiness of the people is the sole end of government, so the consent of the people is the only foundation of it, in reason, morality, and the natural fitness of things.

John Adams, proclamation, 1774

Self-criticism is the secret weapon of democracy, and candor and confession are good for the political soul.

Adlai E. Stevenson, speech, July 21, 1952

You Won't Get More for Your Taxes Anywhere Else in the World

★

Does it surprise you to know that two out of three American adults are "fed up with the current tax system"? That's what they told pollster Louis Harris in one recent national survey.[1] It doesn't surprise *me*, either. Ten years ago, two out of three Americans were complaining to a nationwide Gallup poll that "taxes are too high." They were fed up then, too.

One of our most lasting American traditions is that of griping about taxes. We've *always* wanted the tax system changed. Politicians we put into office have spent light-years of clerical time (and even some thought) developing new tax plans for us. Invariably, the only person entirely pleased with the new tax system turns out to be the person proposing it.

One memorable example of this is George Grenville. Remember? He had this great idea to put a stamp tax on things to "secure considerable revenue." That was in 1765, and what he secured instead was the Declaration of Independence and eventually the American Revolution. We took taxation seriously in those days, and some of us still get violent on the subject. Did you know that there were 789 assaults on and threats to IRS people during 1984 alone? Now the IRS marks the taxpayer file of people who have assaulted one of their people, or anyone who "uses weapons or animals to threaten or intimidate an employee or specifically threatens bodily harm" with a little warning code: "PDT" (potentially dangerous taxpayer). If you've earned a PDT, next time you get called in for an audit, an armed agent may sit in on the meeting.[2] That's how "fed up" some taxpayers can get.

Even Thomas Jefferson got fed up with federal financing methods. That was when Alexander Hamilton came up with a new program to handle the federal budget during George

254

Washington's administration. The press labeled it the "Hamiltonian System." One thing it called for was an excise tax on domestic goods, "especially distilled liquor." You can imagine how that went down with taxpayers. Even Thomas Jefferson distilled his own schnapps in those days.

So when Jefferson took over as president, one of the first things he set out to change was federal money management. He was fed up with Hamilton's system. Jefferson wrote a letter to his own secretary of the treasury, Albert Gallatin, telling him what he thought of Hamilton and his system.[3] Parts of the letter sound like he could be griping about our federal finances today:

I think it an object of great importance . . . to simplify our system of finance, and bring it within the comprehension of every member of Congress.

Hamilton set out on a different plan . . . he determined so as to complicate it as that neither the President or Congress should be able to understand it, or to control him. He succeeded in doing this, not only beyond their reach, but so that he at length could not unravel it himself.

He gave to the debt . . . in funding it, the most artificial and mysterious form he could devise . . . the whole system was involved in impenetrable fog, and while he was giving himself the airs of providing for the payment of the debt, he left himself free to add to it continually as he did in fact instead of paying it. . . .

When Jefferson wrote that letter about Hamilton's system for financing the government in 1802, our federal debt was just $80.7 million.[4] That's only about 1/125th of what we all owe today. But, of course, in those early days they were only beginning to learn how to owe millions without tensing up about it.

The fact is, when it comes to taxes, we Americans today don't have all that much to gripe about. For one thing, our personal income has been keeping pace with taxes quite comfortably in recent years. Twelve years ago, the Tax Foundation reported that taxpayers would have to work two hours, 37 minutes each day to earn enough to cover their federal, state, and local taxes.[5] That was for 1974. This past year, in a similar report, the Tax Foundation announced that in order to pay their 1985 tax bills, taxpayers would have to work two hours, 38 minutes a day[6]—just one more minute of work a day than we worked in 1974.

When you stop to think about the fact that the federal debt has gone up roughly $1 trillion just since 1974, working an extra minute a day to help pay it off doesn't seem too much to ask of us, does it?

We can also comfort ourselves on April 15 with the knowledge that the United States still is one of the lowest-taxed nations in the world. We American taxpayers pay out only 29 cents in taxes, at all government levels, for each dollar of our national output. Among 20 other leading industrial nations, only two have lower tax rates than that, based on 1983 tax rates: Japan and Spain.[7]

Percent of Taxes Paid in Comparison to Total National Output*

Sweden	50.6	West Germany	37.3
Denmark	47.2	Finland	37.0
Norway	46.3	Canada	34.8
France	45.4	Greece	32.9†
Netherlands	45.4	Switzerland	32.2
Belgium	45.4†	Portugal	31.2
Austria	42.0	Australia	30.0†
Italy	40.6†	United States	29.0†
Ireland	40.0	Japan	27.7†
Great Britain	38.6	Spain	27.2†

*Tax levies for 1984 at all levels of government, except those marked †, which are 1983.

SOURCE: Basic data from Organization for Economic Cooperation and Development

It should be mentioned that among the 20 major industrial nations listed in this table, only one has *reduced* its tax levies as a share of total output since 1975: the United States. All the other nations are taking bigger tax bites now than in 1975.

"Fiscal Skinny-Dipping" in Sweden

Sweden has the highest proportional tax rate of all 20 nations in our list. But in all fairness to the Swedes, it should be pointed out that Swedish taxpayers swap tax dollars for fantastic social services. They do pay 70% of their income to the government in taxes, according to Per-Martin Meyerson, senior economist for the Federation of Swedish Industries. But in return, the Swedish taxpayers get what they themselves describe as "wall-to-wall social welfare services."[8] A few examples:

In Sweden, everyone receives free health care. Also free education. The state pays parents a basic allowance for each child they have, no matter what the family income may be. (Half an extra allowance is paid for a third child, and a full extra allowance for the fourth. Sweden wants to raise its lagging birthrate.) The state also pays *both* parents to take nine-month maternity/paternity leaves, in order to give their new youngster the best possible start in life. When the parents go back to work, they may get free day care for their child. It should also be mentioned that the Swedish workweek averages only 28.8 hours, lowest in the industrialized world. To rest up from this rigorous schedule, a five-week annual vacation also is mandatory for all workers.[9]

Sounds like your cup of coffee, in spite of the high rate of taxes? Okay, but wait just a minute before you pack for Göteborg or Hälsingborg—while I remind you of the *Taxeringskalender* in Sweden; because if you are squeamish about what might be called "fiscal skinny-dipping," then Sweden definitely is not for you. Since 1914 Swedes have been able to buy an annual copy of the *Taxeringskalender* in much the way we can buy the *Statistical Abstract of the United States*. The difference is that the *Taxeringskalender* lists *private* financial data, for all the world, your neighbors, relatives, fellow workers, friends—and enemies—to see. It lists the gross and taxable income and assets of every qualified citizen in Sweden. The *Taxeringskalender* for your county might include, for example, every individual who earns more than $15,000 a year, plus every couple making $20,000 or more a year, as well as anybody who has $63,000 or more in assets.[10] Doesn't that give you second thoughts about picking up and moving to Sweden?

Wherever you look around the world, the same thing is true about government services that's true about the "free lunch"—there's no such thing as a free public service. And the comparative figures show that for a bearable balance between government benefits and burden of taxes, we can't do any better than where we live right now.

"Loop-Holing" in America

It's true that one can turn temporarily livid while reading about those 40 huge American corporations that made $10 billion in profits in 1984 and not only didn't pay income taxes but even got rebates on what they didn't pay.[11] But disclosures like that are the stuff Congress uses to plug up loopholes in future years. Besides, the more those publicly held corporations take in in profits, the more they pay in dividends. If you are in a pension plan, own a bit of mutual fund stock, or even have life insurance with a cash value, chances are you also gain by those corporate dividends, through investment by your pension fund, mutual fund, or insurance company in common stocks.

We also read about the 30,000 Americans who each took in $250,000 a year or so in income and yet paid less than 5% in taxes.[12] Our first impulse is likely to be (1) writing our congressperson; (2) looking for more loopholes in the law ourselves; or (3) both. But here's another way to look at it:

One fifth of all the tax money the IRS collects from individuals (20%) comes from the 1.04% of Americans earning $100,000 or more a year. And more than half of what the IRS collects from individuals (52%) comes from the 13% of Americans earning over $40,000.[13] It looks to me like most of those upper-income folks must be carrying their full share of the tax load, at least.

Edward A. Filene, who started business as part owner of two little 20-by-20-foot retail stores in Boston, became one of the world's leading merchants. He also became a world leader in the consumer-cooperative and credit-union movements and is remembered for his enlightened and innovative programs of employee and supplier relations. Along the way, Filene also made a lot of money. Asked how he felt about taxes, Filene said this: "Why shouldn't the American people take half my money from me? I took all of it from them!"[14]

I can't help feeling that there's a lot of that spirit among Americans at all income levels. We gripe about the infuriatingly complex system of tax collection in our country. We're "fed up" with all the paper-saving, loophole-searching, and computer correspondence connected with paying our taxes. We've always said we'd like to see the system changed. But when it comes right down to it, I believe that at least 99% of

Americans realize that whatever we shell out for taxes, we couldn't get more or better for our money anywhere else on earth.

NOTES

1. Associated Press, "Tax System, Deficit Vex Most in Poll" (April 5, 1985).
2. "Dangerous Taxpayers Are Identified by a New IRS System," *The Wall Street Journal* (July 24, 1985).
3. Thomas Jefferson, letter to Albert Gallatin (April 1, 1802).
4. *Historical Statistics of the United States*, vol. 1 (Washington, D.C.: U.S. Department of Commerce, Bureau of the Census, 1975), table Y-493.
5. Associated Press (March 18, 1974).
6. "The Tax Tithe," *Forbes* (May 20, 1985).
7. Basic data from Organization for Economic Cooperation and Development quoted in Albert Zanker, "If You Think Your Taxes Are High," *U.S. News & World Report* (September 16, 1985).
8. James M. Perry, "Swedes Ponder Nonsocialist Alternatives," *The Wall Street Journal* (September 10, 1985).
9. *Dow Theory Letters* (January 23, 1985).
10. Laura Saunders, "Royal Swedish Envy," *Forbes* (February 25, 1985).
11. Laurie McGinley, "No U.S. Income Taxes Were Paid in '84 by 40 Big Profitable Firms, Study Says," *The Wall Street Journal* (August 29, 1985).
12. "$1,000,000+ Income—Little Taxes," *USA Today* (August 3, 1985).
13. Basic data from Internal Revenue Service percentages quoted in Leonard Wiener, "Warning! IRS Is Getting Tougher," *U.S. News & World Report* (April 1, 1985).
14. Louis D. Brandeis, "Business Should Seek More Than Profit" in *The World of Business*, vol. 3, ed. Edward C. Bursk, Donald T. Clark, Ralph W. Hidy, Harvard Business School (New York: Simon & Schuster, 1962), pp. 1615–16. The quote from Filene is from *Advertising Age* (August 29, 1985).

More Voters, More Representative Voters, and More Representative Candidates

★

Do you worry about the fact that the percent of eligible voters who turn out in our presidential elections has fallen steadily with every election since 1960? Maybe I should, but I don't.

For one thing, the total number of Americans who do vote has gone up in every presidential election. That's because of population growth, to be sure. But the bottom line is that more Americans stepped into a polling booth, pulled the curtain shut, and expressed their free opinion about who should be president and vice president in 1984 than in any American election. We had the biggest total voting turnout in 1984 ever. That's my "glass half full" way of looking at it. The "glass half empty" view is that more eligible voters stayed home than ever.

But unlike some nations, where you are penalized if you don't vote, one of our freedoms in this democracy is the freedom *not* to vote. If people really feel, "My vote doesn't count, anyway," how valid would their vote become if they were forced to vote? I personally believe in quality of citizen participation as well as in quantity. And so I give more weight to the vote cast by a citizen who is informed and concerned enough to travel to the polls than to any votes not cast.

Voters today are more representative than ever. Voters come from a broader representation of the American electorate than they used to, even a generation ago. Most Americans didn't get a chance to vote until this century.

• Blacks couldn't vote until the 15th Amendment in 1870. After that, hundreds of thousands of both black and white Americans were still denied the right until the Voting Rights acts of 1957 and of 1965.

260

• Women couldn't vote in most states until 1920, even though there were 31 million of them aged 20 or older in the country—nearly as many as there were men.

• Native Americans couldn't vote in some states until 1948.

• 18-to-21-year-olds couldn't vote until 1971 (when there were 10 million of them) and the 26th Amendment.

So the people who do go to the polls in America today are more truly a representative cross section of our people than they used to be.

The candidates are more representative, too. We have had a revolutionary change, a great and wholesome broadening of our selection of candidates, even in the past decade or so. In a country where almost all elected officials used to be (1) male and (2) white, just look at what has been happening:

• More blacks in office. In January 1984 we had 5,654 black elected officials in America—almost two thirds more than in 1975. We had 396 blacks in the U.S. and state legislatures—a third more than in 1975. [1]

• More women in office. In August 1982 we had 16,881 women elected officials in America—more than twice as many as in 1975. [2] We had 934 women holding U.S. and state legislative office—roughly a third more than in 1975. [3] In fact, the Democratic woman candidate for vice president and her running mate got almost 1 million more votes in 1984 (36.45 million) than the male Democratic candidates got just four years earlier in the 1980 election (35.48 million). [4]

And the candidates' views are as varied as ever. Thank heavens there still are at least as many Americans as ever who have the commitment, stamina, time—yes, and money—to run for elective offices at all levels of government. Over half a million of these hardy souls are in public office today because they ran to get in. And many more than half a million also are running—hoping to take the office holders' places.

Even the most exalted of all elected offices is up for grabs every four years in this no-holds-barred competitive process. We see the televised debates for the presidency between the leading contenders. We even see the preliminary bouts among primary candidates on their way up to the conventions. But behind all that in the 1984 campaign, did you know that some 200 different citizens filed with the Federal Elections Commission to run for president in 1984? They represented just about every shade of political coloration under the sun, and they *all* got at least some votes, from someone. For instance, there were:

• A Libertarian candidate, the fourth in as many elections. In 1980 the Libertarian candidate got over 900,000 votes for president; in 1984, just 228,000.

• A Citizens Party candidate, the first third-party candidate in the election to receive government funding, and the only feminist candidate for president, got 72,153.

• A Labor Party candidate, making his third try for the presidency.

• A U.S. Communist Party candidate, running for the fourth time. He was the one candidate not required to file a list of his campaign contributors with the FEC, even if he received more than $5,000. The U.S. Supreme Court ruled in 1983 that such listing would subject his supporters to harassment and violate their First Amendment rights. He wound up with 35,561 votes in 1984.

• A Populist Party candidate, who got 62,371 votes.

• A Prohibition Party candidate.

This is just a sampling from the field of some 200, but you see what a smorgasbord of candidates voters could choose from if they just went to the polls in 1984. In spite of that, in Nevada, where voters were given the option to vote for "none of the above" for president, 3,950 voters did just that.

Sure, I'd like to see a higher percent of registered voters get really serious about issues and candidates and go out and caucus, ring doorbells for candidates, poll-watch, and vote in elections. I also worry about people picking candidates the way they pick a soft drink—by choosing the one with the sweetest commercials. But to come right down to it, I'm willing to settle for the widest possible representation—a true All-American range of voters and candidates, and a growing number of voters each election who make up their minds firmly enough about what they believe to go all the way to school or firehouse and vote, not only on presidential election day but on local issues as well. As long as that combination holds up, I think democracy will, too.

What's *your* vote on this?

NOTES

1. *Statistical Abstract of the United States 1985* (Washington, D.C.: U.S. Department of Commerce, Bureau of the Census, 1984), table 418.
2. Ibid., table 420.
3. Ibid., table 413.
4. Ibid., table 401.

We Have More Free Media Than Most of Us Even Use

★

We have more free media, more availability of ideas and information in America than exist in any other country in the world—more than most of us are aware of, or even care to exercise. We simply don't know "how good we have it."

David P. Shipler lived in the Soviet Union between 1977 and 1979 as bureau chief for *The New York Times*. He suggested, "We are bathed in information until we no longer feel its force":

> A Catholic priest in Lithuania told me that he had once visited America and was shocked. In New York subways people read and read the huge, great newspaper *The New York Times*, and then threw it away. *Threw it away*. All that precious information, just scattered in the subways, left on seats, dumped in trash barrels. If just one copy got into the Soviet Union, he said, it would be passed through hundreds of hands until it had disintegrated.[1]

We take our great wealth of free information for granted. We assume that it is there for us 24 hours a day, like water waiting in our bathroom taps. And we assume that it will always be there. For that very reason, our freedom of access to ideas and information always is in jeopardy. Of 69 decisions put before the Supreme Court of the United States to decide during 1985, a total of 14 involved some kind of possible change in our rights as Americans under the First Amendment to the Constitution. This single sentence in our Constitution can make the difference between the freedoms we enjoy and the kind of government oppression people labor under in the USSR and other totalitarian nations:

Congress shall make no law respecting an establishment of religion, or prohibiting the free exercise thereof; or abridging the freedom of speech, or of the press; or the right of the people peaceably to assemble, and to petition the Government for a redress of grievances.

A lawyer who specializes in issues involving freedom of the press, Floyd Abrams, called those 14 cases going to the Supreme Court in 1985 "an extraordinary array." Each and every one involved each and every one of us. Our freedom to *know* was being weighed in the balance.

The worst part of it is that you can lose your freedom to know without knowing it. People in countries where the media are muzzled have no way to know what is being hidden from them. Even editors who feel "free" in many countries don't have access to the news. If they do, they dare not publish it.

The editor of a major progovernment newspaper in Egypt, where there is more press freedom than in any other Arab nation, said that compared to conditions during previous regimes in his country, now "The party papers are free. They have no censor." When Gamal Abdel Nasser's government was in power, newspapers were nationalized, and "when Nasser did not like what you wrote he would hang you. When Sadat did not like what you wrote he would dismiss you." Today there is "no censorship," but:

. . . it is the government that appoints the editor in chief and can dismiss him. Some have courage, some are afraid. But overall, the loyalty of the editor in chief is not to the people; it is to the government. . . . It picks an editor without any discussion with the newspaper's staff. Sometimes we like the choice; sometimes not. But we have to accept it.[2]

Where the editor is told what to write, how can the reader know what he is missing? This is why freedom of the press is so fragile. It can be taken from you while your back is turned, and once gone, you have no way to know how much is being taken.

Even in Great Britain today the freedom of a proud press is under siege. In a major speech at the 1985 conference of the International Press Institute, the editor of the independent weekly *Observer* of London reported "a hardening of political and judicial attitudes toward the press . . . mostly a result of the barely perceptible accretion of case law, the slow creep of bureaucratic regulations. . . ."[3]

Later in 1985, the *Observer* reported, "Hiring and promotion of British Broadcasting Corp. staff is secretly controlled by M15, Britain's domestic-security service" and that a five-person department "to liase with M15" was operating at the BBC's headquarters, "monitoring personnel decisions" and was "headed by a former army-intelligence officer."[4] In our country, this would be like having the headquarters of National Public Television taking its daily direction from the FBI.

The BBC's external radio services go out in 37 languages to 125 million people outside Britain. That makes a lot of people in a lot of places around the world whose news is being "adjusted" to fit whatever the five persons "liasing" with M15 think they ought to know. How will they ever know what they are missing?

Even the Unfit News Is Fit

What we get in America (if I may borrow *The New York Times*'s motto for a moment) is not only "all the news that's fit to print" but also a lot of stuff that most of us reject at first sight as *unfit*. That's as it should and must be if full freedom is to prevail. For one famous example, take the case of *Near v. Minnesota* (1931):

Jay M. Near and Howard Guilford were publishers of *The Saturday Press*, a Minneapolis weekly newspaper. The two men were "self-admitted scandalmongers and occasional blackmailers," according to First Amendment historian Fred Friendly. In a series of articles, *The Saturday Press* charged that Jewish gangsters were behind gambling, racketeering, and bootlegging in Minneapolis. ("Practically every vendor of vile hooch, every owner of a moonshine still, every snake-faced gangster and embryonic egg in the Twin Cities is a JEW. . . .")[5]

A district court and then the state's highest court decided that *The Saturday Press* could be ordered not to "produce, edit, publish . . . sell or give away" its paper, under the provisions of a so-called 1925 Minnesota Gag Law designed to protect people against "public nuisance."

The Saturday Press case finally wound up in the U.S. Supreme Court. There Justice Louis Brandeis, the first Jew to sit on the Court, questioned the legality of the Minnesota law on the ground that it threatened our freedom of the press. In the majority opinion of the court, Chief Justice Charles Evans Hughes quoted the great English jurist Sir William Blackstone:

> The liberty of the press is indeed essential to the nature of a free state; but this consists in laying no *previous* restraints upon publications, and not in freedom from censure for criminal matter when published.

In other words, let the publisher be free to print whatever he will, however "unfit to print" it may seem to people who read it. But once he prints it, let him be open to suit on the grounds of whether it's true or not.

That's the spirit of America's free media today. We saw it in 1971 in the "Pentagon Papers case," *The New York Times Company v. United States*, when the U.S. Supreme Court told *The Times* and the *Washington Post* that they could publish the highly controversial and sensitive papers because (as Justice Hugo Black and Justice William O. Douglas noted) in the First Amendment,

> the Government's power to censor the press was abolished so that the press would remain forever free to censure the Government. The press was protected so that it could bare the secrets of Government and inform the people.[6]

We have seen this same spirit again recently in press revelations of waste and corruption in military spending, and in cleaning up hazardous-waste sites around the country. We must see it in the future. The freedom of the press includes the obligation and freedom to tell us things some people—maybe even most people—don't want us to hear.

Which Way Does News Slant?

People have always been angry about the press. Thomas Jefferson often was infuriated by the vituperative editors of his day. Jefferson wrote a lengthy letter to his friend John

Norvell, letting off steam about the press: "Nothing can now be believed which is seen in a newspaper," he wrote. "Truth itself becomes suspicious by being put into that polluted vehicle."[7] Even so, it's on record that Jefferson spent a sizable amount of money each year for newspaper subscriptions. He didn't want to miss anything, and besides, he liked to read the ads.

Today people still doubt the truthfulness of the media. In a television discussion of possible "bias" in CBS television news, Norman Podhoretz, a magazine publisher, noted that "most people who charge bias say it's a matter of liberal ideas, attitudes. I think there's a certain truth in this. . . ." However, far from charging *false* reporting, what bothered Podhoretz was "a kind of mindless neutralism" in reporting the "Soviet-American conflict."[8] Podhoretz wasn't saying the media were *slanted*. What bothered him was that they weren't slanted in *his* direction!

Another media-doubter, a congressman, said of CBS News that *he* felt "its coverage of Vietnam leaned disproportionately toward critics of our policy." Again, someone would prefer that the media "lean" in the direction he favors. In the same interview, Don Hewitt, an executive producer at CBS, said on the lean-slant-tilt subject:

> The left think we're right, and the right think we're left. The National Council of Churches thinks we're a bunch of fascists, and the National Rifle Association thinks we're all a bunch of Communists. We like it that way.[9]

Then Hewitt added another thought:

> Being believed is quite another matter. If we're not believed, why are the networks doing so well? The highest-rated show in television which gets a blockbuster 60 percent share of the audience every night, is a show called "the Evening News. . . ." If so many people are turned off, how come so many people are tuned in?

Why Not Turn Around?

Personally, I don't worry about the media so much as I worry about *us*. The media are doing only what they have always done, and doing it even better today than in the past.

A national survey sponsored by the American Society of Newspaper Editors in 1985 found that three out of four Americans questioned the credibility of newspapers and television news. A fifth of them distrusted the media deeply, in part because they think the press is "arrogant, and more sympathetic to the rich than to ordinary people."[10] Considering the fact that the poll was taken just after a national political campaign in which the press was constantly charged with inaccuracy and bias by the winning candidate, and that historic libel suits of General William Westmoreland against CBS, and former Israeli Defense Minister Ariel Sharon against *Time* magazine had also been going on, it seems remarkable that even *one* in four Americans believed in the truthfulness of the press in 1985. By dutifully reporting all the bad news *about* the press, the press had been shaking people's faith in the press itself!

An earlier national survey taken in 1985 found that 58% of Americans considered network TV news "neutral and objective." While 22% felt it "tilted" left, another 10% felt it "tilted" right! So, as someone has said, "there you go again"; tilt is in the eye of the beholder. All three major noncable networks received almost identical approval ratings from viewers, with seven in 10 at least "moderately favorable" toward each network.[11]

The question raised by Don Hewitt remains: "If so many are turned off" on the print and broadcast news media, "how come so many people are tuned in?" Is it because they are too lazy to take the trouble to change the source of their news? To switch channels for the evening news, for example? Are they *forced* to sit in front of the screen and watch the same news, or sit at the breakfast table and read the same news every day? They are not. Not in America.

We Americans have the widest, richest choice of media in the world. We have just under 1,700 daily newspapers, of every political persuasion, read daily by two out of three adults.[12] (On the editorial pages of our Phoenix daily papers a dozen or more columnists are rotated regularly. They represent just about every viewpoint, from leftish liberal to ultra-conservative. I try to force myself to read even those I disagree with most violently occasionally, even if it does threaten my breakfast.) America's newspapers include at least a few world-class national dailies—*The New York Times*, *The Wall Street Journal*, the *Christian Science Monitor*, and the innovative new *U.S.A. Today*. If you don't like your local paper, or if you simply want a contrasting approach to the news, you can get any of these national dailies home-delivered, right in your mailbox.

We have over 1,100 television stations in America today, nearly twice as many as in 1965.[13] There are over 6,000 cable television systems—almost five times as many as in 1965—with 30 million subscribers.[14] There are over 4,700 AM radio stations, more than twice as many as in 1965.[15] Public television has grown from just 115 stations nationally in 1966 to nearly 300, broadcasting an average of 104 hours a week.[16]

There are more than 11,000 different magazines and periodicals published in America today—over 2,000 more than in 1965.[17] A lot of those are highly specialized publications, of course. But if you want to counterbalance any bias you sense in your regular news source, or if you want to know more about what is going on in the world, there are at least 40 national magazines of politics and world affairs to pile up on your coffee table. They range politically from far left to far right, with every shading between.

Where else in the world could you find *The Nation, The Guardian, In These Times, The Progressive, Nuclear Times, The Freeman,* and *The New Socialist* selling side-by-side on the same newsstand with *The New Republic, National Review, Inquiry, Public Opinion, Review of the News,* the *Conservative Digest,* and the *Conservative Register?* Where else could you find them in your public library?

Where else in the world could you tune in 24 hours a day to watch lengthy, unedited proceedings of Congress on cable TV? You can, on C-Span cable TV network, now reaching over 20 million viewers across America. This free-enterprising network operates without either federal sponsorship, protection, or subsidies. It lets us sit in on Congress, important meetings in Washington, and public-issue call-in shows without leaving home.[18]

Where else could you subscribe to the weekly newspaper of Congress (*Roll Call*) and the *Washington Monthly* to maintain an insider's view of your government's carryings-on? Where else would the nation's top executive stand in front of reporters, television cameras, and microphones for a wide-open press conference?

Where else could you subscribe to a new regular issue of *Pravda* in English, or a monthly digest of news and commentary reprinted from all of the world's leading newspapers in English—as you can in *World Press Review*? *Where else* can you listen to any of the world's shortwave radio newscasts without jamming by your government? And where else does a citizen have a Freedom of Information Act that gives her or him a key to much of the information held by the federal agencies—what they have on file about you, for example?

Where else can you watch and hear leaders in government and critics of government being questioned by the press in the kind of open give-and-take of opinions and ideas we enjoy on *Meet the Press, Washington Week in Review, 60 Minutes, Issues and Answers, Face the Nation,* and other free-swinging shows?

Nowhere else in the world could you have so much news and information delivered to your home without censorship, with such diversity and frequency. The record shows that we Americans spend an almost unbelievable amount of time with various media: Most of our media time goes to television (252 minutes a day) and radio (124 minutes), with newspapers (31 minutes) and magazines (15 minutes) taking less than an hour a day. But put it all together and we spend over seven hours a day (more than some of us sleep) among the media.[19]

And yet the record also suggests that most of us take all or most of our network television news from the same source every day. During 1985, three out of 10 adult Americans didn't even know enough about NBC News and ABC News anchor people to rate them for a national survey. Americans slip into the same comfortable network news every night like a pair of old slippers. As for Public Television evening newscasters, seven in 10 Americans hadn't seen them often enough to know if they do a good job of presenting the news or not.

Actually, the *MacNeil/Lehrer News Hour* on public television is far and away the most complete news presentation on the air. Theirs is the only daily newscast where the biggest news issues are not only reported, but also debated and discussed at length by top national authorities who represent differing viewpoints on the same issue. It's the most searching, thorough, and authoritative broadcast of national and international news available each evening of the week. Unfortunately, most Americans don't even bother to try it on for size. Similarly, Public Radio's *Morning Edition* of the news, and *All Things Considered* deliver the most complete national and international news on radio—a fact most Americans probably don't even know, since the buttons on their car radios are set for their "old familiars."

"One who reads only his local paper will, in all probability, grow up without an understanding of the present-day world," said former U.S. Supreme Court Justice William O. Douglas. He worried that the press, radio and television tended "to skip the controversial or touch it only lightly," leaving us uninformed in depth.[20] But the fact is, the press is *not* failing to deliver the news in depth to any American willing to take the trouble to reach out for it. No other people on earth have free access to more news and information; no other people have more varied and uncensored sources of news and information. The trouble is, most of us don't use the media as fully as we should. The *danger* is, if we don't use them fully, we may lose our freedom.

Efforts to Shut Off Information

The Reporters Committee for Freedom of the Press, a news media legal-defense and research group, listed 51 different attempts by government officials or agencies to "intrude on editorial freedom and restrict access to information by the public and the news media" between March 1981 and January 1985.[21] The group also listed congressional legislation that had been introduced that could shut off access to information about our government. In addition, an administrative proposal during 1985 placed authority over all federal agency information-gathering efforts under the authority of the Office of Management and Budget! One of our government's traditional responsibilities has been to collect, compile, and disseminate information to its citizens. But under this new arrangement, the OMB can arbitrarily restrict or even cut off funds for making vital information, such as labor and health statistics, housing data, economic and trade figures, and environmental reports available to the public. Thus the power of government officials to classify information, cut back on the collection of statistics, and end many government publications was strengthened.

All these moves by government politicians to reduce available information may serve *their* purposes, but they don't serve our purposes, as citizens. Such moves threaten our rights to know what is going on in our government. "How the government should be run is the people's business," said Justice Douglas.[22] It's the business of the press to bring us enough facts so we can make up our own minds about how the government is handling our business. Our responsibility is to take the time and trouble to seek out and weigh the facts, then use them to change the government if it is not serving us.

American history is full of instances when the electorate acted on the basis of its information to change the course of government. When Congress passed the Sedition Act of 1798, early in our history, one section of the act made it punishable by fine or imprisonment to speak or write against president or congress "with the intent to defame" or to bring them "into contempt or disrepute." The act was wrongly administered and became a tool for putting down political opposition. Several outspoken citizens were arrested and sent to jail under the act, including one member of Congress and several Republican editors.

Thomas Jefferson (who was often so scornful of the newspapers and editors) was appalled by the act. He and James Madison both considered it an open threat to freedom of speech and the press. Jefferson spoke out against it and declared himself "for freedom of the press, and against all violations of the constitution to silence by force and not by reason the complaints or criticisms, just or unjust, of our citizens against the conduct of our agents."[23] Two years later, Jefferson was president. One of his first acts was to free those who had been jailed under the act.

The relationship between the press and those in power in our country has *always* been an adversarial one. In 1936, newspaper opposition to Franklin Roosevelt was carried on by 85% of the nation's press. He never tried to muzzle the editors. In 1964, when Lyndon Johnson was elected president with the biggest popular margin in history, and in 1967, when only 36% of Americans supported his handling of the presidency and when the country's most powerful newspapers, *Life, Look, Time, Newsweek*, CBS, and NBC all turned against his administration's policies, he never tried to muzzle the press, although he certainly made every effort to influence them.[24]

Pull and tug between those in power in our government and the press is integral to the working of democracy. When one factor begins to apply too much pressure in our system of balance of powers, others shift to offset it. So we still hold on to the freedoms other Americans won for us over 200 years ago, because we have access to the facts through free media. The American electorate has a kind of collective common sense about government. We have elected great presidents, very mediocre presidents, and even potentially dangerous presidents, but with our free access to information, we correct our errors as we go along.

This is why we must continue to demand the most complete and honest news in the world from our media, even when it is painful and upsetting. We enjoy the fullest freedom of speech and press in the world today. But unless we *use* it, history warns us that we'll lose it.

NOTES

1. David K. Shipler, *Russia: Broken Idols, Solemn Dreams* (New York: Penguin Books, 1984), p. 295.
2. Mustapha Amin, "Egypt's Progress," *World Press Review* (May 1985).
3. "Varieties of Censorship," *World Press Review*, May, 1985.
4. "Autonomy of BBC under Fire," United Press International, August 18, 1985.
5. Nat Hentoff, *The First Freedom: The Tumultuous History of Free Speech in America* (New York: Delacorte Press, 1980), p. 188.
6. Neil Sheehan, Hedrick Smith, E. W. Kenworthy, and Fox Butterfield, *The Pentagon Papers, as Published by The New York Times* (New York: Bantam Books, 1971), p. 663.
7. Thomas Jefferson, letter to John Norvell (June 11, 1807), quoted in *Versions of Censorship,* ed. John McCormick and Mairi MacInnes (Chicago: Aldine Publishing Company, 1962), p. 129.
8. *The MacNeil/Lehrer News Hour* (April 18, 1985), Transcript 2494, p. 8.
9. "Does Television News Tilt to the Left?," *U.S. News & World Report* (May 13, 1985).
10. "75% in Survey Doubt Credibility of Newspaper and TV Reports," *Washington Post* news service (April 15, 1985).
11. Roper Poll basic data quoted in William L. Chaze with Daniel Collins and Ron Scherer, "What America Thinks of TV," *U.S. News & World Report* (May 13, 1985).
12. 1984 American Newspaper Publishers Association (ANPA) survey (reported May 2, 1985).
13. *Statistical Abstract of the United States 1985* (Washington, D.C.: U.S. Department of Commerce, Bureau of the Census, 1984), table 924.

14. Ibid., data on cable TV from *Television & Cable Factbook*, Television Digest, Inc.

15. Ibid.

16. *Ayer's Directory of Publications* data quoted in Belinda Hulin-Salkin, "Viewing the Future in a New Light," *Advertising Age* (October 3, 1985).

17. Ibid.

18. John Herbers, "The World According to C-Span," *The New York Times* (August 13, 1985).

19. R. H. Bruskin Associates survey data reported in *The Wall Street Journal* (April 19, 1985).

20. William O. Douglas, *Freedom of the Mind* (Garden City, N.Y.: Doubleday & Company, 1964), p. 7.

21. "Reporters Group Assails Media Curbs," *The Wall Street Journal* (March 15, 1985).

22. Douglas, op. cit., p. 8.

23. *Thomas Jefferson: A Biography in His Own Words* (New York: Newsweek Books, 1974), vol. 2, p. 292.

24. Doris Kearns, *Lyndon Johnson and the American Dream* (New York: Harper & Row, 1976), pp. 223–24, 336.

A Day in Court if We Need It

★

"The trouble with lawyers is, they breed too fast," a friend complained, "and the same is true for legislation. One law leads to another. We're becoming a litigious society."

That could be. We had just 273,000 lawyers nationally in 1970. A decade later, suddenly there were 502,000.[1] One lawyer for each 485 adults in 1970; one for each 318 in 1980. While one lawyer for 318 people may not seem too much, *two* lawyers for 636 may generate a lot of action in court.

But now let's look at the bright side. If your government hassles you unfairly, you get yourself a lawyer and take your case to court. In fact, you can take it from court to court, up the legal ladder to the very top—the Supreme Court of the United States. There any American citizen has a right at least to seek to have his or her day in court. And many of us do just that, every year. Since 1980 the Supreme Court has had a little over 5,000 cases on its docket each year,[2] nearly half of them "pauper cases" sent there by people who couldn't afford to retain their own lawyers to plead for them at the Supreme Court level and needed court-appointed counsel.

The other U.S. courts across the land—U.S. courts of appeals, and U.S. district courts—average well over 325,000 cases on their dockets.[3] A lot of action, indeed.

But what if you didn't have this great legal apparatus available to you as a citizen? I'm not talking about life in a dictatorship, now. What if you were a citizen in the home of the Magna Carta, Great Britain, and the government tramped on your rights unfairly? Would you go to Her Majesty's courts to have your rights protected, the way we do here?

You would not. We Americans have "unalienable rights" all set out for us in black and white as part of the highest law of the land, the U.S. Constitution. Britons have no such statement of their rights. They have no written constitution, no guarantee of the rights of ordinary folks like us against any act of Parliament. In Britain, Parliament has absolute power. What they say, for right or wrong, is law.

In Britain you can petition for your rights, but no court in the land will hear your case. You'll have to take your petition to the European Court of Human Rights, in Strasbourg, France. There the judges (many of whom don't speak English) will hear your case and deliver an opinion. But even if the court in Strasbourg decides in your favor, Parliament may choose to ignore its judgment. You'll be left "across the Channel with no paddle."

Now, how does that make you feel about an oversupply of lawyers and courts in our country? I'll tell you how it makes me feel: like taking a lawyer to lunch!

NOTES

1. *Statistical Abstract of the United States 1985* (Washington, D.C.: U.S. Department of Commerce, Bureau of the Census, 1984), table 673.
2. Ibid., table 302.
3. Ibid., tables 303–5.

Freedom of Religion—or No Religion

★

We've all seen pictures of our Pilgrim forefathers and foremothers trudging through the snow on their way to worship, presumably at "the church or synagogue of their choice." They were staunch believers. They had come to these strange shores in search of religious freedom after having been persecuted in Europe. But they *didn't* bring religious tolerance with them.

The Puritans' Massachusetts Bay colony was an ironbound theocracy. Either you worshiped their way, or else. The Puritans ran both church and government, and they tolerated no deviations from their own belief. The Quakers in the colony were denounced as "madmen, lunatics, demoniacs,"[1] and in 1658 the United Colonies recommended that Quakers and all heretics were to be banished from each of the colonies "under pain of death, and if afterwards they presume to come again . . . then to be put to death as presumptuously incorrigible." The beliefs of both Quakers and Catholics were banned in Massachusetts Colony as "damnable heresies." And for several generations after the Pilgrims landed at Plymouth there was probably about as much religious freedom in America as there is today in Iran.

In Maryland there was a substantial Protestant population, although it had originally been planned as a Catholic colony. The 1649 Toleration Act in Maryland sounded tolerant enough; it stated that no professed Christian should "be anyways troubled molested or discountenanced . . . for his or her religion, not in the free exercise thereof . . . nor any way compelled to the belief or exercise of any other Religion against his or her consent." However, anyone who denied the Trinity or the divinity of Christ in Maryland was to be hanged.

Anyone who insulted the Blessed Virgin, the Apostles, or the Evangelists should be fined or whipped.[2]

In Virginia, Quakers were banished, Catholics forbidden to hold public office, and

> every person in the colony, or who should come into it, was required to repair to the Minister for examination in the faith. If he should be unsound, he was to be instructed. If any refused to go to the Minister, he should be whipt; on the second refusal he should be whipt twice and compelled to "acknowledge his fault on Sabbath day in the assembly of the congregation"; for the third refusal he should be "whipt every day until he makes acknowledgement."[3]

In Pennsylvania, William Penn, who had been thrown into prison in England for his Quaker beliefs, designed a "Frame of Government" in 1683. It specified that anyone who believed in "One Almighty God" could worship as he liked. However, you couldn't hold civil office unless you believed in "Jesus Christ, the Saviour of the World"—which didn't leave a lot of choice for Jews or agnostics, much less atheists.

Rhode Island was one of the most tolerant colonies. The 1663 charter specified that no person in the colony should "be in any way molested, punished, disquieted, or called in question for any difference of opinion in matters of religion." Every person was permitted to "freely and fully have and enjoy his . . . own judgments and consciences, in matters of religious concernments." However, by 1762, when two Jews applied for naturalization in Rhode Island, they were turned away. The court decided that giving Jews full citizenship in the community would be "inconsistent with the first principles on which the colony was founded."

So much for religious freedom in the early American Colonies.

The men who drafted and debated the Constitution of the United States, beginning at the federal convention of 1787 in Philadelphia, were well aware of our history of American religious intolerance up to then. They knew their history and knew it well. Two were college presidents; three were, or had been, college professors; and more than half (26) were college graduates, in an era when very few men ever saw the inside of a college. Not only did they know the history, they also had practical experience with government. Twenty-eight of the 55 drafters of the Constitution had served in Congress, and most of the others had been in legislatures. They knew the good and the bad that governments are capable of, the strengths and the weaknesses of power.

The men who drafted and debated our Constitution were also church members. Most belonged to one of the traditional churches in their part of the country. There were Congregationalists and Presbyterians from new England; Episcopalians from the South; a range of beliefs, from Quaker to Catholic, among delegates from the middle states.

And yet the original draft of the Constitution had not one reference to God, or to religious freedom.[4] The Bill of Rights, with its specific pledge right up front, "Congress shall make no law respecting an establishment of religion, or prohibiting the free exercise thereof . . . ," was not written until *after* the Constitution went to the states for debate and ratification. Why was there no mention of religion in the original draft of our Constitution? No Bill of Rights?

The distinguished historian Samuel Eliot Morison suggests simply that it was because "the Constitution set forth limited and specific powers for which no bill of rights was logically necessary," and moreover, it was "mostly because members were worn out and wanted to go home when they got around to the subject."[5] After all, they had spent all summer, with no air conditioning, debating and drafting the Constitution in Philadelphia.

During the 10 months between September 1787, when the exhausted drafters finally signed their original document around the big table in Independence Hall (and then "adjourned to the City Tavern, dined together, and took cordial leave of each other") and July 26, 1788, when it was finally ratified by all the states, the Constitution was debated, word by word and thought by thought, "all across the map of America." One question was raised in each state: "Should it not have a bill of rights?"

The drafters of the Constitution, sophisticated men, learned men, men of a "highly rationalist and even secular . . . spirit," men who—most of them—"could take their religion or leave it alone,"[6] in spite of their nominal church attendance, had been inclined to *assume*, in their century of the Enlightenment, the natural rights of men, including the right of freedom of religious belief. They didn't think such things had to be spelled out.

But the people of the colonies were not prepared to take such precious rights for granted. They knew how political power can corrupt people and governments. And they wanted their freedoms as citizens of the new nation to be set down in writing, "chapter and verse."

So, as it turned out, the single most significant action of the first session of the first Congress was to respond to the urging of the people by approving the Bill of Rights. Even to James Madison, who drafted it (as he had much of the Constitution), the Bill of Rights was something of an afterthought. But in response to demands from what he called "the interested majorities of the people" and arguments in favor of a bill of rights coming to him from Thomas Jefferson (who had been in Europe during the early stages of the French Revolution and fully believed the need for "sovereign guarantees" of the people's personal liberties), Madison set down the words that ever since have stood at the very beginning of our most basic American laws:

> Congress shall make no law respecting an establishment of religion, or prohibiting the free exercise thereof; or abridging the freedom of speech, or of the press; or the right of the people peaceably to assemble, and to petition the Government for a redress of grievances.

This is why we have all the hassle about whether kids will pray out loud, silently, or not at all in public schools. All that hue and cry that we've been hearing about "separation of church and state" is as American in spirit and as vital as the Constitution itself. It is a continuation of the argument that swept all across the 13 little original states before they even became the United States of America. It continues to be a sign of just how seriously we value our own religious freedom, and how determined we are that no government official in his temporary seat of power will lay a bureaucratic hand on it.

A World of Religious Persecution

Half a billion or more people in our world today are living in nations where active religious persecution is part of gov-

ernment policy. They are a reminder of what can happen if
government steps across the line to control religious beliefs:

The government of South Africa imprisoned Jehovah's
Witnesses because they are conscientious objectors to military service. Children of Jehovah's Witnesses are expelled
from school because their religious convictions do not permit
saluting the flag and singing the national anthem. Jehovah's
Witnesses have lived in Africa since the beginning of this
century; about an eighth of all Jehovah's Witnesses in the
world now live in Africa, but they are persecuted there for
their religious beliefs by several African nations. The government of Cameroon has banned Jehovah's Witnesses since
1970. The governments of Ethiopia, Tanzania, and Zaire have
made the religion illegal. The government of Mozambique
has suppressed Jehovah's Witnesses, along with many other
religious groups. The government of Malawi has made it
illegal to hire Witnesses and gives orders that Witnesses living
in the villages should be "chased away" from their homes;
homes of Witnesses have been burned, Witnesses lynched.
The Zambian government drove some 20 thousand Malawi
Witnesses who crossed its border for sanctuary "back into the
fire" in Malawi, where they were further persecuted.

The government of the People's Republic of China has
discouraged practice of the Tibetan Buddhist religion since
taking over Tibet in 1950. About a fourth of all Tibetans were
Buddhists, since the religion has flourished there since the
seventh century. Chinese Communists directed the destruction of Buddhist monuments in Tibet, and Tibetans are no
longer permitted to ask blessings for the sick, solicit contributions for religious purposes, or take children to religious
services.

The government of Iran has officially designated members
of the peaceful Bahai faith as "corruption on earth," taken
over their shrines, and confiscated the savings and pensions
of some 15,000 Bahais. Many Bahais have been killed or
imprisoned.

The government of the USSR allows only a few "authorized"
churches and hand-picks their clergy. Some 10,000 Russian
Orthodox churches and about half of all Baptist churches in
the USSR were closed during the 1960s and remain closed.
Moscow, with half a million Jews, is allowed only one synagogue, and Jews are no longer permitted to study Hebrew.

The governments of many Latin American countries have

taken steps to muzzle the clergy and control churches in recent years. In Cuba the government has closed all Christian schools, and religious services have been forbidden since 1959.

A World of Religious Freedom

Meanwhile, here in America 14 million adults and children freely practice their faiths as members of some 219 different denominations, including Primitive Advent Christians, Bahais, Old German Baptist Brethren, Christadelphians, Buddhists, Christian Scientists, Albanian Orthodox, Jehovah's Witnesses, Bickertonites, Latvian Evangelical Lutherans, Mennonites, Fundamental Methodists, New Apostolics, Pentecostal Free-Will Baptists, Schwenkfelders, Spiritualists, Swedenborgians, Muslims, Vedantists, Social Brethren, Friends, Grace Gospelites, and Sikhs, as well as all the major denominations, all worshiping in their own ways—not without argument and disagreement, but certainly without bloodshed or government interference.

There is no other country on earth where so many members of so many and so varied religions live and worship side by side in peace.

"As to religion," Tom Paine wrote in 1776, "I hold it to be the indispensable duty of all government to protect all conscientious professors thereof, and I know no other business which government hath to do therewith."[7]

That's the spirit that's kept us free to worship as and if we please.

NOTES

1. George F. Willison, *Saints and Strangers* (New York: Reynal & Hitchcock, 1945), p. 376.
2. Samuel Eliot Morison, *The Oxford History of the American People* (New York: Oxford University Press, 1965), pp. 84–85.
3. Leo Pfeffer in *Religious Freedom* (Skopie, Ill.: National Textbook Company, 1977), quotes "Lawes Divine, Moral and Martial" adopted by Virginia in 1614.
4. Nat Hentoff, *The First Freedom: The Tumultuous History of Free Speech in America* (New York: Delacorte Press 1980), p. 164.
5. Morison, op. cit., p. 314.
6. Clinton Rossiter, *1787: The Grand Convention* (New York: New American Library, 1968), p. 126.
7. Thomas Paine, *Common Sense* (1776).

We Keep Our Native Terrorists in Check

★

"We're lucky in this country," murmured a cocktail-party guest, reaching for another appetizer. "We don't have the sort of terrorism they have over *there* . . . bombing, hostages—all that violence. . . ."

Wrong. "Violence . . . is as American as cherry pie," as one militant American radical of the 1960s put it.[1] We do have active terrorist groups in America. We've had armed terrorist groups here for well over a century. A lot of people today seem to think terrorism started with the airplane, or that it's like one of those newly discovered diseases that plague humankind. In fact, terrorism goes back centuries before Mao, Hitler, and Stalin. As Albert Parry wrote in his monumental study of international terrorism: ". . . the terrorizing of humans by fellow humans on political or political-ethnic grounds goes much further back [than the 18th century], in many different forms."[2]

In our own country we've had violent confrontations between groups since the beginning. Puritans and Pilgrims shot it out on the Kennebec River one day in 1634, over an infringement of territory. One Pilgrim and one Puritan died. Fighting might have spread, but fortunately, community common sense prevailed. A meeting of magistrates and ministers was called to settle the dispute. This ended with everybody embracing amid "love and thankfulness . . . their love and concord renewed."

But love and concord didn't last. As the country expanded, adding more differences of people, beliefs, and backgrounds, there were many political and religious mob scenes during America's colonial period.

In the 19th century, mobs killed abolitionists, Mormons (including the founder of the Mormon religion, Joseph Smith, and his brother Hiram), Irish immigrants, Roman Catholics, native American Indians, and blacks. However, these bloody mob killings were not terrorist acts committed by groups with a continuing program of violence to other Americans. The nation didn't develop its first homegrown, organized terrorist movements, with classic terrorist characteristics, until the mid-19th century.

What Terrorists Believe

What separates a "classic" terrorist group from a spontaneous mob? The members of a terrorist group seem to share three basic beliefs, according to Parry, who has studied such groups all over the world for many years. Terrorists believe that:[3]

1. Society is sick and can't be cured by half measures of reform.

2. The state itself uses violence; it can be countered and overcome only by violence.

3. The truth of the terrorist cause justifies any action that supports it.

These are basic terrorist attitudes that are generally shared by terrorist groups all over the world. In this country a variation was added. Some American terrorist groups see themselves as performing a sort of vigilante role—"righting wrongs" the government isn't addressing. *True* vigilante groups were an American invention. They were originally created by frontier Americans as a temporary "law-enforcement group" to protect property and enforce laws in remote areas where law-enforcement officers were few and far between. But the American terrorist groups went far beyond the original impulse of frontier vigilantism. They became an underground army plotting against the government, dedicated to changing it through stark terror practiced on a continuing basis. "When such an order as this moves in and takes over the police power," said Attorney General Richmond Flowers of Alabama, "you are completely at their mercy, and their violence can be visited on anybody that disagrees with them in any given situation."[4]

The three basic beliefs shared by terrorists of every stripe can be traced in their history from the 19th century to today:

In leftist radicalism. The anarchist Mikhail Bakunin taught terrorists in the 19th century that the true terrorist "despises and hates the existing social ethic in all its demands and expressions; for him, everything that allows the triumph of the revolution is moral, and everything that stands in its way is immoral."[5] Maoist teaching quoted by young leftist terrorists in America during the 1960s was that "Political power comes from the barrel of a gun." A Weatherman group song lyric crowed: "He's a real Weatherman/Ripping up the mother land . . . Trashes, bombs, kills pigs and more: The Weatherman!"

In far-right radicalism. This same terrorist disdain for "the existing social ethic" runs through the history of Nazis and Fascists in Europe and neo-Fascists and neo-Nazis here during the 1940s and 1950s. In the fall of 1985, a member of a rightist group called The Order admitted in federal court that members of his group were each assigned a prominent American to assassinate. Included among these candidates for death were heads of three television networks. Why? The Order had decided they were "responsible for indoctrinating our race, poisoning the people."[6] Again we see a terrorist group that "despises and hates the existing social ethic" and was plotting to overthrow it—but this time a group from the radical *right*.

The record shows that Klu Klux Klan leaders appeared and spoke at American Nazi Bund meetings during World War II, and the two groups took part in joint meetings. Today Klan groups and members of such far-right neo-Nazi groups as the Aryan Nations, The Covenant, and the Sword and Arm of the Lord, all goose-step in the same direction to the themes of white supremacy and anti-Semitism.

So What?

Knowing that we do have organized terrorist groups in America right now and that whatever name they may go by, they are out to overturn and stamp out *our* rights as free Americans is *one* thing. Knowing that their membership numbers are small just now, compared to the past, but that American terrorists are much more sophisticated and well armed today is *another* thing. Groups like the Aryan Nations and branches of the Klan have set up computer links; they use cable television to recruit members, and they run computerized "bulletin boards" in some cities. Klan groups and neo-Nazi groups are into paramilitary training and camouflage outfits; members of The Order have been charged by our government with stockpiling weapons, robbing armored cars for funds, counterfeiting, arson, and murder.[7] Members of another far-right American terrorist group had their compound stocked with machine guns, hand grenades, an antitank weapon, and had a minefield that could be detonated electronically.[8]

The most *puzzling* thing is: What can *we* do, as plain, ordinary, nonaggressive citizens, to protect America and our own freedoms against such crazies?

"That's the responsibility of the feds," you may be thinking. "I don't really want to . . . I don't really *need* to get involved." It's true that in the past, whenever the Klan began to gain massive power (as it did in 1922, when it signed up over 1 million members across the country, and Klan candidates were winning elections to state and national offices), the basic democratic common sense of millions of Americans turned on the Klan and it withered like a weed. But terrorist hate groups like the Klan grow back like weeds whenever times turn tough, people are troubled, and millions look around to see who is to blame for their troubles. If that happens again, will our Bill of Rights protect us as it has in the past? Will that good old American common sense come to our aid again?

Martin Niemoeller, a German theologian and pastor, spent seven years in the Sachsenhausen and Dachau concentration camps during the Nazi regime. He left a message for us in this matter:

In Germany, they came first for the Communists, and I didn't speak up because I wasn't a Communist.

Then they came for the Jews, and I didn't speak up because I wasn't a Jew.

Then they came for the Catholics, and I didn't speak up because I was a Protestant.

And then they came for me, and by that time, no one was left to speak up.

Even a quick look at the history of the Klan, our oldest, most persistent American terrorist group, will give us information we need to protect us against them. The Klan has had a very consistent and recurring pattern of growth and decline during the past 130 years. It has a consistent "party line" it shares with other neo-Nazi terrorist groups, so it's easy to recognize once you pin it down. History also shows us the kind of environment Klan membership grows in and the kinds of citizen and government action that make the Klan wither and creep away. Here, in brief, is a life history of the Klan's sources and the Klan itself.

First Came the Know-Nothings

Twenty years before the Klan was born, the Know-Nothing party was born in the urban North. *Its* mission was to keep foreigners and especially Catholics out of public office and to turn off immigration. Because of similarities, and because the Know-Nothings seem to have helped prepare the way for the later spread of the Klan, it's interesting to look at the brief but spectacular history of the Know-Nothings.

They didn't call themselves "Know-Nothings" at first. (Who *would*, given a choice?) When these native terrorists first appeared in New England in 1845, they paraded under ringing patriotic names: Order of the Star-Spangled Banner, Sons of the Sires of '76, and the Native American Party. All terrorist groups try to shroud their operations in secrecy and oaths. This new group instructed its members always to answer, "I know nothing" when questioned about its principles. Soon this caught on with *non*members, and the group became best known as the Know-Nothing party.

The Know-Nothings were oathbound to "preserve America for Americans." During the party's growth, between 1845 and the end of 1854, 3,095,774 immigrants flowed into the United States from other countries, most of them landing at northeastern ports.[9] Most of those immigrants had no working skills; 54% reported "no occupation."[10] That put competitive pressure for jobs on workers at the lower end of the work force. At the same time, there was heavy migration from the South to the North.

Thus the mission of the Know-Nothings was to hold the immigrants down and at the same time prevent them from gaining political strength by voting. In the cities Know-Nothings organized local terrorist street gangs with threatening titles: Plug-Uglies, Rough Skins, Rip-Rap, and Blood Tubs. (The latter got their name because they made their mission in life capturing Irishmen; the hapless captive was dunked in a tub filled with blood collected from local butcher shops, then chased down the street by gang members brandishing knives.) Know-Nothing thugs created election day riots to keep immigrants away from voting. During the period from 1830 to 1860 there were at least 35 "major riots" in Baltimore, Philadelphia, New York, and Boston alone, plus riots in midwestern and lower Mississippi Valley cities.[11] The period has been called possibly "the era of the greatest urban violence that America has ever experienced."

This is precisely the kind of environment where terrorist groups flourish—where insecure people feel somehow threatened by newcomers, and the general political situation is shaky, as it certainly was during the Civil War and Reconstruction periods. The Know-Nothings' efforts to exclude newcomers from jobs and votes caught on.

In 1854 the Native American and Know-Nothing parties elected a governor and most of the state legislature in Massachusetts; 40 New York state legislators; and the governor and some legislators in Pennsylvania. They also elected Know-Nothings to Congress from those states.

In 1856 the Know-Nothings did even better for themselves. They elected their own candidates for governor in Massachusetts, Connecticut, Rhode Island, New Hampshire, California, and Kentucky. Know-Nothings also grabbed control of legislatures in all those states except New Hampshire. Although there were no races for governor in New York, Texas, and Maryland that year, Know-Nothings swept into other offices. In Maryland, New Hampshire, and Tennessee, Know-Nothings joined forces with Whigs to control legislatures effectively. There were also strong Know-Nothing minorities in the legislatures of New York, Virginia, Georgia, and Louisiana. Besides all this show of power, Know-Nothing party members moved into many municipal offices and went to Congress.

After making all this progress in just two elections, you'd think it would be "tomorrow the world!" for the Know-Nothings. In fact, after 1856 it was all downhill. Citizens who refused to be ruled by Know-Nothing bullies got together and reopened the polls to *all* voters. Meanwhile, an expanding America needed more of the kind of cheap, hardworking labor provided by immigrants, and the slavery issue became more important in the minds of most Americans. By 1860 "hostility to immigrants was everywhere a dead issue."[12] The Know-

Nothings just faded away by 1860 as a potential national political force.

What stopped the headlong growth of the Know-Nothings in such a brief period? Partly the fact that Americans generally realized that the Know-Nothing aims were only the aims of a minority; there were bigger issues to be faced. But very largely, what killed the Know-Nothings was the "continuing strength of traditional American values," to quote historian Maldwyn Allen Jones.

American leaders and Amerian citizens actively opposed the Know-Nothings. Abraham Lincoln spoke against them. He reminded people that what the Know-Nothings preached was pure intolerance. "We began our nation," he said, "by declaring that all men are created equal," but "when the Know-Nothings obtain control," he added, "they will change that to 'All men are created equal—except Negroes, foreigners, and Catholics.' "[13] Other American leaders also defended our traditional American ideals against the terrorists; some newspapers ridiculed "No-Nothingism." Citizens forced an end to Know-Nothings' interfering with the election process. And people voted against the Know-Nothing candidates. All these were perfectly democratic, nonviolent steps—and they completely defused the Know-Nothing party.

As we look at the history of the Ku Klux Klan, we'll see similarities. The Klan, like other terrorist groups, thrives on bad times and recruits people who are feeling threatened by competition from newcomers. When times get better and jobs are plentiful, the Klan loses members. When citizens and the media speak out against it and government agencies catch it breaking existing laws, the Klan shrinks.

The Klan

The Ku Klux Klan got its start in a small Tennessee town a year after the Civil War ended. It was started by six bored young Confederate veterans looking for ways to liven up their social life. Th founders were well off financially: One was the editor of the town's only newspaper; others were lawyers; all came from prominent families in the community. They decided to form a secret society "just for fun." They took the Greek word *kuklos*, or "circle," and turned it into "Ku Klux," which then became an alliterative "Ku Klux Klan." Still in a spirit of fun, they created fanciful costumes—sheet robes;

high, pointed "wizard hats"; and masks. They gave themselves fanciful titles (Grand Cyclops, Grand Magi, and Grand Exchequer), enrolled friends, and had parties.

Meanwhile, out in the real world of the postwar South, agriculture had collapsed, the economy was in ruins, the 13th Amendment to the Constitution had abolished slavery, and by 1866 the 14th Amendment would give blacks the vote. Tennessee, where the Klan was born, was he first southern state to give black men, including recently freed slaves, the vote. It was precisely the kind of environment to nourish the growth of terrorist groups. Within a year after it was started as a social club, the Klan had become an organized and fast-growing center for resistance to the laws governing the Reconstruction. It started out simply trying to frighten blacks and their Republican sympathizers, but as the Klan spread out across the South its methods became increasingly murderous. In a single Florida county in 1871 the Klan was involved in murders of 163 black citizens; in parishes just outside New Orleans, 300 blacks were murdered. Thousands of blacks and also white Republicans were beaten or murdered. Schools and churches were destroyed to keep black children from learning to read and write.

Then the federal government finally stepped in, and massive arrests and some convictions of Klansmen broke the fever of massive terrorist violence across the South. The Klan officially disbanded, but individual groups continued as clandestine terrorists. From 1882 (when official records began, kept at first by the *Chicago Tribune*) to 1903 there were at least 100 lynchings a year in America, except in 1890, when there were 96. In 1884 and 1892 there were over 200 such killings.[14]

Nearly 400,000 blacks served in the armed services during World War I; black civilians invested over $250,000 in Liberty Bonds and stamps; but when the war ended and the men came back from service, Klan members were determined to keep blacks out of jobs in American industry. When the Klan began to grow again after the war, it had broadened its scope: Now it was out to exterminate all blacks, Roman Catholics, Jews, and foreigners and to break up organized labor in America.

We're inclined to think of the 1920s now as the "Jazz Age," a pre-Crash party time of flappers, fast cars, flasks, and fun. It's true that business profits were up almost 80% during the decade, and the national income rose by 44%. But it was a "parfait" economy—big money in one layer of the population and poverty in the other. Estimates range from 4 million to almost 6 million unemployed; manufacturing, mining, the Deep South, farming—all had bitterly hard times during the 1920s. Newspapers were full of stories of corruption in business, government, and Hollywood, and of big-time gangsterism. It was an ideal environment, again, for recruitment by the terrorists, and the Klan began to grow very rapidly. At the peak of the decade, the Klan itself claimed to have over 5 million members, and they were pouring $75 million a year into its treasury.[15]

What sort of people were these Klan recruits under the protective sheets and masks? Klan Imperial Wizard Hiram Wesley Evans described them as "hicks and rubes and drivers of second-hand Fords . . . plain people, very weak in the matter of culture." They were also of "old pioneer stock, the Nordic race." They wanted their children taught "the fundamental facts and truths" in school. And they were aiming for the "return of power into the hands of everyday, not highly cultured, not overly intellectualized, but entirely unspoiled and not de-Americanized, average citizens of the old stock." Imperial Wizard Evans announced that the Klan would re-create "a native, white, Protestant America."[16]

Again the Klan seemed to be sailing along to national power. They moved into party politics in the Midwest and the Far West. They swept the 1924 election in Colorado. Soon a third of the Klan's total membership was in the heavily industrialized states of Ohio, Indiana, Illinois, Michigan, and Wisconsin. When the grand dragon of Indiana saw the Klan-supported candidates win the major offices in his state at general elections in 1924, he crowed, "I am the law!" It seemed a great time to be under the sheets. But once again, the American instinct for self-preservation of democracy was quietly at work. The Klan's membership had already peaked.

In August 1925, a total of 40 thousand Klansmen and Klanswomen paraded to a rally at the Washington Monument in Washington, D.C., wearing their hooded sheets. A crowd estimated at 200,000 lined their parade route and were reported to have "applauded" as the hoods marched by to the tune of "Onward, Christian Soldiers."

But the parading Klan was marching downhill again. Times were leaving them behind. The economy was booming, employment was up, and people were drifting away from the Klan. Besides, the Klan itself had been getting a lot of bad press, as a result of illegal practices by its leaders and open dissension in klaverns, klonciliums, koreros, and konklaves across the country.[17]

"An Organization of Traitors"

All through the 1920s newspapers around the country warned their readers against the Klan. Not *all* papers, by any means; there were many weak editors, and there were editors who belonged to the Klan. But many of the most influential, widely read newspapers in America attacked the Klan and all it stood for. Even when Klan candidates were elected mayor and to other important offices in Emporia, Kansas, the world-respected editor of the *Emporia Gazette*, William Allen White, continued to urge all citizens to oppose the Klan. One of White's editorials began: "The Ku Klux Klan is an organization of cowards. Not a man in it has the courage of his convictions. It is an organization of traitors to American institutions." It ended: "This Klan is preaching terror and force." White's articles against the Klan were reprinted all over America. He won a Pulitzer Prize, but even more importantly, he helped to unseat the Klan.

In Georgia, the editor of the *Columbus Enquirer-Sun* attacked the Klan all during the 1920s, in spite of canceled subscriptions and advertising, and personal threats against him. Soon other papers around Georgia joined Julian Harris and his paper in exposing the Klan, and the Klan's influence there dwindled.

In Alabama, Grover Cleveland Hall, editor of the *Montgomery Advertiser*, also led a continuing attack on the Klan in his paper.

In Memphis, Tennessee, the *Commercial Appeal* ridiculed and exposed the Klan with editorials, cartoons, and news. All three of these courageous newspapers and their editors also won Pulitzer prizes for their service to readers and their country.

By the end of the tumultuous 1920s, most Klan members had folded their sheets and silently stolen away. In 1930, the Klan had an estimated 40,000 members nationally—about 1/25th of its membership eight years before.

The Great Depression seemed an ideal environment for

Klan recruitment. One in four workers was out of a job. Almost half of the nation's factories were closed. Millions of Americans went to bed hungry every night. But people who couldn't afford food were also too broke to pay dues. Besides, there were so many different kinds of fringe organizations competing for members during the Depression, the Klan became just one in a crowd clamoring for support. It could only claim 50,000 to 100,000 members during the 1930s.

Dozens of new hate groups were preaching the same line as the Klan, including Father Coughlin's National Union of Social Justice, which spread anti-Semitism on a weekly nationwide radio hookup until church superiors put an end to the program. Native Fascist and Nazi groups were also active in those decades, including the Silver Shirts, Khaki Shirts, Blue Shirts, White Band, Christian Mobilization, Christian Front, and German-American Bund. Besides the various Fascist groups, there were the populist Share the Wealth movement, the utopian socialist EPIC movement, and the Socialist and Communist parties—all clamoring at the same time!

The Klan joined hands with Nazi Bund groups to hold joint mass meetings amid burning crosses and burning swastikas! "The principles of the Bund and the principles of the Klan are the same," Bund leader August Klapprott explained.[18]

America's entry into World War II caught the Klan "under the sheets" with the Nazis. Bund leaders were indicted by our government for sedition. It became known that the Klan had been dealing with many of the 30 or so Americans indicted. Klan membership continued to shrink during World War II. Finally, the IRS filed suit against the Klan in 1944, claiming unpaid taxes of $685,000. The invisible empire called a hasty klonvokation of knights, and decided to disband officially. At the end of the 1940s, a federal government estimate of Klan membership was set at no more than 10,000.

In the 1950s and 1960s, as the civil-rights movement gathered momentum, white supremacists again crept under the Klan's sheets. Local branches of the Klan sprang up all over the country. Klan membership increased to from 10,000 to 15,000 nationally in the 1950s, and membership edged up to an estimated 16,000 in the 1970s.

Ater that, Klan membership shrank steadily. The Klan was again getting bad press all over the country. There was a congressional investigation of the group and its high-living leaders. There were federal court trials and monitoring by the FBI. Klan members were exposed as terrorists and murderers all over the country. By 1976 there were only 2,200 members of the United Klans of America.

In the 1980s Klan membership has floated up and down at a low level. It rose to nearly 11,500 in 1981; but as employment and incomes increased nationally, Klan membership dropped again, to about 6,500 in 1984.[19] This size is minuscule in a population of over 181 million adults, but we can't afford to kid ourselves. Any terrorist group of any size is a threat to any decent society. Moreover, expert Klan-watchers say that the Klansmen who survive today are "hard core—and a desperate hard core."[20]

White supremacists of the mid-1980s have put away the traditional highly visible white sheets, slipped into camouflage suits, and become paramilitary terrorists, under new labels such as the The Order. The Klan-member head of the White Patriot party said recently, "We are working toward an all-white nation."[21] In the meantime, personal assaults and threats against Jews, blacks, and Oriental Americans have been growing; Jewish and Roman Catholic places of worship have been vandalized or bombed; hundreds of homes and business places of black, Jewish, Catholic, and Oriental Americans have been invaded and destroyed by native terrorists across America since 1983.

A young, university-educated Klan leader of the "new breed" said this about his cadre:

The Klan is the type of organization that grows and decreases in cycles. The cycle now is inflation, unemployment, crime. You've got everything the Klan can grow on today. You go to a small town and people are out of work. The mood is restless. They'll grasp the first thing that can help.[22]

In this brief review of the life and time of the KKK we have seen that it feeds on fear and uncertainty. It recruits people who feel so frustrated, they are ready to "grasp the first thing" that seems to offer a promise of help. Our society has *some* people who feel this way at any given time. Fortunately, our free society gives even the most frustrated citizen the right to voice his or her frustration and "get it all out," so it can be addressed. Oliver Wendell Homes wrote:

If there is any principle of the Constitution that more imperatively calls for attachment than any other it is the principle of free thought—not free thought for those who agree with us but freedom for the thought that we hate.[23]

That is why our native terrorists have never been able to recruit more than a comparative handful of sympathizers. People who are frustrated by society but can express their frustration openly have no need for secretive, terrorist movements. They can make their wants and needs known peacefully and within the law. We give even the groups whose "thought we hate" freedom to express themselves; that becomes freedom to show themselves for what they really *are*. And like worms exposed to direct sunlight, they simply "dry up and blow away."

NOTES

1. Richard Hofstadter and Michael Wallace, eds., *American Violence: A Documentary History* (New York: Vintage Books, 1971), p. 35.
2. Albert Parry, *Terrorism from Robespierre to Arafat* (New York: Vanguard Press, 1976), p. xl.
3. Ibid., p. 12.
4. Milton Meltzer, *The Truth About the Ku Klux Klan* (New York: Franklin Watts, 1982), p. 70.
5. Parry, op. cit., p. 15.
6. Associated Press, "Group Planned Killings, Former Member Says," (September 14, 1985).
7. Sam Meddis, "The Order: Seattle Case Sent a 'Signal,'" *USA Today* (September 9, 1985).
8. Ted Gest, "Sudden Rise of Hate Groups Spurs Federal Crackdown," *U.S. News & World Report* (May 6, 1985).
9. *Historical Statistics of the United States*, vol. 1 (Washington, D.C.: U.S. Bureau of the Census, 1975), table C-120.
10. Ibid., table C-130.
11. Hofstadter and Wallace, op. cit., pp. 14–15, quoting Richard Maxwell Brown.
12. Maldwyn Allen Jones, *American Immigration* (Chicago: University of Chicago Press, 1974), p. 160.
13. Michael Kraus, *The United States to 1865* (Ann Arbor: University of Michigan Press, 1959), p. 454.
14. *Historical Statistics of the United States*, op. cit., table H-1168.
15. Meltzer, op. cit., p. 47.
16. Ibid., p. 37.

17. Robert P. Ingalls, *Hoods: The Story of the Ku Klux Klan* (New York: G.P. Putnam's Sons, 1970), p. 120. This very informative and readable little book is classified as juvenile literature for libraries but should not be scorned for that reason by adults. It is an excellent example of the sort of material our youngsters should have access to in the classrooms. These various "k's" are selected from the book's "Glossary of Klan Terms," and each refers to a different kind of Klan meeting.

18. Meltzer, op. cit., p. 58. Also see Sander A. Diamond, *The Nazi Movement in the United States 1924–1941* (Ithaca, N.Y.: Cornell University Press, 1974), p. 319.

19. Sam Meddis, "Far-Right Ranks Are Thinning," *USA Today* (September 9, 1985).

20. Ibid.

21. Gest, op. cit.

22. Ingalls, op. cit., p. 113, quoting David Duke.

23. Oliver Wendell Holmes, quoted by Nat Hentoff in *The First Freedom: The Tumultuous History of Free Speech in America* (New York: Delacorte Press, 1980), p. 315.

Organizations to Contact for Further Information

Klanwatch: Southern Poverty Law Center, 1001 South Hull Street, Montgomery, AL 36101.

National Baptist Convention: 52 South Sixth Avenue, Mt. Vernon, NY. 10550. The Convention adopted a resolution on the Klan in 1980 that could serve as a model for other kinds of groups.

National Conference of Catholic Bishops: 1312 Massachusetts Avenue, NW, Washington, DC 20005.

Anti-Defamation League of B'nai B'rith: represenative in your area.

Does Big Business Run America?
(Is the Pope Moslem?)

★

This is a quotation from a Populist Party political manifesto, back in 1880:

> On the one side are the allied hosts of monopolies, the money power, great trusts and . . . corporations, who seek the enactment of law to benefit them and impoverish the people. On the other are the farmers, laborers, merchants, and all other people who produce wealth and bear the burdens of taxation. . . .[1]

The manifesto is long since forgotten. But its spirit—a deep-dyed suspicion of big money and big business—still is strong among American people. Perversely, we admire success—but we mistrust success translated into big business. A mid-1985 national poll asked Americans in every state if they had ever felt that "Big business runs the country." Better than eight out of 10 Americans said "Yes." Asked, "How do you feel right now?" slightly fewer (78%) blandly declared that yes, "Big business runs the country."[2]

Where have all these eight-in-10 Americans been looking lately? Did they see big business running the country when the Penn Central Railroad came to a shuddering halt a few years ago and went broke? Railroad after railroad that once bestrode the continent like giants quietly disappeared in the face of competition from airlines and truckers. It turned out that big business couldn't even run its own railroads profitably, much less a country.

Was big business in charge of the country when Chrysler Corporation—one of the country's Big Three auto giants—teetered to the brink of bankruptcy seven years ago? Not so you could notice. The other auto giants didn't turn a hand to

298

help Chrysler. Seven out of 10 Americans were against giving Chrysler any help at all.[3] What put Chrysler back on its feet and led it back to join the leadership in its industry again was something even more powerful than government funding. It was what Chrysler's chairman, Lee Iacocca, has labeled "equality of sacrifice"—contributions by labor, management, the company's suppliers, car dealers, each giving something extra of themselves for the common good.

Was big business running the country when Continental Illinois National Bank & Trust Company of Chicago—one of the world's biggest big banks—began to run out of operating capital? Or when all those other once-formidable bankers across the nation got into financial hot water, and wise old Uncle Sam had to go and wring them out?

What about the day the courts broke AT&T up, just four years ago? The biggest communications monopoly in the world suddenly shrank. Seven scrambling individual companies, each with hundreds of hungry competitors, took over its territory. Was big business running the country that day?

Big Steel was a colossus of financial power in America not long ago. Look at it today: U.S. Steel, hoping to save itself by setting up a partnership with Koreans; Wheeling-Pittsburgh Steel, maneuvering to avoid bankruptcy; Bethlehem Steel, trying to diversify itself back to profitability. Is Big Steel running the country? (Is the Pope Moslem?)

How about all those grand old giant companies we see every day now, scurrying like little pigs to keep from being gobbled up by big, bad wolves who are much smaller than they are, or captured single-handedly by corporate pirates? Who's running whom?

And take Coca-Cola: the century-old reigning giant of the multibillion-dollar beverage industry decreed a change in the flavor of its own product a year or so ago. Who turned out to be calling the shots there? We did. Every little consumer with two bits for a soft drink had something to say about that. And what they said was, "Oh, no you *don't*." Coca-Cola did what the populace ordered.

It's enough to make me wonder, sometimes, "Where are the economic royalists of yesteryear?" And yet eight in 10 of my fellow Americans look around them and say, "I see big business is still running the country." How do they *get* that way?

A History of Mistrust

A couple of pages of capsulized American history may help answer that question. The deep-rooted conviction that big business is running everything goes back a long way in our country—as far back as the American Revolution and the first days of the infant American republic.

Bonds were issued by the new republic during the American Revolution to pay farmers, discharged soldiers, shopkeepers, and others. But during hard times after the war, the value of the bonds went down and down. When the farmers, soldiers, and small shopkeepers sold them, it was at a ruinous discount. By 1789 most of the public debt was held by monied interests in the big cities—Philadelphia, New York, Charleston, and Boston. Alexander Hamilton pushed through Congress a scheme to pay the bonds (which had been selling for 25 cents on a dollar) off at *full value* using taxpayers' money. To make matters even more divisive, Hamilton proposed to raise the cash to do this by an excise tax on whiskey. This would wring the money right out of small farmers in the interior of the country—they turned much of their corn into this highly exportable and profitable commodity.[4] The direct result was an uproar that ended in the Whiskey Rebellion of 1794.

When furious Pennsylvania farmers mobbed tax collectors and started a march on Pittsburgh, President Washington called out the militia. That cooled the rebellion. But the suspicion that big money and the industrialists were out to take over government was firmly implanted. American political history from that time until 1865 was a constant battle for control of government between farming-planting interests and the mercantile-shipping-financial interests of the big cities. Even Thomas Jefferson suggested, in 1791, that Congress was being controlled by "stock-jobbers."[5]

In 1832 President Jackson vetoed a bill to recharter the Second Bank of the United States with these words to Congress:

> It is to be regretted that the rich and powerful too often bend the acts of government to their selfish purposes
> . . . to make the rich richer and the potent more powerful . . . [at the expense of] farmers, mechanics, and laborers—who have neither the time nor the means of securing like favors to themselves. . . .[6]

Actually, for all his rhetoric, once Jackson killed the bank by withdrawing its government deposits, he tucked them into selected state banks. Wildcat banks sprung up all over the West. Money in circulation grew threefold, and loans outstanding grew fourfold. An inflationary spiral began that came crashing down in financial panic—shortly after the president left office.

During the years before the Civil War, the myth that business is out to take over the government began to look like it could come true. Businessmen flocked to Washington to "put the arm" on Congress. One reputable economist of the time seriously suggested that "the friends of domestic industry should meet annually and prepare a schedule of legislation" that Congress could then turn into law!

Still, up to about 1870, there was no big business in the country in the sense that we know it today. In the 1840s there were not 20 millionaires in the whole country. The United States still enjoyed a comfortably widespread distribution of wealth and power. Local merchants, manufacturers, lawyers, editors, and preachers were the "powerbrokers" in a nation of small towns.

Later, in the post-Civil War era of rapid industrialization and growing urbanization, immense money and power began to accumulate. With it came growing public fear of concentration of wealth.

Between the end of the Civil War and the beginning of our century, business interests did very nearly take over in the seat of government. More businessmen than ever before entered Congress. Senate seats were bought outright by industrialists, and almost no legislation to control business even reached the floor of Congress for debate. One U.S. senator actually suggested that congressmen should be elected according to the industry they represented, rather than their geographic constituency.

The Balance Swings

The incredible expansion of America following the Civil War, opening up of vast natural resources, steadily automating industry, new communication means, a growing population hungry for goods, and the development of "pools" and "trusts" all worked together to raise the specter of "big-business monopoly." But, as often happens in America, when the pendulum swings too far in favor of one sector or another, the people themselves move in the other direction, as if on signal, counterbalancing overweening power.

The 1880s saw the formation of a great national labor federation, the American Federation of Labor. It drew together various national unions of skilled workers and would give organized labor a single voice and great political force in years ahead. Farmers also organized. There were dreams of uniting farmers and organized labor, and the Populist movement was born. As a unified political movement, the Populist party came to its fullest bloom in the national election of 1892. It withered in the same election as both Republicans and Democrats won far more votes. Even so, the Populist *idea*, the notion of social dualism—big money and big business vs. the people—was in our national bloodstream and remains there today.

In our own century, there's been a fairly steady side-by-side growth of business and government. The dynamic expansion of American business has been matched by creation and strengthening of governmental agencies to balance and control it. This intensified during the 50 years between the stock-market crash of 1929 and the beginning of the 1980s. Herbert Hoover began it by approving the Reconstruction Finance Corporation. This was created to bail out with direct federal loans large corporations that got into financial trouble. Franklin Roosevelt enlarged it with a whole series of innovations. The monetary system was reformed and management put into the hands of the government. Citizens' bank deposits were guaranteed by the government for the first time. The Farm Credit Administration was established, along with the HOLC, to provide federal credit for farm and home mortgages. Social Security was initiated. Government created jobs for the unemployed at a time during the Depression when industry could not. The whole Keynesian notion of government spending to stimulate demand and employment was put into practice. The Securities and Exchange Commission laid a restraining hand on investments. And TVA and REA brought light, power, and new industry to parts of the country that had been neglected before.

By the time America entered World War II, government and business were working together rather than in an adversarial mode. Since that war the relationship has continued, and it has intensified more than many people might wish. In recent years, with "unbundling" of industry controls, government has sought to stimulate enterprise and step away, in effect, from such close relationship but without letting business "run wild." The result has appeared to be a growth of entrepreneurship. New-business starts in 1984 were at the highest level since 1978—102,329 new firms in a year.[7]

Presidential Populism

So when we look back over two centuries of give-and-take in our country, during which we've become the most powerful and dynamic economic force in the world, the theme of a threatening big business trying to dominate democracy weaves back and forth all through our history. Not only the people but also our leaders have kept it going from generation to generation. Hamilton may have started it in the federal convention of 1789 when he remarked, "All communities divide themselves into the few and the many. The first are the rich and well-born; the other the mass of the people . . . turbulent and changing, they seldom judge or determine right. Give therefore to the first class a distinct, permanent share in the government."[8] But Jefferson worried about "the rage of getting rich in a day"[9] that he saw in the speculative scramble for stock in the Bank of the United States. In our century, Theodore Roosevelt complained of "the dull, purblind folly of the very rich men; their greed and arrogance . . . and the corruption in business and politics"; he berated the "malefactors of great wealth."[10]

Woodrow Wilson (who also believed "Every great man of business has got somewhere . . . a touch of the idealist in him . . . love of integrity for its own sake")[11] nevertheless complained of the development of trusts, that it gave "to a few men a control over the economy of the country which they might abuse to the undoing of millions of men, it might even be to the permanent demoralization of society itself and of the government."[12]

Franklin Roosevelt told the Commonwealth Club in San Francisco (1932) that "Just as freedom to farm has ceased, so also the opportunity in business has narrowed . . . area after area has been preempted altogether by the great corporations . . ." and warned that "Put plainly, we are steering a steady course toward economic oligarchy, if we are not there already."[13] Even Herbert Hoover used Populist terminology in a backward swipe at Franklin Roosevelt during the 1936 presidential campaign: "I rejected the nation of great trade monopolies and price fixing through codes. That could only stifle the little business man by regimenting him under the big brother. That idea was born of certain American Big Business and grew up to be the NRA."[14] And Harry Truman berated McKinley as "one of those who was good for the rich and bad for the poor";[15] Cleveland's second term in office as "more interested in the big-money people than he was in the common people . . ."[16]; and Truman, himself, believed "people have to keep their eyes and ears open at all times or they'll be robbed blind by the Mugwumps in politics and by the big-business interests." When Merle Miller, author of an oral biography of President Truman, remarked to him, "You sound like a Populist," Mr. Truman said, "Maybe I do."[17]

Philosopher of business Peter Drucker has written that he considers "the claims on business by American populism," which he believes require that "business subordinate economic performance to non-economic performance and non-economic goals . . . are even less compatible with business performance than the European 'Socialist' hostility toward 'private enterprise.' " In fact, he considers it "basically hostile to economic performance altogether."[18]

In spite of all our two centuries of push-and-shove about whether or not big business is "taking us over," the American people generally enjoy the highest standard of living in the world. Fewer of us who are employed are working for "big companies" than in 1976 (32% worked for a company with over 250 employees in 1976; 30% in 1982, the latest year for which figures are available).[19] And more new little businesses open their doors hopefully every day to compete with giants for our favor—and maybe grow up to be big companies themselves someday.

Big business doesn't run the country. The unions don't run the country. Even the government doesn't run the country, when it comes right down to it. We all maintain an intricate, delicate, and often painful balance among us. In the midst of this endless dance of the giants, the American citizen goes about his or her daily life in an environment of personal freedom and opportunity that's unique in the world today.

NOTES

1. Ray Allen Billington, *Westward Expansion* (New York: MacMillan Publishing Company, Inc., 1949).

2. Leo J. Shapiro & Associates special national survey done for this book (August 1985).

3. Leo J. Shapiro & Associates national consumer survey, "What should be done to help Chrysler Motors?" (August, 1979).

4. As a farmer himself, President Washington owned a "particularly profitable" still on his home plantation, from which he "carried over" 755 quarter gallons of whiskey, after selling most of his rye-and-Indian-corn liquid dynamite, in a single year, according to Paul Leicester Ford's *The True George Washington* (Philadelphia: J.B. Lippincott Company, 1902), p. 123.

5. Letter to George Mason (February 7, 1791).

6. Message to Congress (July 10, 1832).

7. Dun & Bradstreet figures (1985).

8. Samuel Eliot Morison, *The Oxford History of the American People* (New York: Oxford University Press, 1965), p. 324.

9. Merrill D. Peterson, *Thomas Jefferson and the New Nation* (New York: Oxford University Press, 1970), p. 436.

10. Richard Hofstadter, *The American Political Tradition* (New York: Random House, 1948), p. 224.

11. Speech to Chicago Commercial Club (1902).

12. Woodrow Wilson, *History of the American People*, quoted in Hofstadter, op. cit., p. 244.

13. Richard Hofstadter, ed., *Great Issues in American History* (New York: Random House, 1969), pp. 348–49.

14. "Challenge to Liberty" speech (1936).

15. Merle Miller, *Plain Speaking* (New York: Berkley Publishing Corporation, 1974), p. 120.

16. Ibid., p. 118.

17. Ibid., p. 153.

18. Peter Drucker, *Managing in Turbulent Times* (New York: Harper & Row, 1980), p. 209.

19. *Statistical Abstract of the United States 1985* (Washington, D.C.: U.S. Department of Commerce, Bureau of the Census, 1984), table 873.

Congress Still Takes Its Time—
and That's Good

★

People complain more about Congress than even Congress deserves. One of the most common complaints is that Congress talks too much, and "dawdles" over legislation. (Anybody who's ever read even one whole issue of the daily *Congressional Record* might be inclined to agree.)

But all that huffing and puffing and talking and even the outright factionalism in Congress are part of the vital signs of democracy. And the people who criticize Congress most for not moving fast enough have their own axes to grind.

Presidents always want to get their way—and if they don't get it pronto, they accuse at least part of Congress of conspiring against America and holding up the mighty wheels of progress. The press wants action in Congress because action makes news, and it's very hard to fill up columns and television time when the news that day is thin and they have to fatten it up themselves.

On the other hand, the public is much more understanding and permissive with Congress. As Will Rogers once observed, "This country has come to feel the same when Congress is in session as when the baby gets hold of a hammer." No news from Congress may actually turn out to be good news—at least for our pocketbooks. We amiably accept the folklore that congressmen (not congresswomen, yet) are windbags. In fact, the only reason why people remember President Coolidge is that he "swam upstream" against the flood of rhetoric in Washington and became "Silent Cal."

But we must be careful of judging Congress only by how fast it can churn out legislation, and with how little debate. When Norman Ornstein, a usually very astute political scientist and Congress-watcher, recently chided Congress for being "sluggish" because "Only 46 bills have been enacted this year, compared with 71 at the same time last year, and committees are moving ahead on only about half as many items as last year," I felt a little warning chill on my back. You talk that way about a baseball player: "He's only had 46 hits so far this year, compared with 71 at the same time last year." Not about a deliberative body, which is what Congress was originally set up to be by our Founding Fathers. Maybe Congress has simply been getting more bad pitches thrown at it lately. Maybe the bills are more complex and life-threatening. If so, let 'em talk until they know what they believe, until they get honestly earnest differences ironed out. That's what we hope we sent them to Washington to do for us.

When Premier Gorbachev suddenly stood up in front of the assembled 1,500 or so members of the Supreme Soviet and nominated Andrei Gromyko to be the new president of the USSR, it apparently came as a surprise to everyone present as well as to the rest of the world. But what did the members of the Supreme Soviet say about it? Did they discuss the nomination? Did they even hesitate? Indeed, not. There was no dawdling. No single sign of "sluggishness." They all said just one word: "*Da.*"

Personally, I hope our Congress never becomes that efficient.

Love It and Change It

★

Ten years ago, when I wrote the 1976 edition of this book, there were still bumper stickers on cars with this peremptory advice: "America—love it or leave it." I always felt that was advice from a person given to easy solutions. No country is perfect, ours included. What we really need is more Americans willing to make the effort to change things that *aren't* right, as a true labor of love for the country.

To "leave it" is the easy way out. What I'd suggest is this:

1. Carefully consider other nations on this vulnerable little globe, one by one: how free their citizens are; how secure; how happy; how they live; what their future prospects seem to be.

2. Then get your own hands busy, even dirty, improving things here. Others are already at work, as they have been since before 1776. Your help will be welcome.

Consider the alternatives. Then: Love it *and* change it.

Index

ABOUT THE AUTHOR

This is DWIGHT BOHMBACH'S third published book. For twenty years he was creative director of an advertising agency, then CEO of a national ad agency. He and his psychotherapist wife Ree are now "cottage laborers," working in offices at opposite ends of their Arizona home. Their daughter Anne is an artist and son Michael does creative research in Minnesota.

Bohmbach "never had time for college" until he got his BA at age 65, MA at 67, and now plans a Ph.D. before 70, "God willing." He is working on two new books aimed at "rediscovering America from different perspectives."

We Deliver!
And So Do These Bestsellers.